FAMILY TIES

FAMILY TIES

English families 1540–1920

Mary Abbott

London and New York

Acknowledgement

Thanks are due to Dick Abbott who supplied many of the
photographs reproduced in the plate section.

First published in 1993
by Routledge
11 New Fetter Lane, London EC4P 4EE

Simultaneously published in the USA and Canada
by Routledge
29 West 35th Street, New York, NY 10001

© 1993 Mary Abbott

Typeset in 10/12 pt Palatino by Florencetype Ltd,
Kewstoke, Avon
Printed in Great Britain by Butler & Tanner Ltd,
Frome & London

British Library Cataloguing in Publication Data
Abbott, Mary
Family Ties: English Families 1540–1920
I. Title
306.850942

Library of Congress Cataloging in Publication Data
Abbott, Mary
Family ties : English families, 1540–1920 / Mary Abbott.
p.   cm.
Includes bibliographical references and index.
1. Family—England—History.   2. Social
classes—England—History.
I. Title.
HQ615.A62   1993
306.85′0942–dc20   92–24886

ISBN 0 415 09109 8
0 415 09110 1 (pbk.)

CONTENTS

INTRODUCTION

WHY STUDY THE FAMILY?

I want this book to provide its readers with enough evidence of the experience of the men, women and children who peopled England between 1540 and 1920 to prompt them to find out more. For a number of reasons an investigation of family life is the best place to start.

First of all, curiosity about other people's lives and relationships, past and present, is a powerful human instinct. This fascination helps to explain the popularity of biography and fiction, gossip and gossip columns, soap operas and houses open to the public. The family is a live issue. Debates and decisions about the rights and wrongs of surrogacy, adoption, single parenthood, 'working mothers', couples living together outside wedlock, and the divorce rate impinge on us all. Investigating the experience of families in the past may put some of these issues into perspective.

A more academically respectable reason is that, like most past societies, between the Reformation and the Great War, the kingdom of England was a federation of families, normally headed by married men. The accession of a queen – and there were five queens between 1540 and 1920 – was an expression of dynastic crisis: Elizabeth I was the last Tudor; Queen Anne the last reigning Stuart. Next in the order of precedence to the royal family came the families of landowners, the greatest of whom were peers. The heads of these families enjoyed the lion's share of wealth, power and prestige. Buying landed estates was the means of translating personal wealth into an enduring legacy of social and political influence. Even when land ceased to be a sound investment towards the end of the nineteenth century, the appetite for hereditary titles with territorial connections did not diminish.

There was a strong tendency for the sons of men of all ranks to follow in their fathers' footsteps: there were dynasties of parsons, lawyers, farmers, millers, timber merchants, cutlers. The son of a labouring man was likely to become a labourer in his turn. Many people worked at home, not necessarily their own. Until they married many of the children of the labouring poor lived in their employers' families. Women often spent their entire lives in waged or unwaged work in a domestic environment.

Heads of families had an obligation to maintain and discipline their households, servants included. This duty was all the weightier because, until the second half of the nineteenth century, there were no laws requiring children to go to school, and most communities were policed by unpaid constables. Those who failed to keep their families in order, therefore, failed in their responsibility to society.

People with a strong interest in the past are generally imaginative and argumentative. Yet, and especially at the start of their careers as historians, they are often in awe of the printed page. Students of family history draw on a range of sources – including images, artefacts and buildings – which, though equally challenging, may be less daunting than books, perhaps because they tend to be more strongly associated with 'free time' than with set work. Questioning the meaning of the contents of a graveyard, a display case in a museum, a broadcast documentary, a feature film or a historical 're-enactment' can help to develop the critical skills that should be the historian's trademark. This is a third important reason for looking at the family.

The big questions I set out to answer in this book are about the range of family experience and the extent that it changed over time. These big questions generated a series of others. Where did particular families fit into the social hierarchy? What were their principal sources of income? What were their spending priorities? Which sources yield most information about them? Were boy and girl babies equally welcome? Were firstborn or younger children better placed? How did parents respond to a child's death? Who was responsible for childcare? Were boys treated differently from girls? What contributions, if any, were children expected to make to the family economy? Did young people leave home? If so, where did they go and why? What were the options for women who did not marry? What attributes did young men and women look for in their future partners? Who else was involved in making or blocking marriage plans? How were responsibilities divided between husbands and wives? What caused friction within marriage? How did widowed men and women respond to the loss of their partners?

It is unrealistic to expect to be able to recover the 'truth' about family relationships. This book is devoted to the less profound project of recording and assessing what people did and said. Within the limitations of the source material, I have aimed to give readers access to the actors' own words. As a result, in several chapters, the nineteenth century is in sharpest focus. Since I believe that the family was an institution which changed slowly, this is not a cause for concern.

HOW I HAVE ORGANISED THE BOOK

The book begins with three short chapters designed to put family experience in context. The first reviews the way in which the topic has been tackled: by people curious about their origins or proud of their forebears' rank or achievements; by antiquarians dedicated to amassing material, usually related to landed families; and, in the last thirty years or so, by academic historians who set out to document and analyse family values, structures and dynamics.

The second chapter sketches the history of England between 1540 and 1920, focusing on the episodes and developments that were of the greatest significance for families. Readers who are already familiar with the social and economic history of the period may be inclined to skip this chapter. Think twice. Time invested in reading it could pay dividends by alerting you to what I believe mattered most. Indeed, the last part of the chapter is essential reading. It provides a broadbrush account of the family as an institution, using the human life-cycle as the organising principle.

The chapters which form the core of the book are concerned with the experience of family life at five social levels. These chapters deal with the families headed by: landowners; working farmers and tradesmen; middle-class professional and business men, and their precursors; white-collared workers and labouring men. I decided to organise the book in this way because of the weight I give to rank and occupation as determinants of family experience. Examining families rank by rank is also a safeguard against the natural tendency to allow the testimony of the articulate, privileged minority to dominate.

Although the chapters differ in length, they are planned along similar lines. Readers who want to concentrate on a particular aspect of family history should have no difficulty in pursuing the theme from chapter to chapter. Each of these chapters opens with a section headed DEFINING CHARACTERISTICS. A review of SOURCES follows. The individual life-cycle is the organising principle of the remainder of the chapter. The main headings are:

THE MEANING OF CHILDREN
INFANCY
CHILDHOOD
YOUTH: SONS
YOUTH: DAUGHTERS
THE CHOICE OF A WIFE
WOMEN'S OPTIONS OUTSIDE MARRIAGE
THE CHOICE OF A HUSBAND
MARITAL ROLES

PARENTHOOD
MARITAL RELATIONSHIPS
MARITAL BREAKDOWN
WIDOWHOOD
SUMMING UP
NOW READ ON

In some chapters, two closely related topics may be tackled together, in others there are further subheadings.

Chapters end with a short list of books which will enable you to pursue some of the issues raised. Opportunities to 'read on' will depend to some extent on your pocket and to some extent on the size and scope of the libraries to which you have access. The suggestions I have made are an indication of the sort of books you might look for rather than an exhaustive or exclusive list. As you 'read on', keep an eye open for the original date of publication: research methods and interpretations change over time and some books have been overtaken by events. Be critical of what you read.

My final chapter takes a closer look at the sources which you can explore for yourself.

Historians are sometimes guilty of relying on over-familiar pictures to illustrate their texts. The illustrations in this book have been carefully chosen. As far as possible, they depict people and families as they chose to represent themselves. Many appear in print for the first time; others have appeared only in sale or exhibition catalogues. They are accompanied by commentaries which I hope you will read and reflect on.

1

APPROACHES TO THE HISTORY OF THE ENGLISH FAMILY

TRADITIONAL APPROACHES

The earliest and most persistent strain of family history is that compiled by or for a family concerned to celebrate its bloodline and antiquity. Eminent ancestors were and remain objects of desire. The urge to list and document those who share a family name has also proved powerful.

Woodrow Wyatt's recollection illustrates the desire to embellish a descent by incorporating noble and romantic ancestors.

> When I was a child there was much talk in the family about our being descended from Sir Thomas Wyatt, the poet, and his son Sir Thomas Wyatt the younger who led an unsuccessful rebellion against Queen Mary . . . Was not our Coat of Arms, properly registered and granted to John and James Wyatt in 1780 by the College of Arms, the same? . . . Pictures of both the Thomas Wyatts hung in the hall . . . There was occasional mention of James Wyatt and some of Thomas Henry Wyatt, but the other architects and inventors, manufacturers, sculptors, artists in the family, were never spoken of. In esteem they were far below a courtier of Henry VIII once in difficulties because he was attracted by Anne Boleyn before she met the king.
>
> As I grew more interested in the architects I looked closer at our connection with Sir Thomas. There is none, or if there is it can only be a distant cousinage . . . Even the most desperate genealogical attempt to establish a descent from Sir Thomas relies on someone being married, with progeny, at the age of four or thereabouts.

Woodrow Wyatt's family was by no means unusual. When Sir Henry Harpur (b.1763) married a lady's maid by the name of Nanette Hawkins he kitted her out with the Elizabethan seadog's coat of arms to camouflage her humble origins.

In *Wedgwood Pedigrees*, published in 1925, Josiah and Joshua

Wedgwood, descendants of the eighteenth-century potter and entre-
preneur, set out to reconstruct 'the complete family' which, they
believed, could be traced back to Wedgwood near Tunstall in
Staffordshire, using a combination of archival research and direct communication with 'all existing bearers of that name', who were 'sought
out, written to, catechised and traced back to the parent stock'. The
History of the Battelle Family represents a convergence of these two
approaches. Lucy Catherine Battelle (b.1903), who amassed an extra-
ordinary archive of material relating to her surname, tentatively
identified a pair of brothers who came over with William the Conqueror
as the family's founding fathers. Curiosity about their families extends
to people with very much less to go on. The staff of the Office of
Population Censuses and Surveys recalled an 'old lady' from Lancashire
who came to consult the records of the Registrar General to discover the
'full names' of her fifteen older brothers and sisters and 'the order they
came in'.

Woodrow Wyatt, the Wedgwood cousins, Miss Battelle and the 'old
lady' were concerned with their own descent. Seventeenth-century
antiquarians worked on a wider canvas. The great manuscript collections of medieval family papers held in the British Library and the
Bodleian in Oxford owe much to the industry of men like Sir William
Dugdale, Sir Christopher Hatton and Sir Thomas Shirley. Their enthusiasm was a product of the new style of education which familiarised the
sons of landowners with the traditions of history writing in ancient
Greece and Rome, and a reflection of the unquiet times before the
outbreak of the Civil War.

The nineteenth century saw the application of scientific concepts and
new technology to family history. Francis Galton (b.1822) sought to
apply the results of work on genetics, which his cousin Charles Darwin
had pioneered, to the breeding of human beings with superior intellectual and physical attributes. The starting point for the development of
his eugenic thesis was his analysis of Foss's *Lives of the Judges*, which
suggested that legal ability was an inherited characteristic. Given the
power of patronage, the conclusion that this was a genetic effect was
debatable. In 1882 Galton enlisted the help of amateur photographers in
developing composite portraits which would embody 'ideal family
likenesses'.

RECENT APPROACHES TO THE HISTORY OF
THE ENGLISH FAMILY

Only within the last thirty years have academic historians embarked on
an exploration of family life and behaviour. This activity has provoked,
sometimes bitter, arguments. In *Approaches to the History of the Western*

Family (1980), Michael Anderson reviewed the developments of the two preceding decades. His pamphlet remains a convenient introduction to family historians' preferred sources and perspectives. Anderson identified four lines of enquiry which he labelled the psychohistorical, the demographic, the sentimental and the household economics approaches.

He summarily dismissed the speculations of psychohistorians, who apply Freudian or Jungian principles to the study of relationships in times past. A majority of historians would endorse his verdict. Not only are historians 'usually unable to penetrate the bedroom, the bathroom or the nursery', but most have strong reservations about the value of applying theories developed on the basis of observations of bourgeois subjects in an industrial, urban society to the men, women and children reared in different contexts and cultures.

Peter Laslett, Tony Wrigley and Roger Schofield were the English sponsors of what Anderson described as the demographic approach. They aimed to redress what they perceived as the elitism and sub-jectivity of studies based on literary sources. Building on techniques developed in France in the 1950s, Laslett and his colleagues coordinated the work of a team of professional and lay researchers who transcribed and processed entries from parish registers and local listings. Wrigley and Schofield's *Population History of England* is the most substantial product of this massive investigative programme. The meticulous analy-sis of data from the registers of 404 English parishes has exploded the myth, innocently promoted by Shakespeare's *Romeo and Juliet* and, apparently, confirmed by scattered records of child betrothals and mar-riages in Tudor and Stuart England, that people married very young. Far from it, the average age of a first-time bride was 25 or 26; the average age of a first-time groom a couple of years older. Fertility, life expectancy, the rate of illegitimacy are among other topics central to the history of the family that have been subjected to scrutiny.

Yet the demographers' results must be treated with a measure of caution, both because of the nature of their sample and because of the distorting consequence of averaging. Other things being equal, 404 would be a very respectable sample of the 10,000-odd English parishes. But the 404 were neither selected as representative communities nor pulled out of a hat at random. They were chosen because their registers were reasonably carefully kept over a long run of years. London parishes are among those under-represented. If historians are right in identifying occupation and region as major influences on family life, these gaps may be important. Averages are often misleading because they conceal variations across rank and over time. Thus aristocrats tended to marry young or not at all, business and professional men were often substantially older than their wives, while there is evidence that the age at which poor couples married was strongly influenced by local economic circumstances. Similarly, the conclusion that the average number of people per household remained steady at 4.75 over the best part of three centuries masks the more significant information that gentry households generally far exceeded the average and labourers' often fell short of it.

Historians using what Anderson labelled the sentiments approach have chiefly been concerned with the emergence of an introspective and affectionate 'modern' family. Their inspiration, like the demographers', was French. Philippe Ariès pioneered the study of childhood, drawing on the evidence of art as well as on the more traditional literary sources. Lawrence Stone's *The Family, Sex and Marriage*, which concentrates on the sixteenth, seventeenth and eighteenth centuries, is based on a similar range of evidence. This is one of the most entertaining and thought-provoking books published in the last two decades: it provides an excellent opportunity for a reader to pit her, or his, critical skills against the arguments of an historian of stature. Stone's interest and sympathies lie with the formally educated and articulate. His substantial and continuous work on the aristocracy gives his commentary on their experience particular authority. The character of his source material precluded effective coverage of the poor.

Anderson's preference is for what he describes as the household economics approach, an approach which employs perspectives developed by social scientists. Historians working within this framework see the family as a flexible and responsive mechanism for acquiring and handing on property and for maximising the chances of surviving in hard times. Anderson, whose academic interests straddle the boundary between Sociology and Economic History, is a leading exponent. His account of *Family Structure* in nineteenth-century Preston illustrates the range of sources available for that place and period. The Census enumerators' books for 1841, 1851 and 1861 were Anderson's 'prime source of quantitative material'.

> These quantitative data are supported by a mass of descriptive material abstracted from contemporary sources of all kinds . . . Some use is made of material from novels. Severe limitations were, however, applied to such data. All material used must have been entirely incidental to the plot of the novel. The work must have been by a writer familiar with working class life and, if possible, the work must have been one known to have been read by working class contemporaries.

In spite of his own contribution to its development, Anderson is not an uncritical advocate of this approach. As he acknowledges, there is a 'danger . . . of over-romanticising the picture by exaggerating continuity and cohesion' and neglecting the tension between the interests of the family as a whole and the interests of individual younger members. It is striking that his discussion ignores what is, for us in our own time, the central question of the breakdown of marriages.

Though a useful starting point, Anderson's system of classification is not definitive. Alan Macfarlane's anthropological analysis of the family life of Ralph Josselin (b.1617), an Essex parson, one of the most instructive examples of the application of social science methodologies to the history of the family, does not sit comfortably in any of his categories. Peter Laslett rejected 'the notion of approaches' altogether: 'People may overemphasise demographic fact in the past of the family and so lack balance, but they are not doing so by adopting a demographic approach.'

Anderson's analysis emphasises sources. Alternatively, and perhaps as usefully, historians of the family can be categorised by the stress they place on change and continuity. As Ralph Houlbrooke put it:

> Some historians believe that the Western family has undergone a fundamental transformation in the past few centuries; others, while readily admitting that changes have taken place, believe that they have been, at any rate until recent years, much slower and less profound than in most other human institutions.

Among the changes he points to 'during the last century and a half' are dramatic falls in fertility and mortality.

In *The Family, Sex and Marriage* Lawrence Stone claimed to have identified several phases in the evolution of the family between 1500 and 1800, phases which reflected the decline in the importance of aristocratic lineage and the impact of Reformation theology. This ambitious typology found little favour; but his propositions that companionate marriages emerged and that childhood was 'invented' after the Restoration in the families of gentle- and professional men have been endorsed. Randolph Trumbach, who investigated aristocratic kinship and domestic relations in eighteenth-century England, and John R. Gillis, whose survey of marriage in England from 1600 to the present day concentrated on the plebeian experience, both identified the eighteenth century as a period of increasing warmth in family relationships.

Linda Pollock is an advocate of continuity, arguing that parents have always recognised children as in need of special care and protection and instruction, a view recently underwritten by Keith Thomas who has, however, stressed shifts in the methods employed. Alan Macfarlane has argued that a distinctive individualism characterised English behaviour as far back into the Middle Ages as records allow researchers to reach. This is a controversial thesis. Paul Monod posed the question:

Is selection of a spouse 'individualistic' if it takes place within determined social, economic and political boundaries and has to win the approval of parents, friends and community?

and answered himself in the negative. Yet, as Monod's own work indicates, the determination to marry like people or not at all was a prescription for 'gradual extinction'.

In a paper published in 1986, Michael Anderson set an agenda for work on the history of the family:

We need to know much more about the conditions under which households were established, about the minimum resources which had to be obtained before marriage at different periods, and how they were obtained (for example, the relative importance of inheritance, loans and savings from earnings); about courtship and matchmaking, and the role of sex in precipitating or retarding movement into matrimony; about the situations under which remarriages occurred and about the changes in the distribution of ages at marriage. We need, if possible, to explore how these factors varied regionally, occupationally and by socioeconomic circumstances.

It is a checklist well worth bearing in mind.

THE APPROACH ADOPTED IN THIS BOOK

My sympathies lie with those historians who believe that family relationships were governed by customs and practices resistant to change. In this survey I stress the part played by rank, gender and occupation in determining these obligations. Hierarchy pervaded all aspects of life. Until late in the eighteenth century, at formal meals, the host and hostess sat at opposite ends of the table, flanked respectively by their male and female guests ranked in strict order of precedence. With the spread of the fashion for 'promiscuous seating', ladies and gentlemen alternated round the table. The order of service was unaffected: ladies were 'served in order, according to their rank or age, and after, the gentlemen in the same manner'. Ladies who knitted took the opportunity to display the delicacy of their fingers; the priority of working knitters was to produce garments as fast as possible. Until 1962 cricket scoreboards distinguished between the amateur 'gentleman' and the professional 'player'. Railway workers, like their passengers, were divided into three classes.

The precise shape of English society is difficult to discern. P. N. Furbank observed that the seating plan of the parish church at Myddle in Shropshire in 1700, which contemporaries would have recognised as a mirror of the community's social structure, looked 'extremely unlike a ladder, and more like a rather intricate piece of knitting'. Knitted fabric is, I think, a useful metaphor, not just for Myddle, but for English society as a whole. Strands of kinship connected people apparently ranks apart. Samuel Pepys (b.1633) was the son of a London tailor and a former laundress. The relatives he mentioned in his diary of the 1660s range from the Earl of Sandwich to an itinerant musician who scraped a living with his fiddle. Pepys had kin who were lawyers and kin who were farmers. He owed his entry to royal service, and thus ultimately his wealth, to Sandwich's patronage, and, in his turn, he patronised his humbler relatives. He bought his mousetraps from a kinsman and, when his busking cousin's fiddle broke, it was to the affluent, music-loving Pepys that he looked for a replacement.

Pepys's diary is an exceptionally rich source, but the kind of wide-ranging network of active kinship that it records was probably not uncommon in the seventeenth century. Margaret Spufford has plotted the contrasting fortunes of the descendants of Lawrence Butler, alias Johnson, and his wife Johan who farmed in Orwell in Cambridgeshire. Having set his three sons – John, Henry and Nicholas – up with land, Lawrence died in 1558. John died ten years after his father, leaving four sons, known as the Johnsons; their childless uncle Henry (d.1594) left them his land. Nevertheless, this branch of the family remained small farmers. Lawrence's remaining son, Nicholas (d.1601), was an ambitious man. He sent his eldest son to study law at Gray's Inn, endowed all five of his sons, the Butlers, with land and married his daughters well. Nicholas owned the status symbols of the rich Elizabethan farmer – silver spoons and a great gilt cup. His son Thomas (d.1622) also prospered. He acquired land, educated his sole surviving son at Cambridge University and left substantial dowries to his daughters. Neville married an heiress, sold his land in Orwell and set himself up as a landed gentleman in another part of the county. Until his removal the Johnsons and the Butlers, 'the relatively humble and the very prosperous sides of the family' remained in close touch.

> Nicholas Johnson, the churchwarden who died in 1627, . . . acted as rent-collector for his highly successful cousin Thomas Butler, the lawyer, and witnessed his will. Nicholas's brother Richard's son, another Nicholas, in turn acted as witness to wills along with his cousin Neville Butler. Neville, another highly successful man, witnessed Nicholas's own will when he died in 1649 . . . The connection was maintained, therefore, from the time John Johnson died leaving his brother Nicholas Butler overseer of his will and young children in 1568, right through until 1649, and probably

until Neville bought the priory lands of Barnwell, and removed from Orwell.

Sir Anthony Wagner drew attention to the dramatically divergent fortunes of the descendants of the four brothers of Jane Austen (b.1775). James, a clergyman like his father, founded a line in which parsons and academics predominated. Edward inherited his uncle's estates, adopted his surname, and established a line of country landowners. Francis and Charles both went into the navy. Admiral Francis Austen's descendants were professional men. Like John Johnson, Admiral Charles's son died prematurely, his son Charles John was a telegraphist, and his grandsons, a bricklayer, a grocer's assistant and a printer. In the nineteenth century contact between 'the relatively humble and the very prosperous sides of the family' was unlikely to be close. The gulf between Beatrice Webb (b. 1858), brought up as a southern young lady, and her working-class Lancashire cousins was judged unbridgeable; she visited them incognito.

As the histories of the Butlers and the Austens suggest, there was continuous traffic as individual men and women and families moved across the debatable territory which separated rank from rank. The status of groups connected by vocation rather than blood also shifted: for example, the prestige of medical practitioners was significantly enhanced between 1540 and 1920.

For reasons that are often obscure, individual men and women deviated from the expected codes of behaviour. Ralph Sadler (b.1507), an otherwise canny servant of Tudor monarchs, married an uneducated woman of mean birth who was rumoured to have made her living as a washerwoman. The painter John Morland (b.1763) abandoned his claim to a baronetcy, coldshouldered potential patrons, including the Prince of Wales, and fraternised with fish porters from Billingsgate. Privilege could be forfeited. When Edith Lanchester (b.1873) set up home with a working-class Irishman she discovered that there was one law for the propertied and another for the poor: the authorities hounded her for attempting to exercise a middle-class prerogative and educate her daughter at home. Most children learned 'their place' in the social order. Anne Garnett, the daughter of a middle-class literary couple, and Edith Stephens, a farmworker's daughter, played together during the Great War. They looked forward to an adult relationship in which Anne would be the lady and Edith her maid. My chief concern is with those who conformed.

As for sources, I have to admit to a bias towards personal testimony, to images in words and pictures of the actors: daughters and sons, brothers and sisters, husbands and wives, mothers and fathers, as they saw themselves.

12

NOW READ ON

Michael Anderson: *Approaches to the History of the Western Family, 1500–1914* (London: Macmillan, 1980).

Michael Anderson: *Family Structure in Nineteenth-century Lancashire* (Cambridge: Cambridge University Press, 1971).

English Family Life, 1576–1716: An Anthology from Diaries, edited by Ralph Houlbrooke (Oxford: Blackwell, 1988).

John Gillis: *For Better, for Worse: British Marriages, 1600 to the Present* (New York, Oxford University Press, 1985).

Ralph Houlbrooke: *The English Family 1450–1700* (London: Longman, 1984).

Peter Laslett: *The World We Have Lost Further Explored* (London: Methuen, third edition, 1983).

Alan Macfarlane: *The Family Life of Ralph Josselin a Seventeenth-Century Clergyman: An Essay in Historical Anthropology* (Cambridge: Cambridge University Press, 1970).

Alan Macfarlane: *Marriage and Love in England: Modes of Reproduction, 1300–1840* (Oxford: Blackwell, 1986).

Linda A. Pollock: *Forgotten Children: Parent–Child Relations from 1500 to 1900* (Cambridge: Cambridge University Press, 1983).

Lawrence Stone: *The Family, Sex and Marriage in England, 1500–1800* (London: Weidenfeld and Nicolson, 1977; London: Penguin, 1979).

Keith Thomas: 'Children in Early Modern Europe' in *Children and Their Books: A Celebration of the Work of Iona and Peter Opie*, edited by Gillian Avery and Julia Briggs (Oxford: Clarendon Press, 1988).

Randolph Trumbach: *The Rise of the Egalitarian Family; Aristocratic Kinship and Domestic Relations in Eighteenth-century England* (New York: Academic Press, 1978).

2

ENGLAND 1540–1920

Our own experience tells us that families don't exist in a vacuum. Nor did they in the past. Births, marriages and deaths, the vital events which punctuate and define family life, are and were influenced by biological, social and economic forces. The English environment in 1540 was very different from the English environment in 1920. This chapter plots the long, halting and patchy processes of change.

The population grew, at an uneven pace, from around two and a half million in 1520 to something like four million in 1600 and to eight and a half million at the time of the first national Census in 1801. By 1901 the population of England and Wales was about 32.5 million. The poor always far outnumbered the prosperous. The proportion of English people living in towns with a population of at least 5,000 grew from something like one in twelve at the end of the sixteenth century to around one in four two hundred years later. The list of big Tudor towns reads like a heritage trail: Bury St Edmunds, Cambridge, Canterbury, Chester, Colchester, Exeter, King's Lynn, London, Oxford, Salisbury, Shrewsbury, Worcester and York all appear on it. In the eighteenth century these ancient centres, London apart, were overtaken by upstarts. In 1801 Manchester, with a population in the region of 89,000, Liverpool (83,000) and Birmingham (74,000) occupied second, third and fourth places. By 1901 there were more than seventy towns with a population of over 50,000; the population of Greater London topped six and a half million.

By the beginning of the twentieth century there was a mass demand for goods and foodstuffs which had been rare or quite unknown in Tudor England. All the same, until the nineteenth century, most English households continued to depend on naked flames for heat and light; water came from springs, wells or the water carrier who sold his wares from door to door. Cereals, consumed as bread, porridge or in soup, formed the staple diet of the poor. Garments were handsewn from fabric handwoven from handspun yarn. Commercially-produced sanitary towels first became available in 1880. This was a make-do-and-mend society, a society in which, when they were discarded, household goods and clothing were handed down and leftover food was passed on to servants or needier neighbours. The physical appearance of the Edwardian poor would not have surprised a time traveller from Tudor England; under their cast-off clothes which 'fitted where they touched', they were likely to be malnourished. Their smell offended the privileged. The national taste for sugar, acquired before 1700, probably meant their teeth were worse than their sixteenth-century predecessors'.

1485–1642:
THE TUDORS AND THE EARLY STUARTS

The Tudors had grave difficulties in securing the succession to the throne. Henry VII's heir Arthur died before him. His younger son Henry, king from 1509 to 1547, inherited. By the middle of the 1520s it was apparent that his marriage was, from the point of view of the succession, a failure. There is a powerful link between Henry VIII's determination to try his luck in fathering a son on another queen and the severing of relations between England and Rome. The dynastic crisis of the 1520s and 1530s coincided with the emergence of the Lutheran movement in Germany. The king's dispute with the Pope prompted Lutheran sympathisers in England to advance their cause, but with caution – they were wary of the king's violent temper and religious conservatism. Initially, the English Reformation was justified in imperial rather than theological terms.

Christianity coexisted with other beliefs. Astrological readings dictated the timing of coronations; aristocrats' marriages took place when planetary influences were at their most propitious. Most ordinary English people accepted that there were 'cunning' men and women who could harness supernatural forces for good or ill. To the sophisticated, theology and demonology were twin aspects of an absorbing study. Sceptics were rare. England was spared the horror of the witch hunts which blighted other parts of Europe; nevertheless, witchcraft was a capital offence and sharp-tongued women found guilty of ill-wishing their neighbours on what, to us, would appear to be the flimsiest of circumstantial evidence were condemned to death. The assumption of women's capacity for wickedness, which lay behind this outbreak, was an inheritance from the ancient world. The dreadful consequences of Adam's failure to discipline his mate were familiar to readers and hearers of the Bible. Belief in female frailty justified patriarchy and severely restricted women's options.

The Tudor elite came to regard classical learning and the cultivation of the ancient Roman virtues of prudence and sobriety as appropriate

15

complements to the chivalric accomplishments of horsemanship and courtly manners which had marked their predecessors. For boys of less privileged birth, Latin learned at Grammar School served as a passport to honourable employment in church and state. The transformation of the Church had important social effects: the dissolution of religious communities destroyed an approved alternative to family life, and the sanctioning of clerical marriage brought into being a large number of households headed by men well placed to confer on their sons the scarce skills of reading and writing in English and Latin. Informed estimates suggest that by 1640 only one labouring man in ten and one in ten of all women were literate in English.

Henry VIII reigned over the sparsely populated southern portion of a small and underdeveloped island off the coast of Europe. In Tudor and early Stuart England birth and death rates both ran high. The outer parishes of London and the marshlands were particularly unhealthy. In some years in the 1550s, when severe epidemics swept the country, deaths outran births across the nation. People married later and died much younger, on average, than we do today; throughout the period many marriages were second marriages. But, overall, the English population rose.

The growing numbers of mouths to feed and the sale of monastic lands helped to make the sixteenth and early seventeenth centuries an era of losers and winners in the agricultural community. Many of those who farmed on a small scale lacked the reserves to survive a series of bad years and found themselves forced out of their tenancies. As the labouring population increased, wages fell. Young men, unable to find work at home, chanced their luck in the growing towns: England resounded to the tramping feet of the displaced. To the settled population, these masterless vagrants represented a threat which had to be contained by harsh measures. There was no paid police force; no regular army; gaols were reserved for the most potent enemies of the state, alleged traitors and those accused of the heinous crime of witchcraft. For vagrancy corporal punishments – death, mutilation and flogging were decreed.

Drawing on the expertise of engineers from the Low Countries, landowners reclaimed wetlands, destroying the livelihood of the fen-men who supported themselves by fishing and wildfowling and cutting peat turves and rushes. Bigger farmers consolidated their holdings. The most successful acquired the means to live like gentlemen: to purchase the services of schoolmasters, lawyers and medical practitioners; to rebuild their homes with glazed windows, staircases, ceilings and other newfangled comforts; and to fit them out with sideboards to display silver spoons and silver gilt cups.

Technology was primitive. Wind and watermills were the biggest

16

machines, the muscles of men, women and draught animals were the prime sources of power. It was the ingenuity of Dutch and German technicians that produced new devices like the printing press, which crossed the Channel in the 1480s. And in the first half of the sixteenth century it was on German, Italian and Spanish craftsmen that the luxury end of the English market depended for its tennis balls, hawks' bells, buttons, playing cards, looking and drinking glasses. Knives, nails, needles and paper were also listed among imports passing through the port of London in 1559. In the late sixteenth and early seventeenth century schemes to satisfy the domestic market for these and other novelties proliferated. Many poor families were able to boost their income by stocking-knitting, lacemaking and other handicrafts, which required a minimal investment in raw materials and tools. A timber famine, created by the increased demand for fuel and building materials, obliged domestic consumers and manufacturers to make more use of coal. The changeover from wood presented householders and brewers with few problems but bakers, potters and metalworkers had to overcome technical problems and the solutions took many decades to achieve.

Between 1540 and 1640 road haulage was slow and expensive. The pedlar carried small items on his back. Livestock was driven to market. Bulky essentials were conveyed by water: England's long coastline and extensive network of navigable rivers made it feasible to distribute coal and the homegrown and imported cereals which secured England's early escape from the horrors of widespread starvation. Nevertheless, chronic malnutrition and the sharp pangs of unsatisfied hunger were widely experienced well into the twentieth century.

In the wake of Italian, Portuguese and Spanish navigators, Tudor merchant ships struck out for all points of the compass. By 1600, trading companies had been set up to exploit opportunities in Muscovy, the Mediterranean, Africa and the East. Before the Civil War England had colonial toeholds in India as well as in North America and the Caribbean. These overseas possessions were treated as sources of raw materials, as captive markets for English manufactures, as mission fields and as dumping grounds for undesirables.

1642–1714:
THE CIVIL WAR AND COMMONWEALTH, THE RESTORATION AND THE LATER STUARTS

Three hundred and fifty years after its outbreak the Civil War is still a hotly debated episode. Many people instinctively side with King or Parliament. Political radicals trace their roots back to the Levellers and Diggers who challenged the traditional structure of society. At this distance, it is difficult to assess the meaning of the crisis of the mid-seventeenth century to those who lived through it. Baptists, Congregationalists and Quakers were among those who refused to conform when the Anglican church was restored along with the Crown in 1660. Until the nineteenth century dissenters were, like Catholics, excluded from government office and from higher education. It was not, therefore, uncommon for members of prosperous and socially ambitious families to enter or re-enter the Anglican fold.

Latin-educated men increasingly used a vocabulary derived from classical roots which was barely intelligible to those who could only speak and read and write English. The tendency to bracket these less learned men with women reflects social and intellectual chauvinism. As yet no satisfactory dictionaries had been compiled to bridge the linguistic gap. The continuing desire to cultivate Roman virtues led a section of the ruling elite to reject frivolity. Laughing was equated with other lapses in bodily control like belching and farting. Traditional names for plants, animals and landmarks were deemed too crude for polite use.

New optical instruments like microscopes and telescopes opened privileged male eyes to formerly invisible worlds. Experiment promoted a confidence that the world was subject to natural laws, that creation could be classified, and that the forces of nature could be controlled. Once the mysteries of the universe had been reduced to the predictable, sophisticated men came to perceive God less as a vigilant father, intervening to chastise, reward and protect his children, and more as an experimental scientist monitoring his creation. In this climate a discreet hesitation about the operation of satanic forces became permissible. Without openly questioning the existence of witches, magistrates and judges began to demand evidence of guilt which would stand up to objective scrutiny. By the beginning of the eighteenth century witches were no longer brought before the bench and those who tried to take the law into their own hands ran the risk of prosecution.

While England remained a predominantly rural society, urban attractions increased. In his diary Samuel Pepys recorded the political, social and cultural excitement of life in Restoration London. One of his great setpieces describes the heroic struggle to contain the Great Fire which raged through London in 1666 and cleared the way for the reconstruction of the city in the new 'classical' taste epitomised by the Wren churches. London's experience was not unique: provincial towns were frequently rebuilt in stone and brick after fires had swept away the old environment of thatch and timber frames. Country landowners had come to town on private and public business since the Middle Ages. Now improvements in the comfort and efficiency of coach travel encouraged them to bring their wives and daughters and promoted the growth of social seasons in London, in regional capitals like York and Norwich, and in developing resort towns like Bath. Men and women divided by rank in private life mingled in such public spaces as assembly rooms.

Wealthy urban householders proved to be adventurous and competitive spenders and the consumption of 'unnecessary', luxury goods increased in consequence. Pepys's diary reveals the investment that prosperous Londoners were prepared to make to remain at the forefront of fashion. The Pepyses were forever redecorating and re-equipping their apartments. They entertained lavishly, hiring cooks and specialists to dress their tables with elaborate folded napery. Inventories of the household goods of other affluent consumers in late Stuart and early Georgian London log the acquisition of novelties like upholstered seat furniture, barometers and the apparatus associated with the consumption of the newly fashionable coffee and tea, the first hot drinks to come into vogue.

1714–1837:
THE FIRST FOUR GEORGES

By 1714 the most remote and inaccessible parts of the country had been incorporated into the national economy: England was secured against even localised famine. Nevertheless, for most of the period the old-fashioned patterns of birth and death persisted. Conceptions peaked in the spring, burials reflected the toll taken by hard weather in the winter and the late summer incidence of dysentery. A very high proportion of babies died. In spite of this, the population continued to rise and, towards 1800, the gap between births and deaths widened, marking the end of the old demographic regime. Thomas Malthus, writing in the 1790s, a period of particular deprivation for the labouring poor, drew attention to the dangers of unrestricted population growth and argued the case for celibacy, late marriage and abstinence, that most reliable of contraceptives.

In agriculture and industry change was slower, patchier and deeper-rooted than the conventional language of 'revolution' implies. When Daniel Defoe toured England in the 1720s he noted local specialities still familiar today: Norfolk turkeys, Cheshire cheeses and Devon cider among them. Judging by the portraits that farmers commissioned of their prize beasts, size seems to have been the improvers' first priority but, over time, the stockbreeders' objectives were refined. Selection produced breeds of horses adapted for patient, heavy work with the plough; for the power, speed and stamina demanded by the coaching trade; and for the sheer pace needed on the race course. Agriculturalists promoted what they regarded as good practice with missionary zeal.

Prosperous farmers, infected with a taste for gentility, began to distance themselves from their workforce. They brought their sons up as gentlemen and made their daughters young ladies. They preferred to eat apart from their employees and turned increasingly to workers hired by the day. Southern field labourers were worse paid and, existing on bought bread and tea, worse fed than their counterparts in the north. The first moves to mechanise such tasks as threshing, which gave employment in the harsh winter season, provoked a bitter reaction in the 1830s. The threatening letters sent by men for whom the pen was an unfamiliar tool are barely articulate cries of distress.

More fortunate English households developed brand loyalties. Porter proved to be a fountain of prosperity for Truman's and Whitbread's breweries in London and for Worthington's in Burton-on-Trent. Schweppes's mineral waters, Addis's brushes, Pears' soap and Wedgwood's pottery were all Georgian success stories. In the quest for profit, craft skills were undermined. Potters, who had served their time as apprentices, saw their jobs taken over by a production line of small children. In theory, industrial workers had to submit to a new discipline, the tyranny of the clock. They were roused from their beds by knockers up; their day was regulated by bells and hooters. Those who refused to conform were liable to be fined or sacked. In practice, even Josiah Wedgwood (b.1730), who aimed to turn his men into animated machines, was forced to admit that no power on earth could prevent his hands from taking a day off to go to the fair.

Before the end of the eighteenth century, artificial waterways linked the Mersey, the Severn, the Trent and the Thames. As output increased, industry made its mark on the landscape. Wind and watermills had been familiar for hundreds of years; now new industrial features began to appear. By 1700 metalworking furnaces in the Shropshire valley of Coalbrookdale were serving as an image of hell. The first steam-powered cotton-spinning machines came in at the end of the century. The tendency to regional specialisation which was already apparent in agriculture developed in industry in exaggerated form. Cotton manufacturing was concentrated in Lancashire; east of the Pennines, Yorkshire produced woollens and mixed-fibre worsteds. As textile production expanded in the north, looms in traditional clothmaking areas like East Anglia and the West Country were put out of action. Precision engineering became a specialism of the old metalworking districts of the West Midlands. The earthenware manufacturing district of Staffordshire became known as 'the Potteries'.

1837–1911:
THE VICTORIAN AND EDWARDIAN PERIOD

During Victoria's exceptionally long reign England was transformed almost beyond recognition. The population rose and was redistributed to an unprecedented degree. In 1837 the average Englishman was a farm labourer, the average Englishwoman worked as a domestic servant until she married. The balance between rural and urban was to shift dramatically in favour of the towns. Home produce faced the challenge of imported cereals and chilled meat, butter and cheese. The mechanisation of arable farming eroded the field labourers' livelihood and encouraged migration to the towns and across the water to North America, Canada and the Antipodes. The 1870s were perhaps landowners' 'last decade of . . . undisputed and comfortable rule'. The agricultural depression created openings for newly rich men but the acquisition of great tracts of farmland had lost its appeal.

The marks made by labouring brides and grooms in the 1830s, 1840s and early 1850s indicate the persistence of illiteracy: only about a third of marriages were between partners capable of signing the register. But for the new uniformed public servants who became familiar figures in the later decades of the nineteenth century – railway officials, policemen and postmen – reading and writing were essential qualifications. In the latter part of the century, opportunities to obtain employment as a clerk, a schoolteacher or a superior shop assistant increased. All the same, at the turn of the century manual workers still heavily outnumbered penpushers and more girls went into domestic service than any other occupation.

The railways played a big part in the reshaping of everyday life: the look of the country was profoundly altered; distances shrank. Railway locomotives brought steam power into the public domain. The railway station and the railway hotel were new features of the built environment; some termini were edifices of cathedral-like grandeur. Monumental railway bridges and viaducts rivalled the achievements of Roman military engineers. Before the railway age most buildings had been constructed from what lay to hand. The cost of hauling exotic materials ensured that their use was confined to churches, public buildings and the dwellings of the rich: structures designed to proclaim power, wealth and status. Goods trains carried the bricks and Welsh slates which displaced local materials. By 1900 hardly a pigsty wall was built in the old way. Thanks to the train, public executions became national spectacles – in April 1849 the Eastern Counties Railway Company laid on a train to take trippers from London to Norwich to the execution of the murderer James Rush. The Highlands of Scotland became a playground of the rich; Blackpool became the holiday destination of Lancashire mill workers.

The first stage of the London Underground opened in 1863. Electric trams appeared in Blackpool in 1886. The still familiar safety bicycle came in in the 1880s. The motor car established itself as a reliable means of transport for the privileged in the early years of the twentieth century.

21

At sea, steam displaced sail. In 1909 Bleriot flew the Channel. The Great War was to be the first fought on land, on and under the sea, and in the air.

In 1840 Rowland Hill introduced the penny post, slashing the cost of communicating with distant friends and relatives. By 1900 the picture postcard, scenic, sentimental, coy or vulgarly comic, enabled correspondents to express their feelings in images as well as words. By 1910 there were more than half a million telephone subscribers – though the level of use remained low. The 707 survivors of the Titanic disaster in 1912 owed their lives to the wireless messages which brought the Carpathia to their rescue.

Great provincial cities came into their own. City fathers demonstrated their pride in the prosperity they had created by commissioning town halls, monuments to commerce, like the Bradford Wool Exchange; and, those temples to rational recreation, the library, the museum-and-art-gallery and the public park, complete with arboretum, a living encyclopaedia of exotic trees.

In the eighteenth century opportunities to acquire consumer goods were restricted. Well-off Victorians occupied houses cluttered with objects purchased from commercial warehouses or worked at home by their wives and daughters; their infants were wheeled out to take the air in perambulators; their kitchens were equipped with gadgets which minced, chopped, cored and peeled – the time they saved was offset by the time taken to clean them after use. Mass-produced pianos graced the parlours of clerks and skilled manual workers. As photographs of working-class interiors indicate, by the end of the century cheap pressed glass, garishly painted and crudely printed pottery and coloured reproductions of paintings which manufacturers used to promote their soap, decorated the homes of the very poor. At this social level ornament served as an ironic commentary on deprivation. These households still lacked the wherewithal (the table, chairs, dishes, knives, forks and spoons) to serve a family meal. Children still went barefoot out of doors.

In new dwellings running water and flushing lavatories became standard utilities. Some of those with well-staffed households manifested an attachment to the hip-bath and, perhaps more surprisingly, the earth-closet. Deene Park in Northamptonshire had no bathroom until after 1945 when modern plumbing was installed at the insistence of the son of the house. First gas and then electricity, safer and more convenient sources of heat, light and power than the naked flames they replaced, became available to more privileged groups of consumers. Progress was slow – only one house in eight had electric light by 1921. Poor families were worst off, as always.

The pace of change promoted spiritual doubts and divisions. Anglicans lost their monopoly of official posts in 1828; in 1837 civilian registrars assumed responsibility for records of birth, marriage and death. The new University of London gave dissenters access to higher education. For 300 years taking Anglican orders had been a natural step for men who wished to pursue a scholarly, academic or literary career: by the 1870s this was no longer the case. The established church faced challenges at a more popular level too. Of the churches, only the Roman Catholic, which responded with great vigour to the challenge of Irish immigration, successfully addressed the needs of a new urban population. The shock tactics of the Salvation Army, founded in 1870, reached communities which less assertive missioners failed to penetrate. But for many, God's battalions were less powerful reminders of the wages of sin than the novel figure of authority – the police constable on his beat.

Some sought refuge in a pre-industrial ideal. Associations were formed to preserve the remnants of the past ways of life: the commons (1865), ancient buildings (1877) and footpaths (1884). Writers celebrated disappearing crafts and 'folkways'. In *Old West Surrey*, published in 1904, Gertrude Jekyll (b.1843) described a pocket of traditional life close to London. A rich eccentric created a 'practically brand-new . . . little Surrey hamlet' at Upper Woodcote. There a friendly commentator noted 'the musical ring of the blacksmith's anvil' from the forge beneath the spreading chestnut tree, the 'old time air' of the parlour of the village inn and the geese on the green. Artistic craftworkers supplied handmade furnishing, table ware and jewellery to those members of the upper and middle classes who scorned the mass-produced. The Cottage Farm Series, published between 1906 and 1909, was aimed at 'those who dream of a "cottage and a bit of land some day" '. Beatrix Potter (b.1866), who used the profits from her books to buy land in the Lake District, was one of the few in a position to translate fantasy into reality. She gloried in the acquisition of new down-to-earth skills, became an expert breeder of Herdwick sheep and, in 1930, first woman President of the Breed Society. A visitor recalled a 'strong', 'offensive' and 'strange pungent smell' which seeped into her living room from sheep skins hung up to cure. A letter she wrote in 1916 described a daily routine which a seventeenth-century farmwife would have found familiar:

I have poultry, orchard, flower garden, vegetables . . . help with the heavy digging, cooking with the girl's assistance. Mrs C, I and the girl all help with the hay, and I single the turnips when I can find the time.

THE GREAT WAR

Peter Levi has preserved a description of the start of the battle of the Somme which he heard in The Fox at Chipping Norton from an old man who had been there. 'It was beautiful, he said, miles and miles of guns and carriages perfectly in line, and brasses shining, all the horses perfectly groomed, like the Oxfordshire Show, then it started.' It is the comparison with the County Agricultural Show, a red letter day in the countryman's uneventful pre-war calendar, that makes this image peculiarly powerful.

Barabara Wootton (b.1897) recalled her experience on the home front. Her chief memory was the 'endless succession of memorial services in college chapels or Cambridge churches'. Brought up in a circle in which 'very occasionally women perhaps might weep – but grown men never' she was profoundly disturbed by the 'unashamed public grief' of 'distinguished professors and famous men' who had lost sons.

With men away, women took on their work. Photographs in the archives of the Imperial War Museum demonstrate their contributions to the war effort. Some stepped in to keep a job open or a business going: in Kent, Rosanna Forster carried on her husband's trade as a chimney sweep; in Norfolk the towncrier and official billposter of Thetford was succeeded by his daughter. This sort of substitution was the standard response to family crises. Now, in the national emergency, members of the Women's Land Army drove plough horses. Shipyards and munitions works took the unprecedented step of employing women as lathe operators, welders and riveters. Members of the Women's Auxiliary Air Force served as mechanics; civilian women built wooden aircraft propellers. On the railways, which had been slow to employ women in any capacity, there were signalwomen and female porters, guards and carriage cleaners. Women worked as sandblasters and 'on the black-stuff', spreading tar. The overwhelming majority of these women returned to traditional female roles after the war was over. The great gulf which separated the experience of men and women is a powerful continuity across the centuries which separate the Reformation and the Great War.

The cemeteries and memorials erected by towns and villages, schools and colleges and companies acknowledge those who fell (the portico of Waterloo Station is a spectacular example). The spectre of the 'unreturning army' haunted the survivors into old age. According to legend, only thirty-one 'thankful villages' welcomed all their serving men safe home in 1918; the small Lancashire town of Accrington saw almost a whole generation of 'pals' wiped out. Casualties among public school men and members of the ancient universities were disproportionately high. Forty-seven peers lost their eldest sons in the first year of the War and the editorial staff of *Debrett's Peerage* could not keep abreast with the slaughter. The deaths of heirs weakened the aristocracy's already slackening grip on the reins of power. The income of professional men dropped during the War and, when it ended, their self-esteem suffered a further blow when the lawyers admitted their first female colleagues.

The Great War marked the end of an epoch. The old 'table of precedence' was not restored. Cinema and, soon after the War, radio were to create a national culture accessible to all, regardless of gender, class or education. The pace at which formerly 'unnecessary' goods became commonplace accelerated – the wireless is a case in point.

In 1925 Alfred Wallis (b.1855) began to paint the boats, lighthouses and harbours which he had known as a fisherman. He did not paint from life:

> What i do mosley is what use to be out of my own memery what we may never see again as Thing are altered all To gether Ther is nothin what Ever do not look like what it was.

He spoke for England.

THE FAMILY 1540–1920

Through all the profound changes which occurred between the Reformation and the Great War the family remained a dominant institution: the chief provider of care, training and discipline for the frail, the young and the irresponsible. It was an enterprise which united the dead, the living and the yet unborn. The family's welfare took precedence over the individual interests of its members, duty was rated higher than the pursuit of happiness. From birth an individual's prospects depended on gender and the wealth and status of parents.

Before marriage the primary duty was to parents and siblings; after marriage it was to spouse and children, though the old obligations were not extinguished and new obligations were acquired. The extent of family networks reflected their members' resources. It was worth making an effort to maintain contact with quite remote kin who had wealth or influence; the very poor might have difficulty in listing their brothers and sisters. Naturally, it was easier to give or receive help when relatives were close at hand but distance did not dissolve kinship ties and sometimes increased opportunities to offer assistance. Elizabethan youths who went to London as apprentices looked out for suitable positions for their sisters. When they needed extra hands, nineteenth-century factory masters recruited the relatives of existing workers. Men and women who settled in the colonies acted as emigration agents for kin in the 'old country'.

THE LIFE CYCLE

In Tudor England birth was a domestic event, managed by women without formal training. Mother and child were cared for and supported by female kin and neighbours. Although male midwives appeared in the seventeenth century and gradually displaced women from the more lucrative end of the business, births continued to take place at home and the old-style female practitioner was still attending poor women in childbed in Edwardian England. Labour pains were traditionally perceived as one of the penalties paid by women as daughters of Eve, for her part in persuading Adam to surrender to the serpent. Chloroform became available to private patients in the late 1840s. Queen Victoria, Mrs Charles Darwin and Mrs Charles Dickens were among the first women to benefit from its use. Darwin (b.1809), who had observed his wife in labour, described chloroform as 'the grandest and most blessed of discoveries'. Access to obstetric care was determined by geography as well as financial circumstances. In 1627 Grace Wallington, wife of a London woodturner, was attended by Peter II Chamberlen, a member of the dynasty of male midwives who developed the technique of forceps delivery. Two and a half centuries later, in 1874, Winston Churchill, heir presumptive to the Duke of Marlborough, was delivered by the local Woodstock doctor because the London and the Oxford practitioners were unable to reach Blenheim Palace in time. Further into the country, at Charlecote in Warwickshire, at the end of the nineteenth century, the aristocratic Mrs Lucy had twice to rely on the assistance of her mother-in-law; in this district the local veterinary surgeon doubled as obstetrician.

The anatomy of the pregnant human female was described in the middle of the eighteenth century. George Stubbs's earliest prints were produced to illustrate John Burton's *Essay towards a Complete New System of Midwifery Theoretical and Practical*, published in 1751. Reproductive physiology remained poorly understood even by professional medical men into the nineteenth century. Lay people depended on folk wisdom passed on by word of mouth or acquired from *Aristotle's Masterpiece*, a popular and evidently widely read guide to procreation and pregnancy which was in print before the end of the seventeenth century. In 1900 there were at least four variants in circulation.

Births were spaced and limited by late weaning, by abstinence (sometimes practised to a degree we might consider heroic), by withdrawal, by the use of drugs and instruments to prevent conception or terminate an unwanted pregnancy and, to an unknowable extent, by abandonment and infanticide. The rapid rate of reproduction which characterised some aristocratic unions (which are inevitably the best documented) suggests that some families were quite unplanned.

Lactation depresses fertility, and so prolonged breastfeeding helped nursing mothers to space pregnancies. Seventeenth-century herbals like Parkinson's *Theatrum Botanicum* contain information about substances which could be employed to procure barrenness or 'to bring on' a late period. Cases in the Church courts, which dealt with those accused of sexual misconduct, confirm that infusions of savin and 'papers of spice' were indeed popularly recognised means of controlling fertility in the seventeenth century. Commercially-produced remedies for 'female stoppages' were among the patent medicines obtainable by post in Victorian England. Sheaths made of fish and animal membranes were being sold as preventives against the spread of sexually-transmitted diseases by the time of the Civil War but they seem not to have been widely used for contraceptive purposes. Rubber condoms and dia-phragms became available, to those who could afford to pay for private medical consultation, in the 1880s. For fear that it would encourage promiscuity, professional contraceptive advice was denied to the mass of the poor. It was probably not until the Great War that large numbers of working-class men encountered the sheath.

Inevitably, some births were unwelcome. Charles Dickens probably spoke for many when he greeted the arrival of his seventh son and ninth surviving child in 1852 with the observation that 'on the whole I could have dispensed with him'. Edward Bulwer Lytton Dickens, 'Plorn', as he was known, became a favourite. Analyses linking the size and shape of late Victorian families with the occupation of their heads lend weight to the argument that the trend to systematic family planning was set by middle-class couples of restricted means who were anxious to endow their sons with an education which would enable them to maintain or enhance their position. Decisions about the number of sons they could hope to launch and the means of contraception may well have been taken jointly by husband and wife: it is unlikely that wives acted unilaterally. The poor were much slower to limit their families.

The penalties paid by the mothers of illegitimate children encouraged them to conceal their births. Many babies were abandoned – Thomas Coram (b.1668) was moved to endow the Foundling Hospital, which opened in 1741, by the sight of dead and dying infants abandoned on the streets and dung heaps of London. Other unwanted children were dumped on 'baby farmers', a step which amounted to infanticide. The Infant Life Protection Act was passed in 1872 following the trial of Margaret Waters who was convicted of killing babies in her charge; a quarter of a century later further horrifying revelations led to a new, tougher Act to regulate the activities of paid foster parents.

Until the middle of the eighteenth century medical opinion favoured swaddling. Babies were tightly bandaged to keep them warm and help them to grow straight – it was not realised that rickets, which afflicted many children, was caused by calcium deficiency. Until the late nineteenth century, an infant not suckled by his mother or a wetnurse had a poor chance of life. Donkey's milk, the preferred alternative to human breastmilk, was expensive and not readily available; unpasteurised and unrefrigerated milk was alive with bacteria; it was extremely difficult to clean feeding bottles. In spite of this persistent problem, artificial milk became popular with parents who were impressed by its 'scientific' credentials towards the end of Victoria's reign. Weaning from the breast was a worrying episode; those who could afford it might introduce expensive, and sometimes unsuitable, items of diet, including fortified wine, to 'strengthen' the child. The real risks stemmed from the poor standards of hygiene, which reflected circumstances rather than lack of care. Utensils were often dirty and food tainted, especially in hot weather; many young children succumbed to dysentery in the summer.

Bad or inadequate feeding was only one cause of the high rate of child mortality. Many now rare or trivial infections were fatal. The first major preventive became available when vaccination against smallpox was introduced in the first decade of the nineteenth century. Edward Jenner (b.1749), whose research made this breakthrough possible, was handsomely rewarded by a grateful nation. In the years immediately before the Great War infant mortality dropped sharply, but even in 1913 nearly eleven out of every thousand babies born died very young. In consequence parents lived in the expectation of their children's deaths. Writing in 1895, Leslie Stephen (b.1832), a member of the economically-privileged upper middle class, with the means to feed and clothe and shelter his children and pay their doctor's bills, suspected that his second wife, who had had seven children, was 'rather unusual' in rearing them all.

The young baby's hold on life was precarious, its personality indistinct, but emotional investment even in the newborn was often high, and by no means only in families anxious to secure the succession to land and title. Sons and daughters were, for many parents, 'dear second selves'. A child's death was often the cause of great affliction. Elizabeth Wallington was nearly 3 when she died in 1625. Her father Nehemiah was heartbroken. Her mother urged him to

> 'consider what a deal of grief and care we are rid of, and what a deal of trouble and sorrow she is gone out of, and what abundance of joy she is gone into. . . . It is your daughter's wedding day . . . will you grieve to see your daughter go home to her husband Christ Jesus, where she shall never want, but have the fullness of joy for ever more?'

Eddy Charlton, the son of a country landowner, died in 1847. Nearly fifty years later his mother (b.1815) wrote

No language can express our grief. Merely to recall the memory of those sad days and months of sorrow, now as I write in my seventy-eighth year, causes me a sinking of the heart. Although so young, Eddy was a child of the sweetest disposition and great promise, but God – who knows best – took the angel boy into his keeping.

As these responses suggest, death, though painful for the bereaved, was recognised as the event which brought the end of sufferings, which parents could do little to alleviate, and transported the child to heaven where he would be safe in the arms of Jesus.

The sentiments printed on the elaborate embossed card circulated 'In Affectionate Remembrance of Beatrice Mary Ann Folkes, the beloved child of John and Emma Folkes, who died December 29th, 1878, aged 1 year and 10 months' might have been expressed at any time between the Reformation and the Great War:

> Farewell! dear little Beatrice thy spirit has fled,
> A bright crown of glory now rests on thy head;
> To the mansion of rest prepared thee above,
> Thy Saviour has called thee in wisdom and love.
>
> Then shall we repine at God's holy will?
> Dear Jesus say to us hush! peace and be still
> I have folded thy lamb in my own tender breast,
> She shall be forever unspeakably blest.

Mr and Mrs Folkes belonged to the first generation of ordinary people who, thanks to new print technology, were able to combine the verbal expression of their griefs and hopes with the imagery of weeping willows, urns and broken columns, symbolising their mourning, and angels holding 'bright crown[s] of glory', symbolising the consolation – that their child was 'safe in the arms of Jesus'.

Dead children were buried in familiar places. In 1670 the Revd Isaac Archer (b.1641) 'laid' his 11-month-old daughter 'in the dust . . . at the end of its grandmother's seat' in the church at Isleham in Cambridgeshire; Archer buried another child, who died unbaptised in 1675, near his own pew in Freckenham church, a few miles away, confident that he would 'meet it at the resurrection of the just'. The physical remains of children buried in family vaults and in family plots were also on home ground.

As the image of heaven dimmed, mourners focused on the dead child's personal history. Emma and Charles Darwin and their circle sought comfort in the positive aspects of the life and death of their daughter Annie (b.1841), who died at the age of 10. Letters and a 'memorial' written by her father stressed her happy and innocent child-hood and her uncomplaining acceptance of illness. Darwin 'was thankful for the daguerreotype' which preserved her features but not her ani-mation. Few of their correspondents mentioned heaven. Agnostics, who became more numerous towards the end of the period, probably had the greatest difficulty in coming to terms with premature death.

Although Annie left a gap which was never filled, the Darwins had a large family including a new baby whose birth coincided with her death. Preoccupation with the needs of the living frequently distracted atten-tion from the dead. George Crabbe's letters to Edmund Cartwright contain many passing references to his son, Cartwright's godson and namesake, born in 1790. They add up to an affectionate sketch of a lively small boy, capable, in September 1792, of 'making a most rebellious tumult with his brothers'. Even when Edmund, 'or some mischievous creature like him', ruined Crabbe's botanical specimens, the principal theme of his correspondence with Cartwright, the accident was recorded without rancour. Then, on 7 July 1796, 'your godson was suddenly taken from us by a severe and (to me) [and in his youth Crabbe was intended for medicine] unknown disease'. Despite his love for the dead child, Crabbe's chief concern was the welfare of those who sur-vived: Edmund's brother John (b.1787), 'emaciated by a malady of a very different kind, slow and of a nature which promises a late, though I hope not a fatal termination'; his mother, victim of 'the effects of mental distress upon the female frame'; and his godfather Cartwright, himself recently widowed.

Poor parents sometimes referred to a dead child's release from material deprivation and the temptations which went with it. A Victor-ian widow, whose son died from whooping cough, was 'glad he was took from me . . . he could but have lived in the worst kind of poverty . . . and God only knows what might have become of him, if he had lived'.

It was recognised that children were different from adults. Those charged with responsibility for bringing them up (parents, nurses, schoolteachers, employers) had a duty to protect them from moral and physical danger and prepare them to do well in this world and the next. The goal was common but the means by which adults sought to achieve it varied. Though the balance shifted, children in every generation were cajoled, bribed, browbeaten and thrashed into conformity with the expectations of their family and society. These expectations reflected the child's rank and gender – historians debate their relative importance.

To a large extent, men and women inhabited separate worlds and, in consequence, the formal and informal curricula followed by boys and girls diverged at an early stage. A woman's rights in law were inferior and her prospects of inheritance slighter than her brother's. She had poorer access to formal education and training. Strenuous intellectual activity was believed to overtax her. By comparison with man, woman was perceived as weak in body as well as mind. Her value in the labour market was lower. According to the medical theory accepted in the sixteenth century, physical maturity left her at the mercy of her womb, and, therefore, prone to hysteria, a predicament which the menopause did not relieve. Nineteenth-century physicians, in pursuit of fees and professional authority, emphasised the need for the expert medical management of the female condition.

Rank was of profound significance. It divided gentlewomen from their humbler neighbours: delicate health was a 'privilege' confined to those whose families could meet doctors' bills. And it divided men: women shared their economic and legal disadvantages with the great majority of male plebeians. Inherited wealth, booklearning and the training which led to respected and well-paid occupations were the preserve of a minority.

The transition from infancy to full adult status was a staged process. Weaning, the first critical step, has already been mentioned. From the sixteenth until the nineteenth century, until they were steady on their feet and could be trusted to go on their own, children wore leading strings, reins attached to their clothes. Within living memory, breeching, the ceremonial putting on of male garments, marked the boy's formal admission to a masculine world. The timing of breeching varied, according to the dictates of fashion and, among the poor, the availability of suitable hand-me-downs – early photographs show quite big boys in skirts.

In our society the first day at school is an important landmark. Though commoner as time went on, school attendance was neither compulsory nor free until the end of the nineteenth century. In schools of all kinds, from the great boys' schools, which, by the seventeenth century, drew pupils from all over the country, to the dame's school, serving a very local need, the birch was the teacher's badge of office. Corporal punishment may have been commoner at school than at home.

Young children were familiar with the world of work. In the sixteenth century and, in some trades and regions, right up to the time of the Great War, the boundary between home and workplace was ill-defined. Small boys shadowed and mimicked their fathers. Girls and, failing girls, boys minded younger children. Among the poor, children, who today would be at infant schools, earned money; their small wages were usually paid direct to their parents and were treated not as pocket money but as a contribution to the family's livelihood. The child who failed to make the expected contribution risked displeasure – or worse.

Households and workplaces were hazardous environments. The diary of Ralph Josselin (b.1617), a Puritan parson and farmer, who

31

believed that God stepped in to punish and protect, suggests how frequent accidents and providential escapes were. With industrialisation, children were employed in mines and factories. The physical and moral risks they faced there were probably no more serious than those run by earlier generations, but they excited concern which led to legislation restricting and, eventually, prohibiting child labour. Legislation to prevent cruelty to children at home was introduced in the 1880s.

Until the end of the eighteenth century most young people left home in their teens to study, to undertake apprenticeships or to work as farm or domestic servants, the girls' usual destiny – grammar schools and universities did not admit women until the nineteenth century and few trades took female apprentices. In their teens and early twenties young men and women developed the skills and, in many cases, built up the resources on which their future prospects depended. Yet youths were regarded as irresponsible and unruly. In Tudor and Stuart England 'masterless' young men were treated with particular suspicion; if they fell foul of the authorities, they were liable to be flogged and returned to their home parish.

Most men and women waited until their mid-twenties to marry and set up home. This was a major undertaking. Heads of independent households were the people who counted in the small community of the parish and the great community of the nation; until the twentieth century property-holding was an essential qualification for the vote. Householders were responsible for socialising children, for training young people and overseeing their behaviour. Until the nineteenth century they participated directly in the policing of their community and in the management of the parish budget. With these burdens in prospect, prudent men and women did not enter into marriage and housekeeping without due consideration. As Queen Victoria put it: 'Marriage is a solemn holy act *not* to be classed with amusements.' Betrothal, the engagement to marry, was treated very seriously. Until 1753 a solemn pledge, confirmed by intercourse, amounted to marriage. Parents, who frequently underwrote the enterprise, and neighbours, who had to bear the ultimate responsibility for poor households which came to grief, attempted to exercise caution on behalf of those they regarded as feckless; ratepayers intervened to prevent the marriages of the very poor. Charged with fornication in 1615, Widow Patrick and Richard Sizer of Terling in Essex explained that their plans to marry had been frustrated by 'the parish'. Inevitably control over the marriages of the labouring poor diminished with large-scale urbanisation. Romantic passion was not a justification for marriage. In 1638, following his marriage, in defiance of the wishes of his guardian, King Charles I, and his wife's father, the Earl of Suffolk, Lord George Stuart (b.1618) framed his apology in a portrait commissioned from Van Dyck. The supplicant leans on a rock inscribed: 'ME FIRMIOR AMOR' ('Love is more power-ful than I').

The ideal life partner, male or female, was of a suitable rank and age, physically fit and attractive, even-tempered, held compatible religious and/or political views, possessed useful kin and other connections and brought appropriate material resources and skills to the marriage. Most people had to settle for less. Imperatives varied. A landowner burdened with debts and dependants might rank money above everything else. The working farmer might prioritise physical fitness and the ability to manage the house, the dairy and the poultry yard. Widowers, who often remarried within months of their wives' deaths, to make good the loss of helpmate and mother, clearly chose from a restricted field. Women, whose capacity to sustain an independent existence was ad-versely affected by law, custom and low earning power, may often have come to the conclusion that any husband might be better than none. Nevertheless, perhaps one in ten of those who survived to adulthood died unmarried. At some times and in some groups the proportion was higher. Perhaps 20 per cent of men and women born in the middle decades of the seventeenth century never married. 'Surplus' women were conspicuous in middle-class society in Victorian and Edwardian England.

Official attitudes to pre- and extra-marital sex were consistently hostile. Men and women who engaged in sexual relationships outside marriage ran the risk of punishment. Children born to unmarried mothers were often the legacies of serious courtships which had come to grief. Anecdote suggests that both men and women allowed themselves to be manoeuvred into sexual relationships in the expectation that marriage would follow.

Women who had two or more children outside marriage, 'repeaters', as demographers call them, do not form a homogeneous group. Some had several partners; others had a succession of children with one man. Alan Macfarlane has identified two women in this category in Earl's Colne in Essex at the beginning of the seventeenth century: Thomas Allen was the acknowledged father of most of Mary Grant's six children; her son Thomas had several children by Lidia Paine. It is not known whether the men lived with their families but they appear to have been a disreputable clan. The local standing of the family headed by Michael Becker, a man of substance, and his common-law wife Hannah Solly, who lived at Ash-next-Sandwich in Kent in the middle of the nineteenth century is less clear. Their twelve children, censoriously registered as bastards by the vicar, were listed, with their parents, by the, almost certainly local, Census enumerators as a conventional family – it would be interesting to know what the neighbours made of the situation. At Courtaulds' Essex textile mill in the nineteenth century, a woman who had borne a single child out of wedlock and conveyed a proper sense of shame would normally be taken back on to the workforce; the mother of several bastards would not:

> Even more frowned upon than illegitimacy were single women living with men. Perhaps this was because such a lifestyle openly flouted middle class moral ideals whereas an illegitimate birth could be put down to innate and uncontrollable male desires.

Illegitimate children were disadvantaged in law. To some extent, but only to some extent, privilege could override convention. Charles II fathered a generation of sons whom he endowed with wealth and titles but the best that he could provide for his favourite eldest child was a dukedom and a wealthy bride. Monmouth ranked after the princes of royal blood, his uncle James, Duke of York, and his cousin Rupert, Duke of Cumberland. Bastardy, it was believed, bred men and women who were outsiders by temperament as well as in law. Barbara Leigh Smith (b.1827) was a prominent and effective promoter of education, property and civil rights for women. Her older contemporary, Mrs Gaskell, who referred to her as an 'illegitimate cousin of . . . F. Nightingale', attributed her 'noble bravery' as a campaigner to her bastardy: 'she is – I think in consequence of her birth, a strong fighter against the established opinions of the world'.

Law and custom acknowledged the husband's sovereignty over his wife. If she failed in her duties, he had the right and responsibility to chastise her in moderation, as he would a delinquent child or servant, for her own good, the good of his household and the good of his neighbourhood. Her rights as a mother were restricted. Until 1837 the wills of married women, minors, idiots and lunatics were invalid. Until the end of the nineteenth century, if a bride brought property to the marriage, her husband acquired control of it – unless her family had had the foresight to secure it on her behalf. It must be assumed that women, schooled in conspicuous deference by family and society, cultivated the subtler manipulative arts on their own account. However, there were – limited – compensations for a wife's inferior status. Her husband was obliged to pay debts she incurred and a plea that she was acting on her husband's orders was a legitimate defence against a criminal charge.

Effective progress along the long road to equal opportunities and rights for women began in the second half of the nineteenth century. The prime beneficiaries were the wives and daughters of the upper and middle classes. A tiny handful of women became figures of national authority, among them the Queen, ex officio; Florence Nightingale (b.1820), who exploited her invalidity and the chivalry of her male allies to establish nursing as a vocation for respectable women; Josephine Butler (b.1828) and Octavia Hill (b.1838), powerful and successful campaigners for social reform. With respect to their children and their property, women's legal position improved. For the first time girls from enlightened and comfortably-off families had access to schools and colleges offering a curriculum broadly similar to their brothers'. Nevertheless, women who took paid work risked ostracism and, with the exception of medicine, professional bodies refused women membership until after the Great War. The campaign for female suffrage involved those who were ready to defy the law and women and men who were determined to work within it. Nationally, the crucial breakthrough was achieved in 1918 when women of 30 were enfranchised; it was another decade before we got the vote on equal terms with men at 21.

Before the Great War deliberately childless marriages were probably exceptional. Like spinsters, 'barren' women were pitied or despised. Yet pregnant women 'travelled with death': childbirth was a life-threatening event. Miscarriages were even more dangerous. Damage sustained in mismanaged deliveries was rarely corrected and women with prolapsed wombs suffered pain and distress for the rest of their lives. Among the labouring poor many wives and mothers combined childcare and heavy household duties with paid employment. They went out charring or to work in the fields or took in washing, sewing or foster children to help support their family. While washing, sewing and food preparation were done by hand, housewives without a full complement of servants were domestic drudges, as these lines suggest:

> Here lies a poor women who was often tired
> She lived in a house where help was not hired,
> Her last words on earth were: 'Dear friends, I am going,
> Where washing ain't done, nor sweeping, or sewing.
> But everything there is exact to my wishes,
> For where they don't eat, there's no washing of dishes.
> I'll be where loud anthems will always be ringing
> But having no voice, I'll be clear of the singing.
> Don't mourn for me now, don't mourn for me never,
> I'm going to do nothing for ever and ever.'

The Oxford Book of Local Verses attributes this doggerel to Catherine Allsopp, a Sheffield washerwoman who hanged herself in 1905. Allsopp's contemporary, Mrs Dash, a vicar's wife, knew the verse and recognised it as appropriate for her own tombstone too.

The trials of washday are underlined by the question first posed in England in 1888 by W. H. Lever, who paid the American who coined it £2,500: 'WHY DOES A WOMAN LOOK OLD SOONER THAN A MAN?' Lever's advertisement provided the explanation:

Put a man at a washing-tub; let him get heated with the hot suds until every pore is opened; then let him stand over the filthy steam that comes from scalding and boiling clothes, and his health certainly would break down before long.

A predictable solution was to hand:

> Fortunately, this trouble can be avoided. Scalding, boiling and steam done away with, clothes made sweet and beautifully white, and much sooner than the old way, by using SUNLIGHT SOAP – a soap so purifying and cleansing that the dirtiest clothing can be washed in lukewarm water with very little rubbing, and clothes, bedding and linen cleansed without either scalding or boiling, while the work is so light that a girl of 12 or 13 can do a large wash without being tired.

This was a prejudiced and partial answer, of course. Other explanations of women's troubles added inadequate diet and frequent and poorly managed pregnancies and births to the burdens of household work.

Most marriages ended in death and ended early – in late Georgian England the odds on couples reaching their Silver Wedding were worse than three to one. However incompatible they might be, the incentives for married couples to stick together were considerable. Many marriages were working partnerships. Deserted wives might be accorded widows' status but the economic prospects of women who walked out of a bad marriage were bleak, particularly if they had dependent children. Formal remedies for marital breakdown were limited. Divorce, with possibility of remarriage, was virtually unknown before the eighteenth century and remained exceptional even at the beginning of the twentieth century. Until 1857 marriages could be terminated only by means of a complicated process involving actions in the civil and ecclesiastical courts and culminating in the passage of a private parliamentary bill. This obstacle course was expensive and, overwhelmingly, a male option. Of the 325 parliamentary divorces, only four were granted to women, who, in line with the prevailing double standard of sexual morality, had to prove adultery aggravated by a further matrimonial 'offence'. Two of these women cited bigamy and two 'incestuous' adultery, adultery, that is, with their sisters. (The double standard of sexual morality stemmed from a determination to secure property against usurpation: a married woman's child was presumed to be legitimate unless, through absence or proven impotence, her husband was physically incapable of having fathered it.) Although the same grounds applied after divorce became a matter for the secular courts, the proportion of women petitioners rose to one in four. Even so, it was not an easy option: press reports dwelt with salacious relish on proofs of adultery and even the 'innocent party' was stigmatised. The cost of proceedings continued to be a major deterrent. The cheaper alternative of legal separation was popular – at the beginning of the twentieth century about twenty-five times more popular than divorce.

Given the social and financial cost of legal termination, it is worth exploring other yardsticks of breakdown. Taking as his criteria 'notorious marital quarrels', annulments and separations, Lawrence Stone calculated that between 1570 and 1659 10 per cent of peers' marriages broke down. He found 'something of a tendency for marital quarrels to run in families', a conclusion echoed by Allen Horstman, who identified a network of aristocrats, centred on the Pagets, a family which flouted matrimonial convention in the nineteenth century. At the other end of the social scale, among the labouring poor, Keith Snell has calculated that desertion effectively terminated, on average, something approaching 10 per cent of marriages. Want, which forced poor men to take to the road in search of work, led to temporary separations which were sometimes protracted by circumstances beyond the partners' control. Wife sales, a quasi-legal device for transferring the 'ownership' of a woman from one man to another, usually with her consent, excited much interest among readers and hearers of news-sheets from the seventeenth to the nineteenth century, but do not seem to have been common.

Because it was so often in the interests of those concerned to conceal it, the incidence of adultery cannot be calculated. Many wives and some husbands turned a blind eye to infidelity. Quaife's sample of *Wanton Wenches and Wayward Wives* in seventeenth-century Somerset included the wife of the remarkably complacent Robert Richmond:

> When she was in bed expecting a child a John Gilbert stayed with her and comforted her during the preliminaries to travail. He warmed a cloth by the fire and put it around the woman's knees and legs, and brought wine and food. He slept on the bed beside the woman while the husband lay in the same room in some straw.

Richmond's passivity contrasts with Elizabeth Pepys's violent emotional and physical response to her husband's infatuation with her waiting woman, Deb Willet, which began in March 1668 and lasted at least until he gave up diary-keeping at the end of the following May. One night in January 1669 Pepys awoke to find his wife at his bedside armed with 'tongs red hot at the ends . . . as if she did design to pinch' him. Pepys's own attitude is instructive. Although he was clearly very powerfully attracted to Deb and discharged her from his service reluctantly, at his wife's insistence, and 'with tears in my eyes' – though he expressed concern about her future and made efforts to find out what had become of her – there is no evidence that he ever contemplated leaving his wife.

Infidelity was not the only cause of friction. A clash of temperaments uncomplicated by infidelity might be as hard to tolerate, as the journal of the Stuart farmer Adam Eyre makes clear. He spent a sleepless night, pondering the 'question whether I should live with my wife or no, if she should continue to be as wicked as she is'.

Although many died young, 70, the biblical three score years and ten, was regarded as the normal span of life. Old age was not, of itself, considered a disqualification for work either in the home or in paid employment: the 'woodman' James Minns (b.1826) was still working when he was photographed in 1901, though by this time failing eyesight had cut his earning power so severely that only a free cottage and a weekly shilling from the squire stood between him and the workhouse. Handouts, charities and poor rates supported the aged and infirm. Octavia Hill favoured allowances which would keep 'those who have worked hard as long as they were able' in their own 'little home' but she regarded as 'startling' Charles Booth's suggestion 'of pensioning every-body without distinction over sixty-five'. The limited provision of old-age pensions, introduced in 1911, was confined to men and women over the age of 75 who had 'worked hard as long as they were able' and never depended on the poor rates.

Death and burial were perceived almost as a type of sacred theatre. Natural death normally occurred at home under lay management. 'Last words' were recorded. The death of a national hero like Admiral Horatio Nelson (d.1805) was celebrated in popular prints and by the production of commemorative plates, jugs and teapots. One inscription read: 'England expects every man to do his duty'; and below: 'Shew me my Country's Foes the Hero cry'd. He saw – he fought – he conquered – and he died.' Convicts addressed the crowd from the scaffold. Broadsheet posters, like the alleged 'Dying Words and Confessions' of Elias Lucas and Mary Reeder, who were executed (on 13 April 1850 in the presence of 30 or 40,000 spectators) in front of the County Gaol at Cambridge for the 'Wilful Murder of Susan Lucas', fed the popular appetite for sensa-tion. The deathbed was a favourite theme of writers and artists. Victorian technologies made the paraphernalia of mourning, including the jewellery and printed cards which had long circulated among the prosperous, widely available. The labouring poor of Victorian England were prepared to invest heavily in insurance and, in extremity, sell up the furnishings of their home to avoid a pauper funeral. From the seventeenth century, some individuals, well able to afford lavish cere-monial, had opted for a simple committal, but it was the ostentation of Victorian mourning and the fact that the customs of the elite had been usurped by the vulgar that provoked a general reaction. The Cremation Society of England was founded in 1874.

3

THE FAMILIES
OF LANDOWNERS

DEFINING CHARACTERISTICS

For eight hundred years after the Norman Conquest the aristocracy –
peers and landed gentlemen – held political, economic and social sway
in England. To prepare himself for the leadership of the Conservative
Party, Benjamin Disraeli (b.1804) thought it appropriate to acquire a
country estate even though he had to borrow a fortune to do so.
Landowners exercised extensive patronage in Church and State: the
right to appoint the Master of Magdalene College, Cambridge, was
vested in the owner of Audley End in Essex. The catalogues of offices
held and ceremonial duties performed by, for example, the current
Duke of Westminster in the Grosvenor country in Cheshire or the
current Earl of Derby in the Stanley 'kingdom' in Lancashire suggest the
landowners' place in local affairs.

The houses they built, their memorials in parish churches, the
ceremonious conduct of their daily life constantly affirmed the aristocrats' status. Daisy Maynard, later Countess of Warwick (b.1861),
recalled the procession with which church services ended when she
was a child: 'At the close of the blessing "We" filed out first before
the gaze of our humbler neighbours. The estate steward and his family
followed, then the farmers and last of all the cottagers.' As Chapter
6 on labouring families indicates, this ritual demonstration of the social
order burned itself into the memories of the less privileged actors
too.

Sir John Statham (b.1676) painted a word picture of the Derbyshire
estate which came to him through his wife. In it he proclaims the landed
gentleman's independence, his power to command men and resources,
his generosity. Wigwell, formerly 'the chief seat of the great abbot of
Darley' stood

> above seven miles in circumference, a manor without one foot of
> anyone's interfering. In that district is all the convenience of life –

wood, coal, corn of all sorts . . . venison, a warren for rabbits, fish, fowl, in the utmost perfection, exempted from all jurisdiction . . .

Our way of life here is, everyone does that which is right in his own eyes, go to bed, rise early, lie late, all easy, only we are confined to meet at breakfast, and then order by agreement what's for dinner; the pastures are loaded with good beef and mutton, the dovecots with pigeons, the mews with partridges, the canals and stews [ponds] with excellent fish, and the barn doors with the finest white, plump pheasant fowls, out of those you order your daily entertainment.

After this, if you're for shooting, moor game, partridges, wild ducks etc. at the door; if exercise, a good bowling green and many long walks; if reading, a library; if walking, a dry park, with a delicious nut wood, full of singing birds, turtles and guinea hens, a delicate echo, where music sounds charmingly. In it are labyrinths, statues, arbors, springs, grottos and mossy banks, in the middle a large clear fishpond with a drawbridge and close arbor . . .

There's about thirty families in the liberty, and in every house you may discern some good blood. If retirement be irksome, on notice to Wirksworth there's loose hands, gentlemen, clergymen etc. ever ready at an hour and stay just as long as you'd have 'em and no longer, and easy to be told so.

. . . If rainy weather confines you, I have a library and the famous chemist Mr Harris, to amuse you with experiments, and a playwright author of some comedies to divert you.

The decline of the landed interest

Richard Greville Verney, Lord Willoughby de Broke (b.1869), who led the abortive campaign to prevent the gelding of the House of Lords in 1911, dated the country landowners' loss of identity to the middle of the nineteenth century when 'land ceased to be either a profit or a pleasure', town houses were let go, ancestral estates sold up. Legislation of the 1880s made it easier to override family settlements and 'sell off the family silver'. Those who could no longer support life in England retreated to refuges like Pau in the French Pyrenees. Families with other investments, like the Dukes of Bedford with their 'few acres in London', were best placed to weather the storm. Between 1886 and 1905 two-thirds of new peerages went to men without significant landed estates.

Values were changing. Barbara Charlton (b.1815) complained that, by the end of the nineteenth century, 'Any nouveau riche, any scallywag of the present day who can produce . . . yard on yard of smart upholstery is on a social footing with the aristocracy.' She blamed Queen Victoria's widowhood for this lamentable state of affairs, her retirement had given the irresponsible Prince of Wales his head. Willoughby de Broke pointed to the profounder challenge of commerce and industry: his estate at Compton Verney 'was too close to Birmingham to be comfortable for a peer'. Joseph Chamberlain's accusation that the Lords were 'drones in the hive' stung. Willoughby de Broke's forebodings were justified: within three years of the Armistice, Compton Verney had been sold to Joseph Watson, a soap manufacturer from Liverpool. More recently, the house has been divided up to make smaller 'residential units'.

A few eccentrics welcomed the changes. The 'Red Countess' of Warwick claimed that, 'even as a child', she 'used to wonder . . . how God viewed the "table of precedence" in His church, where all men are supposed to be equal'. When she came into her inheritance she was determined to put an end to it:

> At the close of the service, I remained kneeling with my head in my hands, to the discomfiture of the waiting congregation, who at last took the hint and departed . . . After following these tactics for a few Sundays, I succeeded in abolishing the precedence custom.

This chapter concentrates on the experience of the aristocratic family during the years of confidence and prosperity.

Pride in their ancestry

According to his official biography, Earl Mountbatten (b.1900) 'was a man who, for his own amusement, rarely took up any book unless it was one of genealogy, most especially on his own forebears'. In no century before the twentieth would this have been regarded as remarkable.

In 1859, under the resounding title *The Noble and Gentle Men of England, or Notes Touching the Arms and Descents of the Ancient Knightly and Gentle Houses of England*, Evelyn Philip Shirley Esq. MA (b.1812), of Ettington, Warwickshire, and one of the Knights of the Shire for the County, 'attempted' to compile a gazetteer of knightly and gentle families still occupying estates held by their forefathers in 1500. Like Willoughby de Broke, Shirley saw himself as a member of an endangered species; he identified an enthusiasm for genealogy and heraldry 'as one of the distinguishing marks of his kind'. Dating back to the Domesday Book or, better still, having come over with the Conqueror was the status to which landed families aspired. Evelyn Shirley had a descent to boast about. Another of his works, *Stemmata Shirleiana*, traces his ancestry to Saswalo, tenant of Ettington in 1086. The early chapters of the story had been outlined by Evelyn Shirley's kinsman, Sir Thomas, who compiled the family tree in 1632. It was thirty feet long and twelve feet wide, decorated with drawings of family tombs, copies of ancient documents and a great shield with fifty quarterings – a potted history of the Shirleys' descent for those who could read the heraldic code. To the uninitiated, it might look more like a patchwork quilt.

The fortunes of Saswalo's descendants suggest the hazardous course run by landed families. The Iretons descended from Saswalo's elder grandson Henry, who sold his inheritance to his younger brother Sewallis, an unusual and, as Shirley remarked, 'a very curious deed'. Cromwell's son-in-law and Lord Deputy in Ireland, Henry Ireton (b.1611), 'arch-rebel to his prince and country', was among Henry's descendants. 'The Ever Loyal Race of Shirley' descended from Sewallis. Sir Robert, a leading member of the Royalist resistance, built his walled church at Staunton Harold in Derbyshire to symbolise his allegiance to Crown and Church. The inscription over its west door reads:

> In the year 1653 when all things sacred were throughout the nation either demolished or profaned Sir Robert Shirley Baronet founded this church; whose singular praise it is to have done the best things in the worst times and hoped them in the most calamitous.

Cromwell responded by clapping Shirley into the Tower for the seventh time. He died there of smallpox.

The Shirley descent, still unbroken in the 1990s, was at its most vulnerable at the beginning of Henry VIII's reign. When he married for the fourth time in 1514, Ralph Shirley (b.c.1460) was already in his fifties, his only child was a daughter by his first wife. His son and successor was not quite 2 years old when Ralph died but the luck of the Shirleys held, the child lived and the sole survivor of his four sons carried on the name. The death of Robert Shirley (b.1650), raised to a barony in 1677 and promoted Earl Ferrers in 1711, provoked a fresh crisis. Robert Shirley had two large families, seventeen children by his first wife and ten more by her successor. Too many children were almost as big a problem as too few. Disputes arose from the earl's generosity to his second brood which left the heir 'only a moderate share of the paternal inheritance'. The legal contest lasted for twenty years. Saswalo's Domesday estate went to the cadet line to which Evelyn Shirley belonged. The senior branch was sadly blighted. The second Earl Ferrers died without male issue. His brother Henry, the first earl's ninth son and sixteenth child, inherited his titles but, 'his lordship having the misfortune to be a lunatic', the estates passed to his younger brother Lawrence. In 1745 lands and titles were reunited in the person of Lawrence's son. However, 'his ungovernable temper (at times amounting to insanity) rendered him unworthy to inherit and eventually led him to an ignominious death'. He was executed for the murder of his steward. The estates were temporarily forfeit.

Spurred on by attachment to their ancestral lands, men strove to recover estates alienated by their forebears. The Cliftons lost the manor of Clifton in Lancashire through an heiress's marriage in the early sixteenth century and recovered it through another a hundred years later. Henry Antrobus sold the manor of Antrobus in Cheshire at the beginning of the fifteenth century; it was bought back by his descendant Edward in 1808. For Shirley, this was 'an instance of an ancient family who, having gone down in the world . . . recovered itself by means of commercial pursuits, after centuries of comparative obscurity'. Heraldic devices were equally prized. The Grosvenors, deprived of their emblem, the Bend Or, in the fourteenth century, after a hearing at which the witnesses included the future Henry IV and Geoffrey Chaucer, nursed their grievance for five hundred years. In 1880 the Duke of Westminster, head of the Grosvenor family, won the Derby with a horse of that name; his grandson and successor was habitually called Bend Or.

Fear of extinction

Despite these instances of tenacity, a justifiable fear of extinction haunted the aristocracy. In 1417 Sir Thomas Erpingham commissioned a stained glass window to commemorate the eighty-seven East Anglian knights and barons who had died without heirs in the preceding eighty-odd years; Erpingham's list was incomplete – twentieth-century scholarship has added to his reckoning.

Strategies were devised to procure continuity. Entails made it possible to exclude daughters in favour of more distant male kin (most titles descended in this way). Alternatively, property could be transmitted through women to men prepared to trade their family names for landed wealth; this practice became popular under the Stuarts. According to family tradition, the eighteenth-century landowner George Tasburgh, the last of his line, urged his widow to remarry – on condition that his successor adopted the name and arms of Tasburgh. Hyphenated surnames, which first appear in the later seventeenth century, commemorate dynastic unions. The six-segment surname of Evelyn Shirley's contemporary, Richard Plantagenet-Temple-Nugent-Brydges-Chandos-Grenville, Duke of Buckingham, was a litany of submerged families.

The history of the Lyttons of Knebworth in Hertfordshire illustrates the grafting of new stock on to a family tree. The Knebworth estate was acquired by Henry VI's Receiver General, Robert de Lytton of Lytton in Derbyshire. For six generations, until the death of Sir William Lytton in 1705, the estate passed in orthodox fashion from father to son or from elder to younger brother. Sir William's successor was his sister's grandson Lytton Strode; from Lytton Strode Knebworth passed to his cousin

William Robinson; and from William Robinson Lytton to his son John; from John to his sister's son Richard Warburton; from Richard Warburton Lytton to his daughter whose marriage carried the property to the Bulwer family. Knebworth was used to endow her third son (b.1803) who adopted the surname Lytton and took the title Baron Lytton when he became a peer.

Wealth

Great magnates lived in palaces, the houses of minor gentry might be barely distinguishable from the prosperous farmers'. Until the nineteenth century, the grandees were the biggest employers of labour in England; their households were managed like hotels, their environs resembled villages. Modest country gentlemen, in contrast, made do with a handful of indoor and outdoor servants. John Bateman's survey of the *Great Landowners of Great Britain and Ireland* suggests that, almost to the end of the period, there was a close match between the hierarchies of rank and riches. That said, the sons of impoverished gentry families were infinitely better placed to scale the heights of noble wealth and privilege than any born beyond the aristocratic pale. John Churchill (b.1650), heir to a Dorset family hit hard by the Civil War, was buried as a 'high and mighty prince' of the Holy Roman Empire, Duke of Marlborough in the English peerage, lord of Blenheim Palace and 1,500 acres.

Recruitment

The frontier separating the landed gentleman from the rich farmer was frequently negotiated, especially perhaps in the sixteenth and seventeenth centuries. Merchants and lawyers, bankers and brewers also devoted their fortunes to establishing their families in county society. The Jacobean monument to Jeffrey Pitman in St Mary's Church at Woodbridge shows a man in transit. Pitman was an esquire when this title was still a mark of distinction; he was also High Sheriff of his county, thus a significant figure in Suffolk society; and yet, described as a haberdasher and tanner, he had not severed his ties with trade. Normally, successful implantation took time and depended on a steady investment in appropriate domestic paraphernalia, a fitting upbringing for sons and daughters and suitable marriage alliances. Outsiders who burst the ranks of the aristocracy ploughed wealth and energy into camouflaging their origins.

Richard Boyle (b.1566) made his fortune, unscrupulously, in the Irish colonies. As Earl of Cork his ambition to secure aristocratic grooms for his daughters contributed to the inflation of dowries. In his determination to conform, he became so expert in House of Lords procedure that a son-in-law, born to his title, came to him for advice. His houses, clothes and pastimes mimicked those of lords of nobler antecedents. He disapproved of gambling but took to betting on dice, horses and the sex of unborn children. Most upwardly mobile families made slower and less conspicuous progress.

SOURCES

The evidence for the history of the landed family is richer and more extensive than that for any of our other categories. Even so, much has been lost or destroyed. Sir John Statham's description of his estate, quoted at the beginning of this chapter, was 'rescued from the sweepings of an old lawyer's office' at the end of the nineteenth century.

It was after the Reformation that genealogical research became a characteristic pursuit of the English aristocrat. Antiquarians like Sir Thomas Shirley produced elaborate accounts of their own descent and embarked on projects to preserve the documentary remains of landed families with which they had no close kinship; they preserved evidence of the earliest known cases of what had long since become conventional strategies for transmitting property from generation to generation in aristocratic families. Less bookish men expressed their passion with equal vigour. In 1629 Sir John Oglander, whose family had held land on the Isle of Wight for five hundred years, gathered his archives together, tied the parchments with the 'points' or laces used to fasten clothes before buttons came into fashion, and deposited them in a leather box. The inscription he wrote suggests the mystical bonds which united the current representative of a landed family with those who had gone before and those that were to come:

> Those evidences that are here tied up were done so by Sir John Oglander with his own points. Everyone of them have been worn by him, and it may be that in the future some of his successors may wonder at the fashion . . . Evil come to him that taketh them away.

Sadly, the box 'no longer exists, as it got damp rot . . . (the documents were saved)'. Evidences of the kind Sir John preserved lack personality. Cecil Aspinall-Oglander, writing during the Second World War, drew an apt metaphor from his daily life when he described the

> task of retracing the steps of bygone Oglanders of the fifteenth and sixteenth centuries [as] not very different to a journey by car in the black-out. The light that comes from their wills and leases and other formal documents is at best a shuttered headlamp.

45

In Tudor and early Stuart England few of those whose 'evidences' were incomplete had any compunction about bridging the gaps. William Dawkyns, an Elizabethan purveyor of false pedigrees, was charged with nearly a hundred offences. The Oglanders, whose archives dated back to the twelfth century, tacked a mythical companion of the Conqueror to the head of their pedigree.

Gervase Holles (b.1607) sought to reconstruct not merely 'the genealogical part', 'the unspirited dead and useless carcase' of his ancestors 'but their very features and dispositions'. But he was unusual. Evelyn Shirley's account of his own career is impersonal. Even in the twentieth century biography was regarded as 'a vulgar breach of privacy'. George Lambton (b.1860), who broke with convention to become a professional trainer of racehorses, prefaced his memoirs with the disclaimer: 'It is not my intention in these pages to write the history of my life, except in so far as it brought me into contact with many interesting men and famous horses.'

Female students of family history were rare. Few women had the learning. One of the exceptions, Cassandra Willoughby (b.1670), produced an 'Account of the Willoughbys of Wollaton in Nottinghamshire' from the fourteenth century to her own day; it remained in manuscript until the twentieth century. Cassandra Willoughby paid unusual attention to her less distinguished kin, men and women who fared badly. Among them was Winifred, born at the end of Queen Elizabeth's reign, whose mother so abused her that friends feared she might be maimed. A cousin took pity on her and married her 'unknown to either of their fathers'. Like other runaways, the couple lived to regret this presumption; they found themselves 'reduced to very low circumstances', at times 'so deplorable' that Winifred wished she were dead. After her marriage to her cousin James Brydges (b.1673), first Duke of Chandos, Cassandra Willoughby carried on her mother-in-law's less ambitious 'account of the births, marriages, and deaths' of the Brydges from 1642 to 1719. Once again she noted the casualties like her 'unhappy kinsman' Robert Jacob, second son of the duke's sister, who, failing to profit from his uncle's patronage and 'miserable to a sad degree', was imprisoned for debt, then shipped across the Atlantic, with his wife and daughter, to New England where 'it pleased God to send him such a consuming illness as ended his life'. After Cassandra Willoughby's death in 1735 Lady Chandos's Register was maintained by the duke's third wife, one of his daughters-in-law and, finally, his son and heir Henry whose entries cover the period 1759 to 1768.

Documentary evidence is frequently complemented by the evidence supplied by houses and their contents – portraits, furnishings and collections of memorabilia. Interpreted with care, these can add to our understanding of family values, if not practices.

THE MEANING OF CHILDREN

The production of a son and heir was the landowner's *raison d'être*. The wait could be agonisingly long. Sir John Oglander (1642–83) and his wife Mary suffered 'biennial disappointments', as six daughters came along 'with mechanical precision' before the necessary son was born in 1680. Edith Sitwell (b.1887) perceived herself, her parents' eldest child, as a boobyprize. In families short of money and burdened with children, girls were expendable. William Blundell (b.1620) reported the death of his ninth child and sixth daughter as follows:

> My wife hath much disappointed my hopes in bringing forth a daughter which, finding herself not so welcome in this world as a son, hath already made a discreet choice of a better.

Barbara Charlton (b.1815) recalled that her father 'thought a third daughter a superfluous addition to his family'. (There were compensations. She was her mother's favourite child, perhaps because she reminded her of her parents: 'I resembled her father, so much so that I used to be called *little grandpapa* and also, it may have been, because I bore my grandmother's name.' When the other children wanted a favour from their mother *'little grandpapa* was sent as spokesman'.) Women as well as men regarded daughters as second best. In the half century before the Great War 'the only difference in the response between the sexes was that women tended to give thanks for the mother's safety before commiserating on the baby's gender'.

As his father's apprentice, the heir was set apart from birth. In the sixteenth and seventeenth century he was often the only member of his generation to leave a distinct impression in the family archive. In the upper ranks of the peerage he was known by his father's senior secondary title – thus Earl Ferrers' heir had the courtesy title Viscount Tamworth; in other families the heir was known as 'Brother'. Family portraits emphasised his special status: in Joshua Reynolds' likeness of the family of the fourth Duke of Marlborough (b.1739), painted in the late 1770s, the duke's hand rests on his heir's shoulder; Marlborough holds a Roman cameo, epitomising his classical education, wealth and taste; his son Blandford holds the case, representing its descent. In 1905 the ninth duke (b.1871) commissioned John Singer Sargent to paint a companion piece; the duke and his heir hold a sword between them. The distinctive Blenheim breed of spaniels features in Reynolds' study and in its twentieth-century pendant.

The loss of a promising successor was the cruellest blow a man could suffer. When George Oglander (b.1609) 'died in Caen, in Normandy, of the smallpox, the 11th of July 1632', by his father's reckoning, 'five hundred and sixty six years since his ancestors came with William the

Conqueror out of the same town', Sir John recorded his death 'with tears
. . . instead of ink' in spite of the 'good and dutiful sons' who survived.
Such tragedies were not uncommon in Sir John's day. Preaching at the
funeral of another victim of smallpox, Anthony Walker observed: 'Most
children die before their parents.' Even a clutch of boys did not guarantee continuity. When the first Duke of Chandos's only surviving son fell
'very ill with his teeth' in 1702, the duke was frightened into a 'very odd'
dream in which this child died. His experience justified his fears. His
first wife bore nine children and miscarried four times. When she died in
1715 only John (b.1703) and Henry (b.1708) survived.

Premature deaths from natural causes diminished but the Great War,
which left a generation with the sense that they knew more dead than
living people, was a corporate bereavement which left the ranks of
landowners indelibly scarred, financially as well as emotionally, as
families were faced with two or even three bills for death duties in rapid
succession.

Distinctions between sons and daughters and the heir and his
brothers became increasingly sharp as they passed from infancy to
childhood, from childhood to youth and from youth to full age.

INFANCY

Tudor and Stuart ladies so rarely breastfed their babies that to do so was
interpreted as a mark of poverty or an out-of-the-ordinary commitment to the child. Cary Gardiner (b.1626) lacked the means to pay a
wetnurse when she was widowed by the Civil War. According to Lucy
Hutchinson (b.1620), it was unusual affection for a frail daughter, born
after three sons, which persuaded her mother to nurse her. Dorothy
McLaren's recent research into the differential fertility of aristocratic and
plebeian women supports the view that mothers whose children were
wetnursed were more likely to conceive quickly than those who
breastfed. Prodigious reproduction, like that of Earl Ferrers' first wife, is
an indication that a woman put her infants to nurse. Maternal nursing
seems to have become commoner in the eighteenth century. From about
1840 press advertisements for nurses declined fairly steadily; by the end
of the century there was a widespread distaste for what Lady Salisbury
called 'the old fashioned folly of a wetnurse'. But even the development
of a substitute for breastmilk did not make the wetnurse entirely redundant. As Nicholas Mosley (b.1923) recorded, 'My mother did not feed
me: it was not the custom at that time for upper-class mothers to feed
their children. A wetnurse was hired.' The research needed to establish
whether women of Lady Mosley's rank and generation habitually
employed wetnurses has not yet been undertaken.

Wetnursing is not of itself evidence of neglect. The source of nourishment did not dictate the frequency or quality of contact between parent and child. Nicholas Blundell recorded regular visits to his small daughters (b.1704 and 1706) at nurse in the village near his home. When her baby son failed to thrive, Katherine Everett, born in the 1870s, refused to accept the monthly nurse's verdict that he was doomed and, on the recommendation of a friend, fed him on asses' milk sent from London at 6 shillings (£0.30) a bottle. She called it 'Ba's champagne'. 'I . . . would have sold my wedding ring or anything else to procure it, seeing him gain weight and sleeping peacefully.' (Convinced of the strategy, she bought a milking donkey.) The Mosleys' use of a wetnurse would appear to reflect an abdication of responsibility for the day-to-day care of their infants. They set off for a holiday abroad when their son was a few weeks old leaving him in his nanny's charge.

Infancy seems to have contracted in Georgian England. Sixteenth- and seventeenth-century babies were apparently suckled until they were 12 or 14 months old; as maternal nursing became commoner, weaning occurred earlier.

CHILDHOOD

Babes in arms were dressed alike. Until the twentieth century small boys wore frocks: in paintings, they can usually be distinguished from their sisters by the masculine character of their props and activities. As little boys recognised, the ceremony of breeching marked promotion from neuter infancy to masculine superiority. In the eighteenth century Lady Lincoln's son, who chopped off his skirts when he was 5, announced his determination to distance himself from his younger brother and be 'like a girl no longer'. Breeching, which seems to have occurred when Stuart boys were 6 or 7, happened two or three years earlier under the Georges. The gulf between male and female experience put fatherless boys at a disadvantage. As he noted in his journal, Sir John Nelthorpe (b.1745), who succeeded as sixth baronet when he was a year old, was humiliated and provoked on his first visit to London in 1754 as a result of his mother's ignorance of the conventions of male dress and conduct. At Kensington Palace, he 'was in great danger of being stopped in the ante-chamber for want of a sword which is part of the dress of every-body that attends there, boys as well as men'. 'One of the little pages looked saucily' at him and laughed at his discomposure.

From the sixteenth century to the Great War, whether they were wetnursed or not, landowners' children were brought up by and among servants. Patently concerned parents proved curiously blind to their treatment. In the nursery, the formidable figure of the nanny, who emerged in the nineteenth century, overshadows her predecessors. Some nannies became so closely identified with the families that

employed them that they became part of them. Occasional announce-
ments in the Deaths column of *The Times* serve as reminders of this
tradition: Evelyn Kerr, who died in May 1986 was better known as
Nanny Barr or Nanny Ponsonby.

Parents and nurses treated the children in their charge with all the
degrees of tenderness, concern, neglect and sadism of which men and
women are capable. Some children were spectacularly indulged. Henry
Fox, Lord Holland, was an outstanding libertarian. According to gossip,
his son Charles James Fox (b.1749) was allowed to wash his hands (or
paddle) in a bowl of cream. When a demolition he had looked forward to
took place in his absence, Lord Holland allegedly had the wall rebuilt so
that it could be knocked down again for his pleasure. When Charles
'declared his intention to destroy a watch' his father responded, 'If you
must, I suppose you must.' Fox grew up to be, like his father, a devoted
husband – and an advocate of women's civil rights. Born a century after
Fox, George Cornwallis-West considered that his parents and their
contemporaries looked on children 'partly as a nuisance and partly as a
kind of animated toy'. Some unfortunate children found the whole adult
universe irrational and terrifying. Christian Miller (b.1921) was 'never
quite sure who was in charge' of her. She

> anxiously . . . struggled to find some line of conduct which if
> carefully followed, would ensure at least a reasonable safety from
> smacks and reprimands, but I never succeeded. Whatever I did
> was sure to be wrong in the eyes of at least one of the grownups, so
> the best I could do was to try to avoid annoying my father, whom I
> feared most of all. Nanny would send me down to the kitchen to
> fetch sugar for nursery tea; as soon as I opened the kitchen door,
> Cook would tell me to go away, and then for half an hour I would
> wander up and down the long corridors that separated nursery
> from kitchen, trying to decide what to do. Perhaps I would pilfer
> some from the canisters in the pantry, but if the butler caught me
> he would be sure to reprimand me; Cook might get really angry if I
> dared to go back to the kitchen; Nanny would stand me in the
> corner if I returned sugarless. I stood in the darkening corridor,
> tears dripping into the empty sugar bowl.

Boys frequently formed close attachments to outdoor servants like
gamekeepers, with whom they served a sporting apprenticeship. Lord
Willoughby de Broke's obituary for Jesse Eales (1820–99) conveys the
strength of such relationships. The gamekeeper's cottage was 'a second
home' to the Verney family. As far as his last employer was concerned:

> After my father and mother he was my first and best friend . . . It
> was with him that I saw my first fox killed, it was with him that I
> killed my first pheasant, partridge, duck, hare, rabbit and rook;

also my first fish. He showed me my first rat hunt, and escorted me on my first expedition in quest of birds' nests. In fact, he initiated me into the whole art of venery

– the art and liberty which set an aristocrat apart from those not privileged to hunt. Hunting, which trained boys to ride over rough country and accustomed them to the sight and smell of blood, was almost an aristocratic obligation. When Henry Martin Gibbs of Barrow Court in Somerset had his heir's portrait painted in 1886 he chose to depict Willie (b.1883) as 'A Master of Hounds' with horn and crop and three devoted dogs. And, when war broke out in 1914, the Hon. Freddy Lambton, former Master of Foxhounds, though 61 years old, came out of retirement,

> no one else being available in the country, he took hounds again, hunted them himself, and with the assistance of one old Whip, kept the whole thing going for three seasons. He used to say how hard it would be for the young men who were fighting, if they should find their hunting gone when they came back.

YOUTH: SONS

Landowners' sons were instructed (not necessarily thoroughly) in English, Latin, perhaps Greek, and mathematics. Some parents had their sons tutored at home but there was a growing tendency to send them away to school. Westminster and Eton emerged as the favoured choices of wealthy parents in the seventeenth century; in the longer term Eton's rural location gave it the edge. Residence at Oxford or Cambridge was not uncommon: at Oxford, Christ Church and, at Cambridge, Trinity and St John's emerged as favoured colleges. From the 1630s, those with the means sent their sons to the Continent to finish their education, ensuring that youthful excesses occurred at a discreet distance. The Grand Tour marked young men and the houses they inherited: William Windham (b.1717) transformed the drawing room of his house at Felbrigg in Norfolk into a cabinet to show off the souvenirs of his four years abroad. When, in the eighteenth century, university education went out of fashion, travel, especially to Italy, remained in vogue. Before 1939 a degree was not an important outcome of residence at the university. College authorities recognised the optional nature of academic endeavour. No sooner had George Lambton arrived at Trinity than his tutor asked him whether

> I had come to Cambridge to work or to amuse myself; if it was for the former purpose he would put me in the way of getting the best instruction possible . . . but, if my wish was for the latter, he could

also tell me how to do the smallest amount of work, involving the least possible amount of friction with the authorities. Having unhesitatingly chosen the path of pleasure, so good was his advice that during the whole of that term I never attended a single lecture or did a stroke of work.

Younger sons

If he survived, the heir's future was assured. His younger brother's was frequently uncertain. With estates earmarked for them, the younger sons of the first Earl Ferrers and the future Lord Lytton were fortunate. More often younger sons could look forward to allowances which would support a single man. Many had no choice but to earn a living. Convention restricted their options. Overt envy of the heir was perhaps at its keenest in the seventeenth century. In Warwickshire, between 1620 and 1660, few of the lesser landowners were in a position to endow their younger sons 'in any real way and in most cases only the heir would continue to be considered a gentleman'. In the 1650s the surge of sympathy for Freeman Sondes, who had killed his elder brother, was so strong that their father was driven to defend his dead son's character in print. Many modest gentry families, like the Oglanders, habitually put younger sons to a trade. Sir John (b.1585) put his philosophy on record:

> Be sure to give all thy sons a vocation. Without this they will hardly live in this or the next world. Keep not thy children idly at home to be bird catchers or dog drivers [as he contemptuously described those who gave themselves up to sport] settle them in a course of life.

He apprenticed his son Richard to a London mercer who traded 'at the sign of the Hen and Chickens' in 1615.

By 1700 the soaring cost of apprenticing a boy to a merchant in the overseas trade and subsequently launching him into business on his own account put this possibility out of the reach of many. In the eighteenth and nineteenth centuries Oglander cadets entered academia, the Church and the Army. Geography may have influenced the younger sons' choices. The Oglanders were south country men from the Isle of Wight. Francis Hurt, who was born in the 1720s, the seventh son of a Derbyshire landowner, went in for lead smelting. When, against the odds, he inherited the family seat, complete with the aristocratic appurtenances of deer park and vineries, he chose to have himself painted with a specimen of lead ore at his elbow. It is probable that the edge of resentment was blunted as the younger son's horizons widened. By the beginning of the nineteenth century the Gentleman's Club provided those without an establishment of their own with a cheap and congenial facsimile of the aristocratic town house. India offered the possibility of a lavish lifestyle on a limited budget.

The heir

Along with the life-tenancy of his estates, the heir acquired obligations. Junior members looked to the head of the family for patronage and protection. Lady Chandos's Register illustrates the cohesion of the Brydges clan in the late seventeenth and early eighteenth century. The frequency with which she and her husband stood godparent (he fifteen times in thirteen years, she fourteen times in eleven) underscores the expectations of sponsorship. Eustace Rolfe (b.1845), who succeeded to a modest Norfolk estate at the age of 24, found himself defending the interests of eight younger brothers and sisters and six dependent aunts and uncles against his grasping and litigious stepmother.

By the 1880s the heir's prospect may have been more of a burden than a prize. Sir Henry George Bedingfeld (b.1830) gave each of his sons £1,000 and sent them off 'to seek their fortunes'; his heir (b.1860) became a rancher in Wyoming. Another hundred years on the 'very curious deed' by which Henry, ancestor of the Iretons, made his younger brother 'his lord and firstborn' had come to seem less bizarre: in 1984 Simon Howard, third son of Lord Howard of Henderskelfe, came into possession of the family estate. 'His two elder brothers did not want the responsibility.'

YOUTH: DAUGHTERS

Education drove a cultural wedge between men and women. For girls, domestic crafts and accomplishments were priorities. While boys' horizons expanded, girls remained enclosed in the household. Lady Emily Lytton (b.1874) summed up the abiding sense of inequality and separateness when she described an occasion when she was received at home with such joy that she felt like 'a royal guest or a boy'.

In Tudor and Stuart England daughters, like sons, were often sent away to other households in their teens. The pious Lady Margaret Hoby (b.1571), who had no children of her own, found herself entrusted with the bringing up of a succession of young gentlewomen. To confer an aristocratic polish, Richard Boyle, the 'upstart' Earl of Cork, fostered three of his daughters out with the childless Lady Cleyton; two others were dispatched to live with prospective in-laws when they were 9 and 10 years old. Later, girls were kept cloistered in their own schoolrooms until they were catapulted into adult life. Governesses were employed primarily as childminders. In the twentieth century, the 'tiny wages' of the governesses engaged to teach the Mitford sisters were paid out of 'the meagre profits from the eggs and table birds' produced in their mother's poultry pens. Most girls learned to read and write in English but their 'speling', as Sarah, Duchess of Marlborough (b.1660), confessed, tended to be 'oridgenal'. Lady Diana Cooper (b.1892) described hers as 'atrocious and so phonetic that I write bs for ms when I have a cold'.

Occasionally, girls were allowed temporary access to the masculine universe. Men without sons made companions of their daughters. W. E. Nightingale tutored his daughters in classical and modern languages, history and philosophy. By the time they were in their teens the family had divided into two camps – Mrs Nightingale and her elder daughter Parthenope occupied themselves with feminine pursuits in the drawing room while Mr Nightingale and Florence (b.1820) devoted themselves to intellectual matters in the library. Daughters proved themselves capable of grasping the technicalities of family business. Also in the nineteenth century, Lord St Leonard's daughter drafted his will and recalled its contents in such detail that her statement was admitted for probate in place of the missing original.

However, it was the hunting field that offered Victorian young women the best chance of entering a man's world on equal terms. Hunting dominated the sportsman's winter calendar and, for much of the season, the sons were away at school. Safeguarded by technical advances which reduced, but did not eliminate, the risks of riding across country side-saddle in a habit, girls became familiar figures in the hunting field in the last third of the nineteenth century. The memoirs of an impressive tally of hunting men pay tribute to their skill, courage and fortitude when injured, as they often were. Some hunting couples celebrated their engagement with a lawn meet; Lord Willoughby de Broke's wife was among his most intrepid companions in the field. During the emergency created by the outbreak of the Boer War women were judged competent to exercise the awesome responsibilities of Master of Foxhounds as representatives of men absent on war service.

THE CHOICE OF A WIFE

The heir

The heir was required to marry early and profitably in order to secure the succession without delay. Nevertheless, every generation produced inheriting sons who failed to marry with the expected speed. Some of these men seem to have been scarred by unhappy experiences in childhood or youth; others may simply have been unwilling to shoulder the full burdens of adulthood. Charles Talbot, Duke of Shrewsbury (b.1660), whose guardians were pressing him to consider a bride in 1676, made a late and unconventional choice. In 1705 he married a widow 'without fortune and a foreigner' who sometimes exceeded 'the bounds of decency': she described her bunions to a polite assembly as 'things growing upon her toes like thumbs which made her so lame she could not stir'. According to his daughter Lady Augusta Fane, the second Earl of Stradbroke put off marriage for almost fifty years after being rejected by the Duke and Duchess of Richmond, the parents of his first love who considered him too young. The sixth Duke of Devonshire (b.1790), a conscientious curator of the Cavendish inheritance, whose pride in Hardwick and Chatsworth is evident both in the Guide he wrote in 1844 and in the ambitious outdoor works he commissioned from Joseph Paxton, left it to a kinsman to carry on the line. Like Shrewsbury, whose father died after a duel with his mother's lover, the duke's life was shadowed by his parents' notorious conduct. They shared a *ménage à trois* with his 'crocodile' stepmother. On the eve of the birth of a child by her lover, Earl Grey, the mother sent her small son 'my blessing written in my blood'. Her dying letter, composed when he was 16, warned her 'Dearest, Dearest Heart' against the vortex of dissipation into which she had plunged when she was scarcely older.

From the seventeenth century, the heir's marriage was the occasion of decisions which determined the long-term disposition of property. Marriage settlements curtailed the heir's freedom of action yet they should not be seen as straitjackets forced on reluctant youths. Men whose fathers were dead and who, therefore, negotiated as free agents on their own account – and there were many of them – generally submitted to the customary constraints. The six women paraded before the orphaned baronet Sir Thomas Isham (b.1657) between 1679 and 1681 suggest the conventional options for a man of his rank. Henrietta Maria Wentworth was a baroness in her own right. Barbara Chiffinch was the daughter of one of Charles II's close advisers. Two of the field were from Isham's home ground: Mary Catesby was a Northamptonshire heiress; Ann Wyatt the daughter of a more modest country gentleman who supplemented his income by practising as a lawyer. Elizabeth Dashwood's father was a London alderman and Mary van den Bemde was the daughter of a wealthy Dutch merchant settled in England. Their fortunes, religion, disposition and accomplishments were reviewed by Isham and his advisers. Chiffinch, a papist, was suspect on that account – Anglicans, often on good terms with their Catholic neighbours, rarely married them. Dashwood was reported to be 'of excellent temper . . . brisk and cheerful, a notable housewife and may prove a very endearing consort, if well managed'. Her dowry came from trade but, as the saying went, even the best cultivated land could benefit from manure.

Landowners were happier to negotiate city marriages for sons than for daughters. Isham died of smallpox before he made his choice known.

The dowry was the poor man's acknowledged priority. Among the ancestors whose features and dispositions Gervase Holles sought to bring to life was his mother's father (b.1554) John Kingston who, having wasted his inheritance, married a widow 'towards forty' in the hope of being able to 'bury her', marry a 'young wench and get children'. As it turned out, 'his old widow . . . held him in tug about thirty-eight years' and outlived him by twelve. Nicholas Blundell (b.1669), a Lancashire squire, whose inheritance had been ravaged during the Civil War and afterwards by fines and the demands of his many dependent relatives, set himself a target of £2,000 – and lived to regret his choice. Blatantly mercenary propositions can be found in the twentieth century. In 1901 *The Daily Telegraph* carried a peer's advertisement for a bride prepared to pay cash down for the honour of his hand and title and willing and able to support him in a style appropriate to his rank.

Birth and dowry were high priorities but a good name was beyond price. The slightest blemish might be disastrous. Rumour had it that the young Lady Dorothy Walpole (b.1826) had been surprised alone in a summerhouse with George Smythe MP, heir to an Irish peerage. The story got out of hand. Scandalous reports appeared in the 'low papers'. A prompt marriage to a 40-year-old cousin, 'a kind amicable person and particularly good tempered', with 'an independent pasture of £8,000 a year' and a small estate in Norfolk, failed to rehabilitate her. The Queen refused to receive her. Fortunately, Lady Dorothy's ostracism was not complete. She continued to enjoy Disraeli's friendship and became a correspondent and junior colleague of Charles Darwin whom she supplied with orchids and insectivorous plants for use in his research.

Younger sons

Many younger sons were lifelong bachelors. A fortunate minority married money – widows of property and heiresses were the quarry. Generally, however, those younger sons who married married later and more modestly than heirs. Men who went into business or the professions tended to take wives from colleagues' families. Those who married without consent might look in vain for support from their families. As late as 1857 the Marquess of Salisbury refused to acknowledge his second son's marriage to the daughter of an eminent judge. His heir endorsed the verdict, pointing out that the couple's relative poverty would condemn them to social isolation. There was opposition even where there was money in abundance. In the 1870s Lord Randolph Churchill, the Duke of Marlborough's second son, had to 'plot and intrigue like a second Machiavelli' to wrest his father's consent to his marriage with the handsomely endowed Jennie Jerome. Her American origin was a handicap; as the duke pointed out, it was 'slightly coming down in pride' for the Churchills 'to contemplate that connection'.

WOMEN'S OPTIONS OUTSIDE MARRIAGE

Women relied on their male kin for food, drink, clothes and the capital which would secure a marriage and endow a widowhood. Even the staunchest flouters of convention were trapped in dependency: Lady Eleanor Butler (b.1745) and Miss Sarah Ponsonby (b.1755), the notorious Ladies of Llangollen, who went into picturesque retreat in Wales in 1778, lived on money extracted from grudging and embarrassed kinsmen.

It was in a family's interest to retain the services of a daughter or niece who could be called on to act as companion to a dowager, to support women in childbed, to keep house for a widower, to mother orphan children. But, for the poor spinster, shunted from one relative's house to the next, exposed to malicious innuendo, humiliation might be a way of life. In the 1530s Jane Bassett, poor, in or approaching middle age, ill-tempered and often unwelcome, moved between houses belonging to her married sisters and her stepmother, Lady Lisle, with an entourage consisting of a servant, a greyhound, a horse and a cow or two. Mary Verney (b.1628) spent her late teens and early twenties dependent on meagre handouts, shuffled from one household to another, accused of 'being too familiar' with a brother-in-law when her sister was lying in. Marriage – almost any marriage – was preferable, as she put it: 'a little of my own is better than a great deal of another's'. A pamphlet published in 1698 proposed a 'A Protestant Monastery' to relieve the 'many families . . . so burdened with daughters their parents cannot either for want of beauty or money dispose of in marriage or in any other decent manner provide for'. The women's colleges founded in the late nineteenth century went some way to meeting her prescription.

THE CHOICE OF A HUSBAND

Its daughters' marriages were an index of a family's standing and prosperity. Families in straitened circumstances were reluctant to settle for a husband of inferior rank; from the family's point of view, spinsterhood was a preferable fate. Women who, in the seventeenth-century phrase, 'bestowed themselves meanly', degraded their relatives as well as themselves.

In the sixteenth century an heiress might be treated as a commodity. Elizabeth Trussell, sold to the Earl of Kent by Henry VII in 1501, was bequeathed to the purchaser's younger son, sold back to the king and finally disposed of to the Earl of Oxford who married her. By the middle of the seventeenth century, although mercenary marriages still occurred, it was generally recognised that it was wrong to force a child to marry against her will. All the same, reluctant brides continued to be bullied or blackmailed into acquiescence. Alice Wansford (b.1627), persuaded that her marriage would ease her family's financial problems, wrote of her engagement to William Thornton: 'I thought it rather duty in me to accept my friends' desires for a joint benefit than my own single retired content.' As late as the nineteenth century daughters schooled in habits of submission found it impossible to resist parental pressure. Mary Elizabeth Lucy (b.1803), marrying against her will, 'fainted away' at the end of the ceremony.

The letters which Nicholas Blundell (b.1669) wrote while negotiating his daughters' marriages suggest the limits of tolerance. His 'chief aim' was to 'settle [his] daughters to their own comfort and satisfaction'; he sought 'a personable man, one of sense and good parts and good humoured' and of his own persuasion – a Catholic. Honourable rank and 'a good estate', were 'not sufficient motives': they were taken as read.

As Winifred Willoughby's fate suggests, women who married without the consent of the head of the family were severely penalised. In a letter to a friend, the Duke of Richmond (b.1701) analysed his responses to his daughters' husbands:

> Emelie, our second girl, has married with our hearty approval the earl of Kildare, who I dare say is the equal by birth to anyone in Europe, they have been peers of Ireland since 1205, and as there are no dukes in that kingdom he is the premier peer. He is also an English peer, has a big income, and is the most honest, as well as the most likeable young man of the day. He is 25 years of age and she is 16 and has already got a son, to the great joy of this ancient family for Lord Kildare was absolutely the last of his line.

By contrast, 'the eldest girl Caroline married against our wishes a man infinitely beneath her, so we do not see her'. Caroline was a great-granddaughter of Charles II, her husband was the son of a man who had entered Charles's service as keeper of his dogs and stables; of his grandparents, the best that could be said was that they were 'distinguished from their neighbours by their pious and orderly living'. Nevertheless, the duke conceded that 'this man by his merits and talents is bound to make a name for himself . . . and he holds one of the best appointments that a gentleman could have: he is Secretary of State for War. His name is Mr Fox.' Affection for their daughter and respect for Mr Fox got the better of the Richmonds' pride. Within a couple of years of their elopement Mr Fox had become the duke's 'dear Harry'. His 'merits and talents' were rewarded with a peerage.

Socially ambitious men were willing to invest heavily in desirable connections. The first Earl of Cork bid up the going rate for dowries in his quest for well-born in-laws. The 1640s and 50s were a difficult time for Royalist families who underwrote the cost of the King's campaigns and risked the sequestration of their estates. Daughters of hardpressed landowners like the Verneys competed on the marriage market with the likes of Elizabeth Dashwood whose father had done well out of the war, selling saddles to both King and Parliament.

During the agricultural depression at the end of the nineteenth century, the competition was trans-Atlantic. In the 1880s publications listing English and European men of title who were 'available for matrimonial purposes', their education, marital history, acres, mortgages and income circulated in the United States. By 1915 five hundred-odd American heiresses had married into the European aristocracy. Between 1870 and 1914 roughly 10 per cent of peerage marriages were with Americans. Rumour had it that William K. Vanderbilt spent 'fully $10,000,000' on securing his daughter Consuelo's marriage to 'the Marlborough dukedom'.

Towards the end of the nineteenth century parental perceptions of suitable grooms became less rigid. In 1897, after determined campaigning by a married sister and a clergyman who was a friend of the family, Lady Emily Lytton's mother agreed to her marriage to the architect Edwin Lutyens, who had, in his own words, 'practically nothing to offer beyond [his] income . . . and the possibility of some life insurance'. It may be that Lady Emily's recent entanglement with the flamboyant William Scawen Blunt, a close friend of her father's and father of one of her own school friends, played a part in making up her mother's mind, but her sister's assertion that

> to marry a gentleman in heart, as well as birth, to love him passionately and faithfully and to give up all things to follow him through life . . . seems to me an ideal which can only bring honour to any family which holds it

does suggest a shift in values.

By the end of the Great War the definition of suitability had undoubtedly relaxed. Lady Anne Cavendish, daughter of the ninth Duke of Devonshire, thought that most of her siblings 'ended up married to fairly ordinary people instead of automatically going for the very rich or the very grand'. The Cavendishes' choices, though varied, were 'ordinary' only by ducal standards. The heir's bride was the daughter of the Marquess of Salisbury. His younger brother married the film star Adele Astaire. Among their sisters' husbands were Captain John Cobbold of the Suffolk brewing family; Major Harold Macmillan, publisher and future Prime Minister, whose family packed their side of the church at his wedding with authors from their list to balance the Cavendishes' aristocratic supporters; and Captain James Stuart, later Viscount Findhorn, descendant of a bastard son of James V of Scotland, and a former beau of Lady Elizabeth Bowes-Lyon, who married George VI.

MARITAL ROLES

The bride, uprooted from her childhood home, was not given secure tenure in her husband's. Heirs sometimes brought their wives as boarders to their fathers' households. Often it was a tense experience. In 1646 Sir Richard Strode, enraged by a financial dispute with his pregnant daughter-in-law's family, burst into the young couple's chamber, broke the windows and made off with furnishings including stuff put by for the coming baby. Diaries and memoirs describe power struggles between co-resident wives and mothers-in-law. Nicholas Blundell (b.1669) logged his wife's two-year campaign to dislodge his mother from the chamber she had occupied before his marriage; his aunt, the prop and stay of the family through hard times, was driven from her home. Some mothers-in-law defended their position tenaciously. At the beginning of the nineteenth century, Katherine Cholmeley's mother-in-law treated her as 'a tame animal kept for breeding purposes'. In the 1870s Jennie Jerome, who had married the Duke of Marlborough's younger son, compared life in Blenheim with a 'volcano ready to burst out at any moment'. The robust and self-assured Lady Maud Cecil (b.1858) described the experience of settling into her husband's family as 'worse than new stays on the whole'. Elsewhere the dowager's demotion was instant and automatic. When Mary Elizabeth Lucy (b.1803) returned to Charlecote on the eve of her son's wedding she found the bedroom she had occupied since her own marriage stripped and refurbished for the new mistress. As the Duchess of Devonshire has put it:

> If you are a woman who finds herself married to the hereditary owner of what used to be known as a stately home and is now called a historic house, you soon become aware of the unwritten rules of primogeniture. You live in furnished rooms, surrounded by things which do not and never will belong to you. You are also aware that if you should become a widow you move, pronto, and the familiar things stay.

The landowner's wife had responsibilities which paralleled her husband's. Among grandees housekeeping was the least of them. Great households were managed by professionals. At Cannons, the Duke of Chandos's residence, early in the eighteenth century, the size of the portions sent up to rooms was controlled, glasses and cutlery were regularly counted, visitors' gratuities were earmarked for the purchase of gardening tools and cleaning equipment. The mistresses of more modest households hired, trained and supervised their servants; as late as the nineteenth century spinning and weaving might be done at home. Women took a housewifely pride in their stocks of linen. Margaret Verney, who made her will in 1639, hoped that her household linen would be used by her eldest son, his heir and his son too. Frugal twentieth-century housekeepers were still using bedding manufactured in the reign of George II.

With servants at their disposal, landowners were slow to adopt the domestic technologies. When Mrs Herbert arrived in Ireland in the 1860s she denounced it as 'almost a century behind England in amenities . . . There wasn't a tap or a closet in the house'; instead there was a row of eight privies, which ranged from a 'giant-sized one down to one for a dwarf or an infant'. She 'wanted, of course, to slip out unseen' but 'Patsy the Bucket' was always lurking there 'with an old carriage umbrella as big as a tent and would insist on coming with [her] and choosing which booth [she] should occupy'. The first present her husband gave her was a water closet. Mrs Herbert was fortunate in her experience of English plumbing and optimistic about the date of its introduction. Adrian Verney-Cave, a pioneer aviator, wired his family home, Stanford Hall in Leicestershire, in the 1890s 'with the aid of his father's grooms and two ferrets' which were lured along their route with 'a smelly bit of rabbit'. After 1945, deprived of housemaids to carry slops and water and make up fires, and footmen to attend to oil lamps and candles, the occupants of great houses without bathrooms and electricity were exposed to inconvenience and acute discomfort.

A landowner's wife had duties in her neighbourhood. She might well possess the only medical expertise in the community. Lady Elinor Fettiplace's manuscript book of receipts, compiled at the beginning of the seventeenth century, records 'fifty-six ways of dressing wounds, nearly four dozen remedies for failing eyesight, two dozen plasters and potions to relieve and comfort the stomach, sixteen different cough mixtures and eleven cures for a bad back'. Fettiplace's contemporary, Lady Margaret Hoby (b.1571), regularly dressed wounds, human and animal, and sores. The local people had an awesome confidence in her. One afternoon a child was brought to her,

> one Talliour['s] son, who had no fundament, and had no passage for excrements but at the mouth: [she] was earnestly entreated to cut the place to see if any passage could be made, but, although [she] cut deep and searched, there was none to be found.

During the Civil War, again 'for want of another', Lucy Hutchinson served as surgeon to her husband's troops. The professionalisation of medicine, completed in the nineteenth century, made these amateur practitioners redundant, except in emergency. Janie Ellice's album of recipes, compiled on the recommendations of friends and relations between 1846 and 1859, reflects the diminishing importance of this paramedical role; it contains only a couple of medical prescriptions – one for cough mixture, the other for a 'pomade for promoting the growth of hair'. The generally frivolous tone of her collection is suggested by the instructions for banishing rats: 'Get a big HEELANDER with his bag-a-pipe – he blow his music – all the Rats run away.' In the crisis of the Great War the wounded became a major preoccupation of landowners' wives; they converted their houses into hospitals and convalescent homes.

Women fortunate enough to have the support of efficient servants were able to develop interests of their own. At a time when most top-flight embroiderers were male, Bess of Hardwick, in partnership with Mary Queen of Scots, produced work of professional quality, some of which can be seen at Oxburgh Hall in Norfolk. One of the most striking and detailed representations of a Stuart garden forms the backdrop to the portrait of Arthur Capel (b.1604), his wife and five children. Lady Capel, it seems, was the enthusiast; her son Henry created an important garden at Kew. Between 1837 and 1850 women of the Clifford family collaborated in recording the plants of their neighbourhood. The Duchess of Rutland was a very competent artist; she designed the monument in the chapel of Belvoir Castle commemorating her eldest son Lord Haddon, who died in 1894 at the age of 9. A scattering of aristocratic women were their own architects: 'Building Bess' of Hardwick emblazoned her house with her initials ES (for Elizabeth [Countess of] Shrewsbury) in the 1590s; Lady Wilbraham designed Weston Park in Shropshire in the 1670s and Lady Catherine Parker Saltram in the 1740s. Their architecture, like their spelling, was marked by a certain 'oridgenality', their houses betray them as gifted designers imperfectly acquainted with architectural decorum.

But the wife's chief and peculiar obligation was to deliver an heir. Those who did not were exposed to popular and medical remedies. Elizabeth Blundell's failure to conceive after the births of her daughters Mally (b.1704) and Fanny (b.1706) prompted a succession of pilgrimages to the miracle-working springs at Holywell and the scientifically-approved spas in Flanders, without result: a chain of male succession stretching back to the twelfth century was broken.

PARENTHOOD

Birth was women's work. In 1706 Nicholas Blundell absented himself from the house when his wife 'felt the pains of labour coming upon her' and went coursing with a neighbour. Blundell, concerned as he was about the outcome, recognised that a husband had no place in the birth chamber. The arrival of the male midwife in the seventeenth century signalled the end of female control but access to his services depended on location as much as wealth. Even at the close of the nineteenth century women confined in the country might be out of the reach of professional assistance. In the later nineteenth century husbands were present when their children were born. This practice, which shocked some country doctors, seems to have been a fashion imported from London and perhaps inspired by Prince Albert's example.

Some women immersed themselves in motherhood, others were little more than jewelled apparitions wafting through their children's lives. For such mothers, a child might be a decorative accessory. Sentimental portraits of mothers and infants, which became conventional in the eighteenth century, may be a better reflection of fashion than practice. According to George Cornwallis-West, in the 1870s,

> it was the custom for ladies of fashion to drive in Hyde Park . . . with one – only one – of their children. . . . It was nearly always one of my sisters who was given the place of honour in the victoria. . . . One afternoon, however, Lady Dudley appeared in her barouche with one of her six sons and, as she was a leader of society, this apparently set the fashion for mothers to produce their boys for the daily drive. One day, to my utter astonishment, I was bundled into the victoria, and afterwards drove with my mother for quite a considerable time

– until 'the fashion waned'. The Edwardian socialite Mrs Willie James, setting out for church, would ask their Nanny which of her five children would go best with her dress.

The bringing up of children was a potential cause of conflict between man and wife. The marriage of Ashe Windham (b.1673) and Elizabeth Dobyns (b.1693), which took place in 1709, was constructed on the sound footings of 'liking' and the lawyer's fortune she brought with her. Nevertheless, it was troubled from the outset – the Windhams and their friends blamed Elizabeth's temperament – and it broke down after the birth of their son William. In 1720, when William was 3, his father wrote a letter which, without putting the reader fully in the picture, records the deterioration of their relationship. The persistence of potentially misleading endearments is worth noting.

My Dear

You do not care one jot for my son or me: when all the pain, all the torment which I had the last time you was here, by your cruel usage of him, could not prevent you from using him so but the night was filled with his horrid shriek, terrible to every ear but his mother's; and stabbing every breast in the family but your own . . .

I cannot possibly account for such behaviour to him unless it was out of pure hatred to me, even tho' you greatly indangered the very life of your only child, who to me is more valuable than the riches of the universe.

MARITAL RELATIONSHIPS

Although the intimate relationship between husband and wife is difficult to observe and assess, there is reason to believe that, in practice as well as in theory, prudence was the soundest foundation. Those who married at the order of or with the advice of fathers or friends had lower expectations of emotional rewards than those who married on the basis of 'liking' alone, particularly in defiance of parental advice and in the absence of financial support. A shared religious or political allegiance or a common enthusiasm for foxhunting might help to compensate for the cultural division created by the contrasting childhood experiences of boys and girls. Some husbands made specific efforts to share their masculine interests with their wives. The mathematical seventh Duke of Devonshire (b.1808) taught his wife geometry on their honeymoon. Their, reputedly idyllic, relationship was solidly grounded in their shared religious faith: 'One of their favourite pastimes was reading Wesley's sermons together.'

Ill-suited couples had ample excuse for keeping out of each other's way. The complementary duties of man and wife almost inevitably kept them apart; the pursuit of health was a legitimate reason for separation. Peers' families normally had town and country houses, sometimes more than one. The scale of landowners' houses made autonomy possible under a shared roof. In the nineteenth-century country house separation was, potentially, complete: the master had his study or business room and a dressing room adjoining his wife's bedroom where he could sleep; the lady of the house had her sitting room.

MARITAL BREAKDOWN

Since the transmission of property was a crucial factor in matchmaking and the field of suitable partners was limited, it is hardly surprising that disputes over property and clashes of temperament were often causes of breakdown. The disintegration of the marriage of John and Sophia Musters of Colwick Hall in Nottinghamshire has been traced by art historians and restorers. George Stubbs painted two portraits of the couple on horseback in 1777, the year after they married. As this commission suggests, Musters had sporting tastes – his horse Orion won the Nottingham Gold Cup in 1775, and he kept a pack of hounds. Sophia was more at home in London or Brighton where, according to gossip, she caught the fancy of the Prince of Wales. Finding her conduct insupportable, her husband recalled Stubbs to paint her out. A quarter of a century later the Tasburghs were living separate lives under a single roof, locked in a bitter feud over property. Whenever the opportunity arose, Mrs Tasburgh 'would lean out' of her bedroom window 'and spit on his head'. The negotiation of their daughter's marriage settlement was disrupted by their feud; she broke the deadlock by eloping.

Church courts had the power to grant legal separations but, unlike most churches which broke with Rome, the Church of England made no provision for divorce with the possibility of remarriage. Until the nineteenth century a private Act of Parliament was the only proper method of dissolving a consummated marriage. Sir Ralph Sadler (b.1507), a Crown servant who did well out of the Reformation, promoted a private bill to resolve the difficult situation which arose when Lady Sadler's unsatisfactory first husband, long presumed dead, turned up to threaten the legitimacy of their seven children. In the 1540s Henry VIII's brother-in-law William Parr, Marquess of Northampton, used two Acts to dispose of his adulterous first wife and secure the succession through his second marriage. For over a century no one followed his example. Then, in 1671, Lord Roos introduced a bill to rid himself of a wife who had taunted him with the prospect of his name and title passing to her lover's son. Parliamentary divorce was disgraceful, difficult and expensive. The Duke of Norfolk had to campaign for almost a decade before his bill was passed in 1699: he succeeded only when his wife's family turned against her.

Although it became commoner in the eighteenth century, divorce was normally undertaken to prevent an inheritance passing to a child conceived in adultery. When inheritance was not in question, a civil action for damages could be brought to salve the pride of the outraged husband. In some circles, discreet infidelity, which did not threaten the legitimate succession, was condoned. In late Victorian and Edwardian England a hostess in the 'fast set' was accustomed to accommodate her guests conveniently close to their lovers. The Duchess of Manchester's three-decade affair with the Duke of Devonshire's heir was a secret confined to their own circle. Their marriage in 1892, a decent year after Manchester's death, made her the 'double duchess'. Queen Victoria, who was generally prejudiced against second marriages, declared her as 'not a fit companion' for the Princess of Wales.

Even after divorce proceedings were transferred to the Law Courts in 1857, the termination of a marriage remained a serious business. 'Guilty' women were ostracised; 'guilty' men were hounded from office. There was some sympathy for the 'innocent' female party; in 1887 the Queen, who voiced her disapproval of the 'double duchess' and barred Lady Dorothy Nevill from her court, admitted poor divorced ladies – victims of 'cruelty, desertion, and misbehaviour but . . . in no way to blame themselves' – to her drawing room for the first time.

WIDOWHOOD

The vast majority of marriages ended in death. Displays of violent grief were frequent, though it would be wrong to interpret them automatically as evidence of loving marriages. Most memorials and epitaphs display conventional virtues. This tribute to Alice Pitman (d.1613) in St Mary's, Woodbridge, Suffolk, was commissioned by her husband's second wife.

> Alice his former wife and spouse most dear
> Like fruitful vine grew by him many a year
> To him a Sarah, Martha to his house
> A Dorcas to the poor and piteous
> This Sarah, Martha, Dorcas fell asleep
> Left husband, house and poor for her to weep.

Dame Dorothy Selby's epitaph at Ightam in Kent celebrates similar qualities. Known for her needlecraft, she was 'a Dorcas'; a widow in the difficult years before the outbreak of the Civil War, she showed herself 'prudently simple, providently wary' – 'to the world a Martha, to heaven a Mary'. The biblical heroines and the qualities they embodied – fecundity, fidelity, domestic competence and good works – would have been as familiar and as estimable to the Victorian churchgoers as to the Stuarts who saw the Pitman monument when it was new.

Henry Brydges, second Duke of Chandos (b.1708), praised his second wife Anne, who died in 1759, in the less public pages of his family Register. (Anne's origins were obscure. Rumour had it that she had been a maidservant in an inn, an ostler's mistress, the subject of a wife sale. Gossip of this sort was often exaggerated then, as now.)

Anne, Duchess of Chandos . . . was possessed of every good quality . . . every paper relative to household affairs was left in the most exact order for the use of her surviving lord with directions indexed where to go to each paper, which must have been a work of some months, and plainly showed that she was not insensible of her approaching dissolution.

The memorial to Frederica Stanhope, wife of the Honourable James Hamilton Stanhope, who died in childbirth in 1823, at the age of 22, describes her in her own words as 'what she wished to be' and what her 'afflicted but grateful husband' declared she was:

> a pious Christian, a faithful affectionate and tender wife, a dutiful and grateful daughter, a kind sister, the mother to my children which my mother was to me, the friend of the poor and needy . . . to have true charity, to live a godly life on Earth and to die in the blessed hope that my sins though many may be forgiven and that I shall enter the gates of everlasting happiness, there to meet or wait for those I love: this is the life and end for which I pray.

Stanhope, impatient of waiting 'in humble hope for a united immortality', took his own life.

Remarriage was universally approved only for widowers without sons. Even in these cases, there might well be problems. Sir Justinian Isham (b.1610) acknowledged that, in his case, 'the age, the widower [himself, that is] and the daughters' – he had four – would 'be obstacles, especially the daughters, for his age may pass undiscovered'. Lord Lyttleton, under 40 when his wife died in 1857, looked forward to 'thirty or forty years' of solitary misery. Three years later the marriage of his eldest daughter Meriel (b.1840), his 'great companion' and the younger children's foster mother, plunged him afresh into 'terrible fits of depression' and provoked anew thoughts of marriage. He had twelve children (unrelieved childbearing had been the death of his first wife) and 'very inadequate means compared with [his] position'. Only a mature childless woman with a fortune would do and he 'might as well think of the moon'.

In law, the widow enjoyed greater autonomy than she had as a maiden or a wife. However, her first reponsibility was not to herself but to her children. The memorial to Alice (b.1659), widow of Sir John Brownlow at Belton, Lincolnshire, records the achievements of her widowhood. 'She was chiefly employ'd' in the 'education' and marrying of her daughters: 'three of them she dispos'd in marriage to three noble Peers of the Realm and the fourth to the husband's nephew out of respect to his Memory'. Six years after his marriage 'the husband's nephew' was granted an Irish peerage with the title Viscount Tyrconnel.

The motivation of widows who remarried varied. According to a gossipy letter of 1598, Dorothy Unton demanded, among other things, that she should be left in control of her own income and property and be guaranteed alimony and the right to live apart if 'she and her husband fall out'. Moreover, 'if she chance to find fault with her husband's unsufficiency', she was at liberty 'to choose another bedfellow'. The story tells us less about Dorothy Unton than it does about the Tudor and Stuart conviction that widows were eager for a sexually satisfying mate. Material ambition seems to have moved Bess of Hardwick (b.1527). Born a farmer's daughter, she ended her life as Countess of Shrewsbury, taking her children up the social ladder with her. A few weeks after her marriage to the earl in 1567 her 12-year-old daughter Mary and her 18-year-old son Gilbert married his son and daughter. Widows who remarried often did so in the hope of securing a 'friend' to represent their interests and those of their children in a male-dominated world. Harriot Eliot (b.1714), who was widowed at the age of 34, sought a friend in Captain the Honourable John Hamilton. His presence in an informal picture of the Eliot family, which was painted in her first husband's lifetime, shows him with one of the small Eliot girls riding on his back and suggests a close relationship with her family. Hamilton's gallant record as a naval officer and Reynolds' portrait, which shows him as a dashing figure in the costume of a Hungarian hussar, imply an energy which Mrs Eliot's first husband, who died in his middle fifties, may have lost.

Some widows married beneath them. Their choices included such confidential servants as chaplains and tutors: they were known and, presumably, trusted companions. According to *The Dictionary of National Biography*, the Marquess of Blandford's tutor, John Moore (b.1730), son of an inn-keeping butcher from Gloucester, prudently declined the dowager Duchess of Marlborough in favour of a career in the Church which was crowned, thanks to Churchill influence, by his elevation to Canterbury.

As the letters of Arthur and Honor Lisle suggest, some mature marriages of convenience proved remarkably affectionate. In November 1538, Lady Lisle wrote of a channel crossing, 'I should have been much merrier if I had been coming towards you, or if you had been with me'. A few days later she signed a letter 'by her that is more yours than her own, which had much rather die with you there, than live here' alone. For his part, Lisle 'never loved none so well, neither thought so long for none since I knew a woman'; he claimed that he could not sleep for thinking about her. At the time of these exchanges Lisle was probably in his sixties, his wife in her forties. A century and a half later Lady Willoughby's second marriage to the immensely wealthy Sir Josiah Child, who had made his fortune in trade with the East, proved less satisfactory; she opted to be buried beside her first husband. Her sons' attitude to their stepfather – they left home to live with an aunt – may have undermined her confidence in Sir Josiah.

SUMMING UP

Until the second half of the nineteenth century wealth, political power and patronage were concentrated in the hands of landowners. Successful businessmen, lawyers, soldiers and government servants invested in country estates and the other appurtenances of aristocratic life.

Transmitting an undiminished inheritance to his son and heir was the landowner's priority. In consequence the heir was singled out from the rank and file of younger brothers, many of whom were destined for the professions. Daughters were generally less welcome than sons. Young children were normally consigned to the care of servants. From the sixteenth century Latin and field sports dominated the boys' curriculum; most girls had little formal education.

Marriage and breeding were the heir's prime duties. His choice of a wife was prescribed by family priorities: her connections, endowment and chastity were of the first importance. Younger sons married later, many remained bachelors. The poverty of couples who married without consent was regarded as a self-inflicted condition. Unmarried women were treated as understudies, filling in for missing mothers, daughters and wives. Even in desperate need few sought paid employment. Daughters' marriages were negotiated by parents and guardians but the girls' influence on the choice of a husband gradually increased.

The domestic responsibilities of a landowner's wife reflected the scale of her household. Invariably she was expected to act as her husband's lieutenant, standing in for him during his temporary absences and, if he died before his son was of age, for the duration of his minority.

There was a wide variation in the warmth and closeness of relationships between parents and children and husbands and wives. A good many marriages were soured by property disputes. Ill-feeling led to separation but divorce was normally undertaken only to prevent the succession of a child born to an adulterous wife.

NOW READ ON

Mark Girouard: *Life in the English Country House: A Social and Architectural History* (New Haven, Conn.: Yale University Press, 1978).

John Pearson: *Stags and Serpents: The Story of the House of Cavendish and the Dukes of Devonshire* (London: Macmillan, 1983).

Lawrence Stone: *The Crisis of the Aristocracy, 1558–1641* (Oxford: Clarendon Press, 1965).

Lawrence Stone and Jeanne C. Fawtier Stone: *An Open Elite? England 1540–1880* (Oxford: Oxford University Press, 1984).

Hilary Spurling: *Elinor Fettiplace's Receipt Book* (London: Viking Salamander, 1986).

J. T. Cliffe: *The Puritan Gentry: Great Puritan Families of Early Stuart England* (London: Routledge and Kegan Paul, 1984).

Miriam Slater: *Family Life in the Seventeenth Century: The Verneys of Claydon House* (London: Routledge and Kegan Paul, 1984).

John Cannon: *Aristocratic Century: The Peerage of Eighteenth-century England* (Cambridge: Cambridge University Press, 1984).

Randolph Trumbach: *The Rise of the Egalitarian Family: Aristocratic Kinship and Domestic Relations in Eighteenth-Century England* (New York: Academic Press, 1978).

Jonathan Gathorne-Hardy: *The Rise and Fall of the British Nanny* [1972] (London: Weidenfeld and Nicolson, 1985).

Pat Jalland: *Women, Marriage and Politics, 1860–1914* (Oxford: Clarendon Press, 1986).

Maureen E. Montgomery: *Gilded Prostitution: Status, Money and Transatlantic Marriages* (London: Routledge, 1989).

Plate 1 The Harvey family of Catton, Norfolk, *c.*1821, painted by Joseph Clover

Living models and portraits of their dead kin were the sources for Clover's anthology of Harveys. Families united the dead, the living and the yet unborn. Portraits and other legacies, including given names as well as material possessions, linked the current generations with their forebears. (Reproduced by permission of Norfolk Museums Service (Norwich Castle Museum))

Plate 2 'The Society betwixt Parents and Children' described by Joannes Amos Comenius in *Orbis Sensualium Pictus*

Comenius, born in Moravia in 1592, sought refuge in the West during the Thirty Years War (1618–48). He was the first European to use pictures and parallel texts in Latin and a mother tongue to increase the schoolboy's word power. The first, Latin–German, edition of *Orbis Sensualium Pictus* was published in Nuremberg in 1658. The work was an enduring success. The final version, with texts in Czech, German, French and Latin was issued in Prague in 1845. The editors failed to catch up with scientific discoveries: not until the New York edition of 1810 was the heart recognised as the organ which pumped blood; the heavens continued to wheel about the earth a century after Newton described the solar system. The illustrations changed only superficially from the first edition to the last. This page is reproduced from the twelfth English edition of 1777: the painter's costume has been updated but other elements – cradled infant, the sucking child, the standing stool or walking frame, the daughter's role as surrogate mother – have been retained.

Comenius recognised three domestic societies: *Societas Conjugalis* (the society between husband and wife); *Societas Herilis* (the society between master and servant); and this, the *Societas Parentalis* (the society between parents and children). (Reproduced by permission of the Syndics of Cambridge University Library)

CXXII.

| The Society betwixt Parents and Children. | Societas Parentalis. |

Married Persons,
(by the blessing of God)
have Issue,
and become Parents.

The Father, 1. *begetteth,*
and the Mother, 2. *beareth*
Sons, 3. *and* Daughters, 4.
(sometimes Twins.)

The Infant, 5.
is wrapped in
Swaddling-clothes, 6.
is laid in a Cradle, 7,
is suckled by the Mother
with her Breasts, 8.
and fed with Pap, 9.

Afterwards it learneth
to go by a Standing-stool, 10.

Conjuges,
(ex benedictione Dei)
suscipiunt *Sobolem* (Prolem)
& fiunt *Parentes.*

Pater, 1. generat,
& *Mater,* 2. parit
Filios, 3. & *Filias,* 4.
(aliquando *Gemellos.*)

Infans, 5.
involvitur *Fasciis,* 6.

reponitur in *Cunas,* 7.
lactatur a matre
Uberibus, 8.
& nutritur *Pappis,* 9.

Deinde discit
incedere *Serperastro,* 10.

H 6

playeth

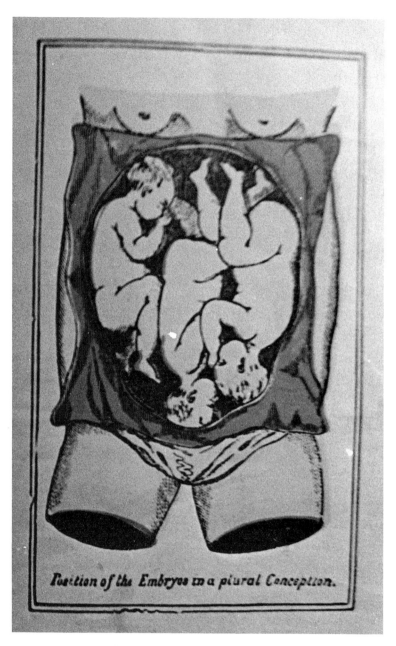

Position of the Embryos in a plural Conception.

Plate 3 Aristotle's Masterpiece

Aristotle's Masterpiece had a long but covert history as a guide to 'married sex'. Neither the name of the publisher nor the date of publication is revealed in the edition from which this plate is taken; the binding suggests that it was produced in the last quarter of the nineteenth century. Earlier versions were in circulation before 1700. (Private Collection)

In affectionate Remembrance

OF

BEATRICE MARY ANN FOLKES,

The beloved child of JOHN & EMMA FOLKES,

WHO DIED DECEMBER 29th, 1878,

Aged 1 year and 10 months.

"Farewell' dear little Beatrice thy spirit has fled,
A bright crown of glory now rests on thy head;
To the mansion of rest prepared thee above,
Thy Saviour has called thee in wisdom and love.

Then shall we repine at God's Holy will!
Dear Jesus say (as we hush) peace and be still,
I have folded thy lamb in my own tender breast,
She shall be for ever unspeakably blest."

Plate 4 Card printed in affectionate remembrance of Beatrice Mary Ann Folkes, 1878

This is a large and elaborate example of the memorial cards distributed in Victorian England. Beatrice's parents selected a blank design to carry the lines they had composed or, perhaps more likely, modified from a stock text. Stuart mourners had been summoned to interments by printed tickets decorated with 'death's heads' (skulls). In the eighteenth century these brutal tokens of mortality were supplanted by the emblems embossed on this card: the urn, the obelisk, the weeping willows, the broken column trailing ivy, the attendant angels poised to wreathe Beatrice's brow with crowns of glory. (Private Collection)

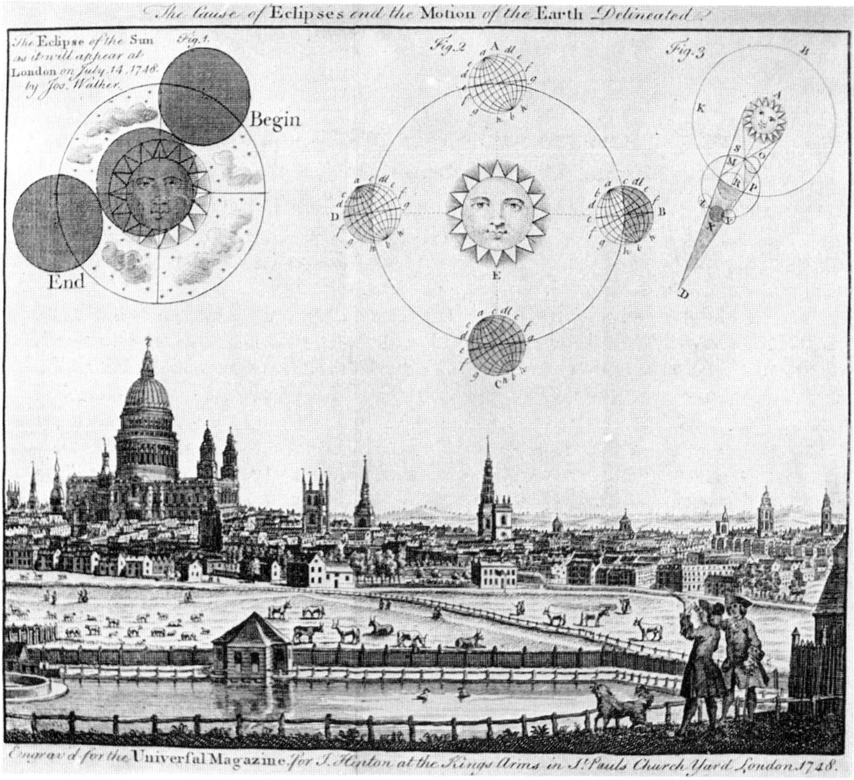

Plate 5 'The eclipse of the sun as it will appear at London on July 14 1768' drawn by Jos. Walker for the *Universal Magazine*

The engraving illustrates the interest in scientific explanations which spread through the male elite from the middle of the seventeenth century, as the telescope and the microscope opened their eyes to hitherto invisible worlds. Illiteracy and poverty meant that labouring men and women had little access to ideas in print.

The skyline of Georgian London was dominated by the dome of St Paul's and the towers and steeples of other churches built to replace those destroyed in the Great Fire of 1666. The riverside pastures are reminders both of the comparatively small scale of eighteenth-century cities and of the difficulty of transporting fresh food before the coming of the railways. (Private Collection)

Joan is supported by her daughters Jane, Elizabeth and Joan; her husband by their six sons, William, Edward, John, George, Essex and Barnard. In spite of William's protective gesture, Death, an arrow in one hand, a wreath in the other, comes between them. The couple's dead children look down from heaven. The Latin text, which few of her female friends and relatives could have interpreted, records the names of her husband and her father, Edward Barnard, and accords her credit for conventional wifely virtues. In twenty-eight years she had borne sixteen children; she was faithful and well-intentioned, a dutiful daughter, a loyal wife, a fond mother and a good neighbour. The design includes no fewer than five shields. The Barnards' bear is shown at the top of the column to Joan's left; the arms of Strode on the column to William's right. The shields in the arches, symbolising the couple's union, show 'Strode impaling Barnard'. (Reproduced by permission of Somerset Archaeological and Natural History Society)

The interior of Belton parish church is dominated by dozens of monuments to the descendants of Richard Brownlow (b.1553), who made a fortune in the legal profession. Brownlow obtained a grant of arms in 1593; two of his sons achieved the novel dignity of baronet; in the 1680s his great-grandson built Belton, 'to many . . . the perfect image of the English country house'; barons and earls adorn the upper branches of his family tree. The church was listed in Domesday Book in 1086, its fabric includes Norman fragments. From this perspective, the Brownlows are newcomers but churches were a favourite medium for family propaganda and it was natural that they should make their mark on this one.

Belton House passed into the custody of the National Trust in 1984. The churchwardens of St Peter and St Paul remain custodians of a sculpture gallery in which the outstanding exhibit is Antonio Canova's monument to the first earl's first wife, set up in 1818, four years after her death. (Reproduced by permission of Belton Parochial Church Council)

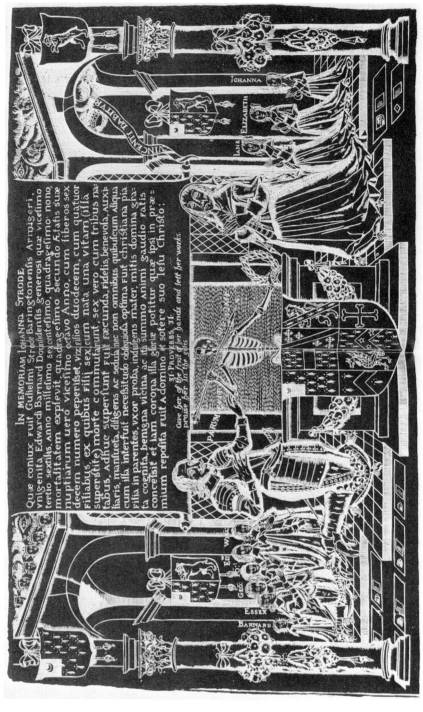

Plate 6

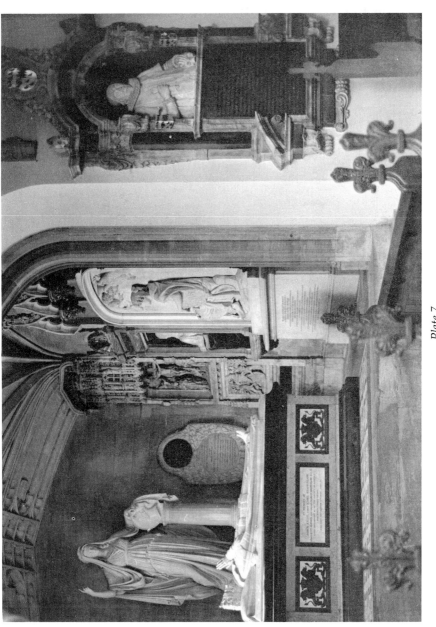

Plate 7

Plate 8 A half-gallon (2-litre) jug celebrating the partnership of David and Ann Davis, 1808

The text around a jug's neck wishes the couple peace, plenty and success. The body is decorated with key components of that happy state: a plough; a thatched farmhouse; well-observed geese, cackling and flapping their wings; cows with their calves; what may be a sheep; and three men off to reap or mow, carrying their drink in harvest barrels, which would have held about half a gallon of ale or cider; one has slung his dinner, wrapped in a checked cloth, from the handle of his scythe. Mrs Davis is presumably occupied indoors. (Private Collection)

Plate 9 War work: Cambridge street cleaners

During the Great War, as in previous crises, women stepped into men's shoes. As this picture demonstrates, not all these roles were glamorous. After the war, most women returned to their traditional spheres. (Reproduced by permission of the Cambridgeshire Collection, Cambridgeshire Libraries)

Plate 10 Postcard sent from Woodlea, Manitoba, Canada to Millie Booth of Halifax, Yorkshire, England in 1908

Literacy, photography and cheap postal rates made it easier to keep in touch. Postcard-size prints of family snapshots were routinely produced with the legend 'POST CARD' and the standard layout on the reverse. Thanks to Gutenberg, Fox Talbot, Roland Hill and her Uncle Ed, Millie Booth was able to put names to faces and follow the progress of her cousins, their dog Khaki and their pony Molly on the other side of the Atlantic. (Private Collection)

Plate 11 'The Royal Family of Great Britain, in memory of the 50th anniversary of the accession of Her Majesty Queen Victoria, the 21st of June 1887'

This Jubilee souvenir celebrates Victoria as matriarch. The designer has reproduced the layout often used in photograph albums of the period. The queen is surrounded by her children and their spouses. Her late husband and her dead children are represented but distinguished from the survivors by the wreathes which circle their portraits, the darker background against which they are depicted and the dates of their decease, which follow their names. In keeping with the code governing the succession to the throne, the next generation is represented by the sons and daughters of Victoria's heir, the Prince of Wales. (Private Collection)

Plate 12 Empire Day, 24 May 1909

Empire Day, the occasion of this photograph, has been dropped from the popular calendar. Mont Abbott (b.1902) recalled the celebrations at Enstone Council School in Oxfordshire:

> We wore a daisy in our buttonholes, and prayed at long length for all the people of the British Empire . . . The whole school 'ud line-up in the playground for 'The Salute'. The old battle-flag, Enstone School Union Jack, 'ud be waft-wafting . . . on the breeze . . . We'd march, we old bwoys leading the little'uns, to the ring of our hobnails . . . right round the yard, looking up at the flag and saluting as we passed.

By 1909 elementary education had been compulsory and free for a generation. Many lower-middle-class parents sent their children to private schools to preserve them from contact with their 'inferiors'. The age of the children and the fact that the boys and girls are sitting together suggest that this is a class of 'mixed infants'; older boys and girls were normally segregated. These children seem to be relatively privileged, those we can see are shod. Leaving aside the teachers' gender, the Edwardian schoolroom bears little resemblance to the environment in which young children of the 1990s spend their 'working lives'. A patriotic print is the most prominent decoration. No examples of the children's work are on display. These children were strictly regimented: they spent most of their day at their desks. The piano was probably used to accompany marching and other orderly activity.

Elementary schoolteaching provided working-class girls with an entry to the lower middle class. Although many women had obligations which tied them to their parents, single schoolmistresses had a better chance of achieving economic independence than most of their contemporaries: in country districts a house often went with the job. Before the Great War married women were permitted to negotiate cover for their maternity leave. Teachers paid a price for these advantages: they and the discipline they imposed were often unpopular in the communities they served. (Reproduced by permission of the Cambridgeshire Collection, Cambridgeshire Libraries)

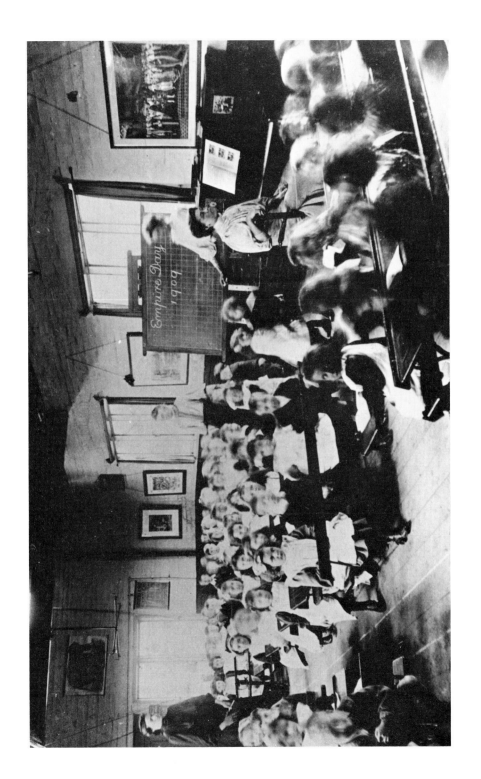

Plate 13 John Geoffrey William Baker (1906–88)

Geoffrey Baker was born in Hampstead. The toy animals shown in this portrait, painted in 1910, suggest the imperial influence on a middle-class nursery. Geoffrey attended University College School, London; he went into the Midland Bank and became Manager of the Chelsea branch. (Reproduced by permission of Mr and Mrs Philip Baker)

Plate 14 Frances, Lady Daresbury's bookplate

Lady Daresbury chose to have herself depicted as a foxhunting woman. Fishing is a secondary pursuit. On horseback, women were able to compete with men on more or less equal terms. (Private Collection)

Plate 15 Lord Haddon, heir to the Duke of Rutland with his younger brother and sister, by James Jesuba Shannon

Lady Marjorie Manners is sitting in a silver punch bowl, weighing 1,979 ounces, made in 1682 in the time of the ninth Earl of Rutland. Lord Haddon died in 1894. His mother, an accomplished artist, sculpted his effigy for the chapel of Belvoir Castle, the Manners family's home. Lord John Manners succeeded his father as ninth Duke of Rutland in 1925.

Shannon painted many portraits of this generation of the Manners family. Another of his models, Lady Diana, remembered Shannon 'whom everybody loved, darting backwards and forwards with palette and mahlstick, delicious smells of paint and turps, a mirror behind the painter in which I could watch the picture grow'. (Reproduced by permission of The Belvoir Estate)

Plate 16 Cheveley Park, Cambridgeshire, by Jan Siberechts, 1681

This painting shows the aristocratic house as a dominant feature of the rural landscape. Cheveley Park was built for Henry Jermyn in the 1670s. John Harris, historian of *The Artist and the Country House*, described it as a 'typical house' of its period: 'red brick, some stone dressings, two main fronts to the walled gardens, and nothing spectacular, just handsome and fine'. Behind it is Newmarket, a town associated with racing even in the seventeenth century. Ely Cathedral, visible for miles across the flat East Anglian countryside, is on the horizon.

Cheveley Park passed to the Manners family by marriage in the middle of the eighteenth century. It has since been demolished. The painting survives in the Duke of Rutland's collection at Belvoir Castle. (Reproduced by permission of The Belvoir Estate)

Plate 17 The Cupola House, Bury St Edmunds, Suffolk

This house was built in the 1690s for Thomas Macro (b.*c*.1649), a successful apothecary and a leading figure in the civic community of Bury St Edmunds. In 1679 he married Susan Cox, the daughter and heiress of the rector of the nearby parish of Risby. Celia Fiennes (b.1662), a granddaughter of Lord Saye and Sele, who visited Bury St Edmunds in the course of her 'Great Journey' of 1698, admired the house: 'except this', she noted, 'the rest are great old houses of timber'. By contrast, the Cupola House was in 'the new mode of building, four rooms of a floor pretty sizeable and high, well furnished, a drawing room and a chamber full of china', a novel luxury. There was also – a traditional sign of wealth and pretension – 'a pretty deal of plate' in Mrs Macro's chamber. The couple's son, Cox Macro, was a noted collector of manuscripts and Old Master drawings. He served as one of George II's chaplains, 'but the possession of an ample fortune placed him above the need for preferment'. (Reproduced by permission of Suffolk Record Office, Bury St Edmunds Branch)

Plate 18 Delft barber's bowl, 1716

Like many other craftsmen and shopkeepers, barbers were expected to give their regular customers extended credit. Quarter Day was the usual time for settling three-monthly accounts. Some barbers had to wait a year to collect their dues.

The bowl held the water and soap (in the well between 'Quarter' and 'Day') which the barber used to lather his client's face before he shaved him. The rim was designed to fit the customers neck. The perforations at the top indicate that the bowl was hung up while not in use. Barbers' bowls were often decorated with the tools of their trade: scissors, razor, comb, brushes, needle and thread and powder horn. A bowl decorated in 1706 shows the barber-surgeon who owned it with the horse which took him on his rounds. (Reproduced by permission of Christie's)

Plate 19 Stoneware tankard recording the dates of birth of John and Margaret Davis of Henley-on-Thames and six of their children, 1740

In the seventeenth century, pottery became a favourite medium of those who wished to celebrate their families but could not afford gold or silver plate. The survival of such fragile items indicates a reverence for heirlooms.

The tankard lists the dates of birth of John, his wife Margaret, and their children, the twins Elizabeth and John, Thomas, William, Mary and Robert. The tankard is discussed in Jonathan Horne's *Catalogue of English Stoneware from the 17th and 18th Centuries* (London: Jonathan Horne, 1985), p. 22. (Reproduced by permission of Jonathan Horne Antiques Ltd)

Plate 20 Harvest

Traditionally, harvest was a protracted labour-intensive task involving teams of men and women of all ages and, when circumstances demanded, of most ranks. Labourers were recruited from the barren uplands and, later, Ireland. Until late in the nineteenth century, cereals were cut, bound into sheaves and loaded by hand. Harvest earnings enable labourers to settle debts and buy clothing. Mechanisation made women and children redundant. They continued to scour the stubble fields for fallen corn; their gleanings made a significant contribution to the household income. (Reproduced by permission of the Cambridgeshire Collection, Cambridgeshire Libraries)

Plate 21 (overleaf) George Robinson's pottery, Brentford, *c.*1840

The chimney pots on the left are impressed with their manufacturer's name. The 'waste not, want not' ethic that prevailed in the home was applied in the workshop. At the Fishley pottery in Devon: 'nothing was wasted. If the clay got dirty, it was made into bricks.' Traditionally, the craftsman's workplace was his children's playground; they became familiar with his trade long before the boys were old enough to be apprenticed. Girls became accustomed to the routines and rhythms of the trade: it made sense to marry a woman who understood the way things were, particularly if, like millers and bakers, your work involved unsocial hours. (Reproduced by permission of Sotheby's)

Plate 22 (overleaf) Mr Norman's farm, Cambridgeshire

This group portrait illustrates the gentrification of farmers, which Cobbett had denounced in the 1820s. Mrs Norman sits in her trap, her husband stands at her side, their son is behind on his pony. Their servants are on parade. Emma Brown has been kitted out with a white cap and pinafore; the pails she carries betray the hard physical demands domestic service made on many women. The boy, Henry Barker, probably did most of the roughest jobs in the kitchen and the yard. The men on the right are outdoor workers. (Reproduced by permission of the Cambridgeshire Collection, Cambridgeshire Libraries)

Plate 21

Plate 22

Plate 23 The Strachey family, c.1895

Sir Richard and Lady Strachey are supported, respectively, by their sons: Richard, Ralph, Oliver, Lytton and James, and their daughters: Elinor, Dorothea, Pippa, Pernel and Marjorie. Their pose consciously replicates that of aristocratic families portrayed on tombs and brasses; they too are divided by gender and ranked by age.

The Stracheys were pillars of the 'intellectual aristocracy'. From the beginning of the seventeenth century Strachey men made their mark in the colonies, academia and the world of letters. William Strachey (b.1572) was educated at the University of Cambridge and the Inns of Court. He moved in literary and theatrical circles; between 1610 and 1611 he was Secretary of the new colony of Virginia. His grandson John (b.1634) was a friend of the philosopher Locke. John's son and namesake (b.1671) was an amateur geologist and antiquarian. Henry (b.1736) revived the colonial motif. He served Clive in India and was rewarded with a fortune and a baronetcy. His younger brother John (b.1737), one of George III's chaplains, edited the records of medieval parliaments. India was the dominant theme in the lives of Sir Henry's male descendants for a century and a half.

Sir Richard (b.1817) had a long and distinguished career in Indian affairs. He was largely responsible for the development of the sub-continental railway system. He also made a substantial contribution to the study of Indian geography, botany and meteorology. Strachey remained remarkably vigorous into old age: he was 70 when his youngest child was born and he played an active part in the management of the Indian railways (from London) until he was almost 90. His first wife died miscarrying her first child. In 1859 he married Jane Grant (b.1840), a member of another family prominent in the history of British India. Lady Strachey was active in the movement for women's suffrage.

The ten children who survived childhood added to the family's honours. Richard Strachey (b.1861) was a professional soldier. Ralph (b.1868) and Oliver (b.1874) kept up the Indian tradition. Lytton (b.1880) was one of the Victorian-born leaders of the assault on Victorianism. In their private lives too, he and his friends the Bells and the Woolfs cast aside traditional family values. James, sometimes known as 'Uncle Baby', became a psychoanalyst. Elinor (b.1859) followed the traditional female calling of marriage and motherhood. Dorothy (b.1865) and Marjorie (b.1882) were writers. Pippa (b.1872) was a leading suffragist. Pernel (b.1876) became Principal of Newnham College, Cambridge. (Reproduced by permission of the National Portrait Gallery)

Plate 24 The Sharp family, 1779–81, painted by Johan Zoffany

Music was an integral element in the portfolio of the cultivated man; the Sharps gave regular Sunday concerts. William played the French horn, John the cello, Granville the flageolet and James the serpent. Frances strummed a theorbo, Elizabeth was the pianist.

Although other relatives are present, this portrait emphasises the relationships between siblings rather than 'the society betwixt parents and children' or man and wife. The group celebrates the bonds of affection and shared tastes that united the Sharps. They were grandchildren of John Sharp, Archbishop of York (b.1645); their father Thomas (b.1693) was a younger son, he also followed an ecclesiastical career. Dr John Sharp, his eldest son, entered the Church in his turn. William (b.1729) was a distinguished surgeon who worked at Guy's Hospital and ministered to George III. James was an engineer. Granville (b.1735) was a prominent campaigner against slavery, an advocate of the founding of Sierra Leone, a colony for ex-slaves repatriated to Africa. His brothers clubbed together to support him and he spent much of his time at William's house in Fulham.

Zoffany depicts the musicians at rest. William is the commanding figure waving his cocked hat to the audience. John is recognisable by his black clerical dress. Their sister Judith is holding the score. (Reproduced by permission of C.G.M. Lloyd-Baker Esq.)

Plate 25 Paul and Sally Gotobed mending fishing nets, Cambridgeshire, *c.*1870

The long basket in the background was used to trap eels. In the sixteenth and seventeenth centuries fishing was an important source of income for the population of the wetlands. Drainage deprived many inland fishermen and wildfowlers of their livelihood, and by the nineteenth century they were a rare breed. Fishermen's wives were among the many women who made an important contribution to their husband's trade. (Reproduced by permission of the Cambridgeshire Collection, Cambridgeshire Libraries)

Plate 26 (overleaf) P.J. Knights' advertisement for shawls and other items of dress

The slogans above the roundels which flank the cartouche proclaiming the queen's patronage convey sentiments which informed policy towards the poor throughout the period of this survey: 'Train up a child in the way it should go / And when old t'will not depart from it.' Daniel Defoe observed working children under 5 when he toured England in the 1720s. In the nineteenth century the primary responsibility for socialising the children of the poor was shifted from the workplace to the elementary school. The copy emphasises the popularity of Knights' goods with people of rank and fashion; royal custom was, of course, the accolade which entrepreneurs prized most highly. Note that Knights' goods carried a trademark. (Reproduced by permission of Norfolk Museums Service (Bridewell Museum, Norwich))

Plate 27 (overleaf) Colour Sergeant Dollery, his wife and son

Mementoes like this were popular with soldiers and their relatives. The variations in the writing of the inscription suggest that the dedication to an aunt was a departure from the norm. The costume suggests that the Dollerys were painted in the 1820s or 1830s. The uniform was instantly recognisable, the names were distinctive – though significantly Mrs Dollery's given name is not recorded – but the portraits were conventional. Artists working in this genre took advantage of the camera to achieve a real likeness of their subjects. Among the examples of late-Victorian military portraits preserved in the Regimental Museum of the 17th/21st Lancers at Belvoir Castle is that of Trooper J. Charles, taken in 1884. A photograph of his head is mounted on a watercolour of a Lancer in Review Order standing by his horse. (Reproduced courtesy of The Kings Own Border Regiment Museum)

UNDER THE PATRONAGE ··· OF HER MAJESTY

Train up a Child in the way it should go

And when Old t'will not depart from it

P.I.KNIGHTS
Shawl Manufacturer
To her Majesty
N.º 2 Colgate Street, S.ᵗ George
NORWICH
Nº 349 Strand, London

Shawls cleand to look

Shawl Bed Furniture Dresses Scarfs Shawls & Fancy Waistcoats equal with New

To the Promoters of Female Industry

P.I.Knights most Respectfully informs the Nobility Gentry &ᶜ of
and its Vicinity that he has prepared for their Inspection at the above place a most
Superb assortment of Ladies Train Dresses, Scarfs Shawls Sashes Turbans and
Habit Shapes. Gentlemens Waistcoat Shapes Riding Cravats &ᶜ &ᶜ The very
near affinity of the above Articles to the real India Shawls, the very great
improvement they recieve by Washing superior to the printed ones & the thousands
of Young Females it gives constant Employment to will he presumes be a peculiar
recommendation.   NB for the Inspection of the curious will be seen a Beautiful Embroidered Counterpane 4 Yards Square without seams, exactly similar to
that presented to her Majesty by Mʳ Knights for weaving of which he was honored with
a Medal from the Society of Arts Manufactures & Commerce Likewise a Child
who at 4 Years of Age wrought before her Majesty will be seen Embroidering Shawl.

The approbation the above Manufactory recieved from the Royal Family & the very
Numerous Assemblage of rank & Fashion at Mʳ Knights Exhibition in London, renders it
unnecessary to pass any further comments thereon.

Every different Article is stampt with a round Label

Plate 26

In many a hardship have I been
      With many a thousand more;
But we will hope soon to return
      To our dear native shore —
Oh grant ye Powers that rule above
      Our Son may grow in grace;
And may he still protected be
      In every dangerous place —

O Dear Aunt accept this trifling Gift
      This token of good will;
For though we now are far from you
      Yet we shall love you still. —

Plate 27

Plate 28 The rod yard, Sutton Gault, Cambridgeshire

In the sixteenth century most things were made in small workshops. This scene is a reminder that, in spite of the spread of factory-produced goods, some small enterprises survived. Baskets were among the commonest traditional containers. They were made entirely by hand; unlike pottery, wickerwork did not need to be fired. It was light and strong – but not waterproof. According to the donor of the photograph:

The rod yard was in the backyard of the Fish Inn at Sutton Gault . . . The rod peeling was carried out in the springtime when the sap began to rise, the job lasted for a month. When cut they were tied into bundles or bunches for transport to the yard, put into a big clamp and watered at night. To peel the rods they were drawn through a clave which bruised the rod to make it easy for peeling, it was hard work, it made our hands sore pulling them through the clave. They were separated at that time into large and small. After being dried they were bunched up again for the basket maker, there was a big demand for skips for the fruit and potato trade . . . The fruit basket held 21 pound and the potato skip one hundred weight. They also made baskets for the clothing trade for transportation on the railway.

The text does not identify the individuals in the photograph. Their poses and clothing suggest their relative status. Presumably it is the 'boss' who takes the chair and the 'missus' who has no need for an apron to protect her clothes. The presence of women workers is a reminder of the largely invisible army of mature women who combined housekeeping with earning. The children of farmers, craftsmen and labourers had firsthand experience of the world of work from infancy. (Reproduced by permission of the Cambridgeshire Collection, Cambridgeshire Libraries)

Plate 29 Men 'slubbing out' a drainage channel in the Cambridgeshire fens
Digging was one of the labourer's principal skills. These men dammed the channel then passed the mud up the bank from shovel to shovel. The ridge half-way up the bank made their task easier. (Reproduced by permission of the Cambridgeshire Collection, Cambridgeshire Libraries)

Plate 30 Tea-packet wrapper

The sketches exploit the common anxiety about the plight of widows and orphans. The second caption, playing on the company's name, emphasises the wife's role as 'Chancellor of the Domestic Exchequer': it was her duty to balance the budget and build up contingency funds; the conversation takes place in the shadow of Nelson's Column. 10/- (10 shillings or £0.50) was a significant sum. Fabian women recorded many respectable working-class households subsisting on *Round About a Pound a Week* at the beginning of the twentieth century. (Private Collection)

Plate 31 Homeworkers

This woman and her six children (she has a baby in her arms) were photographed in the course of a survey of poverty in late-Victorian London undertaken by the Salvation Army. The picture illustrates the way in which money-making activities invaded the working-class family's limited living space. The blanket on the left suggests that this room was used for sleeping as well as eating and earning. The table is hidden by a heap of party streamers (like many other homeworkers, this family made goods associated with the leisure and pleasure of the better off). This was the kind of task at which even young children could lend a hand. Notice that, by the end of the nineteenth century, even the very poor owned teapots and family portraits, the exclusive possessions of the rich two hundred years earlier. (Reproduced by permission of the Museum of London)

4

PLAIN FOLK
The families of farmers and craftsmen

DEFINING CHARACTERISTICS

Manual labour, working clothes and lack of ceremony set the wealthiest farmers and craftsmen apart from landowners. In these households authority, and often age, separated employer and employee but farmers, craftsmen and their wives laboured alongside their servants. And, among servants in husbandry, apprentices and serving maids, a proportion, although a proportion which shrank as time went on, could look forward to becoming their own masters and mistresses. The old ways endured longest in the pastoral uplands.

It was possible for a man to be as rich as a squire and still style himself 'yeoman'. At Kibworth Harcourt in Leicestershire Mr Thomas Ray (d.1559), lawyer, officer of the royal household and bailiff of the manor, had a gentleman's education and appurtenances. The inventory of his goods and chattels hints at recent building; his home, now the Manor House, had old and new parlours furnished with the luxuries of the day: chairs, cushions, hangings and table carpets. His richer neighbour Robert Bryan had the reputation and tastes of a prosperous, thrifty farmer. Two of the six rooms of his house were given over to processing the milk of his herd of cows and storing the cheese – when he died there were seventy cheeses on his premises.

A description of Richard Inckpen, dating from 1638, provides a thumbnail sketch of the 'plain' man. The language is characteristic of its day but the criteria would have been recognised at any time between the Reformation and the Great War.

[He] laboureth in husbandry ordinarily with his own hands, holdeth the plough, maketh hay, selleth corn at market himself, and keeps no man or attendant upon him but such as are employed in labouring and husbandry, and in the parish rates and other writings he is only written Richard Inckpen without the addition of gentleman to his name.

Generosity to the needy was the mark of a gentleman. In 1613 the churchwardens of Great Burstead, Essex, rejected Edmund Blagge's claim to be a gentleman because 'the gates of his house were not greasey with giving alms to the poor'.

Mr Tovell, a rich eighteenth-century East Anglian farmer, rejected social advancement. 'Jack will never be a gentleman' was a phrase often on his lips. In spite of its nostalgic colouring, his great-nephew's description of his establishment serves to suggest the affluent simplicity of a 'first-rate yeoman' of the period.

> His house was large, and the surrounding moat, the rookery, the ancient dovecot, and the wellstocked fishponds were such as might have suited a gentleman's seat of some consequence; but one side of the house immediately overlooked a farmyard, full of all sorts of domestic animals and the scene of constant bustle and noise. On entering the house, there was nothing at first sight to remind one of the farm: a spacious hall, paved with black and white marble – at one extremity a very handsome drawing room, and at the other a very fine old staircase of black oak polished till it was slippery as ice, and having a chime-clock and a barrel-organ on its landing places. But this drawing room, a corresponding dining parlour, and a handsome sleeping apartment upstairs, were all *tabooed* ground, and made use of on great and solemn occasions only – such as rent days, and an occasional visit with which Mr Tovell was honoured by a neighbouring peer. At all other times the family and their visitors lived entirely in the old-fashioned kitchen along with the servants . . .
>
> At a very early hour in the morning, the alarum called the maids, and their mistress also . . . After the important business of the dairy, and a hasty breakfast, their respective employments were again resumed; that which the mistress took for her especial privilege being the scrubbing of the floors of the state apartments. A new servant, ignorant of her presumption, was found one morning on her knees, hard at work on the floor of one of these preserves, and was thus addressed by her mistress: '*You* wash such floors as these? Give me the brush this instant, and troop to the scullery and wash that, madam' . . .
>
> . . . the family dined on this wise: the heads seated in the kitchen at an old table; the farm-men standing in the adjoining scullery, door open – the female servants at a side table . . . with the principals at the table, perchance some travelling rat-catcher, or tinker, or farrier, or an occasional gardener in his shirt-sleeves, his face probably streaming with perspiration.

It should be observed that, while Tovell did not stand on ceremony with visitors – the neighbouring peer apart – his household servants were expected to know and keep their places.

During the working week craftsmen were recognisable by their protective garments: metalworkers and cobblers were among those who wore leather aprons. Cloth aprons were patterned to indicate the wearer's trade: seventeenth-century barbers wore checked aprons; the butchers' and the fishmongers' were striped; the carpenter had trousers with a special pocket to accommodate his rule. Labour left a physical mark. The hands of a farmer's son might be so calloused by his weekend tasks that he could not hold his pen at school on Monday morning. After years of working a kick wheel the potter developed a 'curious shamble or catch' in his walk.

Farming craftsmen and craftworking farmers

Farmers and craftsmen came from the same stock and made their living serving each other's needs. In their make-do-and-mend culture, the repair of farm implements was the bread and butter of the country blacksmith and the carpenter. The eighteenth-century Yorkshire shopkeeper Abraham Dent took payment from his customers in kind; in the 1920s Harry Cramp's father paid the miller and the doctor in grazing and fodder.

Farmers with smallholdings worked at other trades to augment their income. Until the fishing declined in the seventeenth century, many Humbersiders made their living by a combination of fishing and farming. Farmers were part-time craftsmen. Exempt from the restrictive practices of the gilds, countrymen could display a remarkable versatility. Leonard Wheatcroft (b.1627) followed his father into the tailoring trade but he also worked as a carpenter, planted gardens, served as parish clerk, kept a school, *and* he tuned virginals. When they had the opportunity, country craftsmen farmed; lists of their goods made in the seventeenth century provide evidence of stock and crops. Zachariah Day, an Essex carpenter who died in 1705, had wheat, oats, beans and hay in his barn, he owned sixteen sheep and two hogs. In Lincolnshire, in the 1780s, a farmer–weaver combined his craft with work on his own holding and those of his neighbours. Weather and the seasons influenced the rhythm of his day; when it rained, he spent more time at the loom. George Fishley (b.1771), who founded a dynasty of North Devon potters, was sometimes described as 'potter' and sometimes as 'yeoman'. A hundred years later his descendant fattened pigs for his own consumption and sent his surplus garden produce to market. Walter Rose's grandfather, a Buckinghamshire carpenter who died in 1893, sold milk to his neighbours. As Rose remembered it, the cowshed gave the woodyard 'some semblance of a farm'. George Sturt, a

Farnham wheelwright, who retired in 1865, grew hops to brew his own beer. On the Yorkshire moors craftsmen kept a cow or two even after the Great War.

In the Pennines smallholders combined farming and leadmining. When the old partnerships of self-employed miners disappeared in the early nineteenth century, the new capitalist employers found it paid to keep the working week short and honour the customary break of a fortnight or three weeks for the hay harvest. The lead industry finally collapsed in the 1880s but the tradition of part-time farming persisted in Derbyshire for another seventy or eighty years.

In hard times farming families shifted the emphasis from agriculture to craft. Sometimes it was a temporary expedient but the concentrations of framework knitters in Wigston and of tailors and shoemakers in other Midland villages signalled the descent of small farmers into the ranks of the labouring poor. In other parts of the country communities of farming craftsmen contributed to the generation of industrial centres. In the West Midlands at the beginning of the eighteenth century metalworking and pottery were part-time crafts; up to the 1720s farmer–scythemakers were common. Josiah Wedgwood (b.1730) belonged to a potting clan of farming origin.

Waste not, want not

For these families practical considerations were more important than comfort or appearances. Stock and produce were to be found in living quarters. Before he had a fireside of his own, William Stout (b.1665) kept his store of confectionery beside a friend's hearth to protect it from damp. Well into the twentieth century Yorkshire farmers' wives stored meal and flour in the driest bedchamber, the one warmed by the kitchen fire. The working world invaded living spaces by other means too. Alison Uttley (b.1884) remembered 'the smell of the rabbits which were flung under the tallboy by [her] father as he hung up his gun, the smell of manure on boots, of horses and cattle, of stable and byre, all . . . surging into the kitchen'.

Neither newfangledness nor extravagance was admired. As William Cobbett (b.1763) argued in his *Cottage Economy* (1821–2):

> In household goods, the warm, the strong, the durable, ought always to be kept in view. Oak tables, bedsteads and stools, chairs of oak or yewtree, and never a bit of miserable deal board. Things of this sort ought to last several life times. . . . As to bedding and other things of that sort, all ought to be good in their nature, of a durable quality, and plain in their colour and form. The plates, dishes, mugs, and things of that kind, should be of pewter, or even

wood. Anything is better than crockery-ware. . . . When a house is once furnished with sufficient goods, there ought to be no renewal of hardly any of them wanted for half an age, except in the case of destruction by fire.

In Derbyshire, at the end of the nineteenth century, Hannah Taylor, Alison Uttley's mother, used kitchen utensils inherited from earlier generations of farmwives.

As far as possible these families ate and used things that cost 'nowt but work'. From Cumberland in the north to Surrey in the south peat was dug for fuel. In the Yorkshire Dales ling was gathered for thatching, kindling and making besoms to sweep the floors. In eighteenth-century Gloucestershire dairywomen grew the garden orach for its large pale green leaves which they used to wrap their butter. Their 'pailstake' was a 'bough furnished with many branchlets', cut short to form pegs 'to hang a pail upon'. Cowhorns were used as containers. William Hartas recalled in the 1850s that, when he was a lad in the North Riding, plenty of men wore 'their fathers' leather breeches, and more than one . . . had breeks their grandfathers had had for their best, and there was a vast o' good wear in them yet'. Hannah Taylor used red sealing wax to turn outworn darning needles into pins. Women swept the bakstones on which Westmorland oatcakes were cooked with brushes made from horsehair. Goosewings were used to sweep hearths in Cumberland into the 1970s.

Harry Cramp (b.1912) remembered that:

In our house nothing was renewed or replaced until absolutely necessary. . . . When sheets and blankets became holed they were turned sides to middle. When that no longer sufficed, they became bandages, flannels, dusters and polishers, all carefully hemmed. . . . Clothes were handed down. . . . Egg shells and broken pottery were pulverised to provide grit for the hens. Goose grease was preserved to rub on the chest against winter coughs, and anoint hands and toes when we had chilblains. . . . Water buckets with holes became coal buckets, broken metal handles were replaced with cord. . . . When boots finally wore out, tongues and tops were removed to repair harness. Rabbit skins were dried and preserved to make gloves. Household waste went to the pigs. The hens drank their water from chamberpots which had lost their handles. When we killed hens, the soft feathers were used to re-stuff pillows. By such means 'outgoings' were reduced.

Frivolity was spurned: parties were disparaged as 'bun struggles'; balloons and toy windmills were worthless 'knick-knacks'. 'Profitless' work was put off as long as possible: 'when the bedroom windows wouldn't open or close because of the ivy, we cut the ivy'.

Domestic austerity was undermined by a desire for fashionable or pretty rooms: an indulgence in unnecessary frills was often an indication of a shift in values which, if resources were adequate, would translate the family into a new social category. In seventeenth-century Leicestershire the Dands had their walls panelled a generation before John Dand assumed the style of gentleman. During his lifetime (he died in 1858) the walls of the potter William Smith's house were distempered but he had little doubt that, when he was dead, his womenfolk would paper them. 'And sure enough they did.' Hannah Taylor also had a weakness for 'fresh wallpaper'.

Masters and servants

In plain households employers and servants lived on relatively equal terms. Richard Heath, visiting Swaledale at the beginning of the 1870s, heard that, in the remoter communities at the head of the dale, 'the servants [sit] in the same parlour as their master and mistress and call them with the simple familiarity of friends, Tom and Mary'. Alison Uttley witnessed the eclipse of the old ways in Derbyshire in the 1880s and 90s. Although some local farmers still sent their sons into service by way of training, a new space was opening up between master and servant. The whole household ate Sunday dinner together in the kitchen but the labourer sat apart 'at the dresser on a high stool'; an 'ancient pewter saltcellar' and special cutlery were reserved for his use; when the family took tea in state in the parlour at Christmas, the maid was left behind in the kitchen.

Promotions and demotions

Farming

In Tudor and early Stuart England big farmers were regarded as 'gentlemen in ore'; refining normally took two or three generations. Nicholas Butler of Orwell in Cambridgeshire (d.1601) sent the eldest of his five sons to law school in London. Legal expertise gave Thomas Butler an edge over his neighbours – and his brothers – in negotiating leases and building up his holdings. By the time he died, he was a 'gentleman'. He sent his only surviving son Neville (b.1609) to Christ's College, Cambridge. Neville Butler married an heiress, sold up and moved from Orwell to an estate at Barnwell within easy walking distance of Cambridge.

William Cobbett (b.1763) lamented the way in which traditional farmers' families were being 'transmuted' into 'mock gentlefolk' in the first quarter of the nineteenth century. Touring Surrey in 1825, he contrasted the old style with the new: 'Everything about this farm-house was formerly the scene of *plain manners* and *plentiful living*.' But fashions had changed:

> One end of the front of this once plain and substantial farmhouse had been moulded into a *parlour*, and there was the mahogany table, and the fine chairs, and the fine glass . . . and there were the decanters, the glasses, the dinner set of crockery ware.

Meals consisted of 'two or three nick-nacks to eat instead of a piece of bacon and a pudding'. The younger sons of the house would not 'go to the plough'; they were brought up for the soft indoor clerical life.

A. G. Street (b.1892) described the well-off farmer's way of life in his autobiographical novel, *Farmer's Glory*. On his farm the harvest supper was provided by 'a local caterer'. As Street noted: 'The large tenant farmer's social position was peculiar. Definitely he was not "County". . . . But the "county" met him as an equal over rural sport.' In winter he enjoyed the 'pleasures which came almost automatically' to him and the aristocrat but cost a townsman dear, 'to hunt two days a week' and 'shoot two days'.

Unprofitable harvests and the changes in organisation and technology which benefited some Tudor farmers destroyed others. The parcelling-out of the commons and the draining of the wetlands deprived small farmers and craftsmen of the chance to keep stock, fish and trap and reduced them to day-labouring. The 'Fen Tigers'' bitter resistance to the drainage projects of the seventeenth century reflects the threat posed to their way of life. In 1767, about the time that the phrase 'gentleman farmer' was coined to describe those who did well, the Revd William Cole noted that the sons of Buckinghamshire farmers were unable to marry 'for want of places to settle at' as a result of the enthusiasm for 'accumulating farms together'.

The pace of change was uneven. Pockets of the Cambridgeshire wetlands survived into Victoria's reign. Squire Pell of Wilburton (b.1820) recorded the fenman's hunting techniques. He exploited his knowledge of his quarry's behaviour: quail are territorial and responded to a piped imitation of a rival bird's call; the dotterel is insatiably curious and a human figure in 'contortions' would bring 'the inquisitive little creatures within shot'. Jacob Sanderson recalled the revolution brought about by the enclosure of nearby Cottenham in the middle of the nineteenth century:

> old times were to pass away and all things become new. . . .
> Nearly all the old landmarks removed and a new order of things
> substituted in their places. Three old watermills taken down . . .
> fresh roads made through the fens and fields.

Dispossessed farmers fought hard to recover their position. Richard

Gould (b.1800) lost his holding in Dorset in the agricultural depression which followed the Napoleonic wars. His grandson (b.1836) laboured as a hedger and ditcher and worked a coppice until, in the 1880s, he was able to rent a farm and pass a tenancy on to his son. A catastrophic infestation of liverfluke drove Harry Cramp's great-grandfather off the land; his grandfather saved enough from his earnings as a woodcarver to get back into farming.

Crafts

In the boroughs the old crafts were governed by gilds which regulated recruitment, supervised training, restricted working hours and controlled the quality of their members' output. When unemployed London pewterers petitioned the City authorities in 1521, the traditional remedy was applied – the problem of oversupply was answered by limiting the number of apprentices pewterers were allowed to take on. As the gilds' powers declined, the wage-earning journeymen and small masters were exposed to the harsh realities of a free market. Changes in methods of production and distribution which brought prosperity to some craftsmen reduced others to destitution.

The barbers' fate illustrates the way in which the specialisation and increased pretensions of some practitioners affected their more conservative or less commercially-minded colleagues. In the Middle Ages there had been no distinction between barber and surgeon, the man who trimmed and shaved also performed surgical operations. A comparison of three versions of the constitution of the Oxford Barbers' Gild indicates the erosion of their territory. A Latin text, drawn up in 1348, obliged members to undertake that they would not discuss their clients' foul breath or secret ailments; the guarantees were repeated when the charter was translated into English a hundred years later. By the time the Oxford barbers revised their regulations in 1675 their ministrations were apparently confined to shaving, trimming and periwig making. The Master of Pembroke promoted his college as a centre of medical education: strollers in college gardens ran the risk of grisly encounters with skeletons hung out to dry. Medical practice flourished alongside teaching and research – at the barbers' expense. Their responses differed. One Oxford barber made the transition to surgeon; another put up a sign to advertise that he specialised in drawing teeth; several took up innkeeping (barbers were on the fringes of the entertainment business – they often provided music and reading matter for their customers); at least two were licensed tobacco sellers. The Oxford men were early victims of the expansion of the medical profession. In Bristol at the end of the seventeenth century the surgeons retained by the city poorhouse still cut the boys' hair and shaved the old men. In many places the boundaries between barbers and surgeons remained blurred for at least another generation.

In Georgian England, although the majority of families still lived from hand to mouth with no margin to spare for frivolities, the demand for consumer goods rose. To meet it entrepreneurs broke complex crafts down into a series of tasks which could be carried out by semi-skilled adults or children, thus undercutting the prices and eroding the autonomy of craftsmen who could make a timepiece or a jug unaided. Before 1800 watch parts were being mass produced. The sons, grand-sons and great-grandsons of the watchmaker Stephen Simpson (b.1716) exemplify what might be called occupational diversification. Simpsons designed and made nautical instruments, textile-printing and spinning machines, machines for manufacturing gold thread; others worked as engineers in the railway and gas industries – a Simpson invented the coin-in-the-slot gas meter. They prospered.

Thanks to Josiah Wedgwood's flair for marketing and his ruthlessness in analysing the pottery workers' skills, his descendants 'inherited wealth and lived in the country like gentry with horses, dogs and flowers', while their distant potter cousins in Burslem, whom Wedg-wood sought to 'make such machines . . . as cannot err', 'died off like flies'. Half a century later sanitary legislation generated a demand for stoneware drainpipes which enabled Henry Doulton (b.1820) to build a country house and aspire to a baronetcy (that he only achieved a knighthood was a disappointment). Competition from Doulton's mass-produced wares took trade away from William Smith's rural works.

At about the same time the country wheelwright began to lose ground. Wagons had been designed to suit the land they worked: big wheels were used in the flat fens; in hilly districts smaller wheels gave greater stability; on the steepest inclines wheeled vehicles were less useful than sledges. The disappearance of carts and wagons that were recognisably Lincolnshire- or Cotswold-made testified to the village wheelwright's decline. His neighbours the saddler and the cobbler likewise became menders rather than makers of new goods.

In the retail trades the pattern was different. The 1880s saw the development of grocery chains but large numbers of their employees retained their skills of purchasing, packaging and presenting food into the twentieth century. Sugar, currants and other 'dry' goods were sold in paper screws or bags made by shopkeepers and their assistants. Cheese was burnished or dusted with oatmeal, as convention dictated.

A proportion of the wealth accumulated by thriving nineteenth-century craftsmen and shopkeepers in manufacturing or commercial ventures was almost inevitably spent on sending their children to schools which would carry them into another class. The profits of commercial biscuit-making bought an education which transformed the

Quaker Palmers into Tory-voting Anglican landowners. Sometimes the new values triumphed with bewildering speed. Frank Crossley (b.1817) was the youngest son of a man, born in 1772, who had made the transition from weaver to mill owner, and a woman who had worked before marriage as a farmservant, cooking, cleaning, spinning and milking. Crossley revered his mother, he was a a religious dissenter and a radical MP, yet in 1862, perhaps under the influence of his wife, he accepted a baronetcy; in 1863 he purchased Somerleyton, 'a princely residence . . . suited to the requirements of a nobleman, or a gentleman of taste and fortune', complete with sporting rights and the patronage of the rectory. His son was sent to Eton. Jesse Boot (b.1850), son of a herbalist and founder of Boots the Chemist, spoke with a 'rough Nottingham accent' and always thought of himself as a working man yet he educated his son (b.1889) in Cambridge among the middle classes; John Boot bought an estate in Scotland and set himself up as a laird with his personal piper.

SOURCES

In the families of farmers and craftsmen, writing – and especially reflective writing – was a skill less valued than reckoning. Tallies of income and expenditure were often informal. Scores could be scratched on a wall or notched on the timber posts of a mill or barn. Alison Uttley's father

> flatly refused to write anything except his own name. He could handle a gun . . . plough a straight furrow, and mow, and build a barn and break in a colt. He could manage a nervous horse, and doctor sick cattle, but the slim penholder was not his tool. . . . Marks [were] cut into the beams of barns as reminders of important farm duties and dates.

At Woolsthorpe in Lincolnshire, in the farmhouse where Isaac Newton was brought up, the National Trust's restorations revealed a note of a later tenant's seed order for 1897 jotted on a wall.

Inevitably, families like this produced comparatively few journals or autobiographies. In spiritual or emotional distress, men like Nehemiah Wallington (b.1598), a London woodworker, William Stout (b.1665), a Lancashire ironmonger and dealer, and Thomas Turner (b.1729), a Sussex shopkeeper, put pen to paper. Wallington's is primarily an essay in spiritual autobiography but Stout and Turner have a good deal to say about their daily round, family relationships and attitudes to marriage.

Despite their aversion to booklearning, families took a pride in their occupational heritage and descent. Those men and women whose 'industry and frugality' had endowed the family were especially revered. Robert Furse, the Devon yeoman, who compiled a history of his ancestral holdings in 1593 from manuscript evidence, the reports of 'ancient men' and his own memory, singled out those who did most to build up the farm. More than three hundred years later Harry Cramp, son of a Leicestershire farmer, discovered that his father's interest in the family's farming pedigree, which reached back into the sixteenth century, was an antidote to his prejudice against his son's academic ambitions.

In the absence of examples of other forms of personal testimony, the wills in which these men left instructions for the endowment of their widows and surviving children assume a special importance as evidence of family values and strategies. Margaret Spufford's analysis of Stuart wills illustrates the determination of Cambridgeshire men to protect their wives' independence in old age and also demonstrates the powerful influence of the local economy on the provision they could make for their children.

For a flavour of life in these families, we are heavily dependent on the testimony of Victorians and Edwardians who spent their childhood, but less often their working lives, on farms or in family workshops. In attempting to reconstruct the household life of plain families, we must be both alert to the attractions of less arduous occupations, attractions which Thomas Turner hinted at, and beware of the nostalgia which encouraged the urban middle classes to construct the myth of the good life.

THE MEANING OF CHILDREN

To independent farmers and craftsmen, children represented continuity. Property and skills might be handed on to one or several successors. In some boroughs by-laws favoured the youngest son but this was a recessive custom. Old-fashioned men of modest fortune left children and grandchildren a ewe lamb or two, potential founding mothers of a flock. Thomas Wood, who farmed in Melbourn in Cambridgeshire, died in his nineties in 1834. He made small bequests to 'many young relatives' whose prospects improved in consequence. But, from the seventeenth century, there was a tendency to pass farms on intact. Fathers who had the means might purchase holdings to endow younger sons or fund their training in a craft.

The craftsman handed on the tools of his trade as the farmer passed on land and beasts. In 1552 the Stourbridge scythemaker Richard Coles left his 'best anvil to the child that is in my wife's womb, if it be a boy'. At the end of the sixteenth century Richard Grove, an Essex mariner, left his eldest son and his eldest son's son shares in his boat. The nature of their trade influenced parental strategies. In Oxford, canal boatmen could afford to bring several sons up to follow in their footsteps; their fishermen neighbours' fear of exhausting the catch led them to restrict the succession to one. In Leicester between 1580 and 1600 three sons out of four followed their fathers' trades but few family businesses survived for as long as a hundred years. The Norries, tanners from 1494 to 1639, and the Newcombes, bellfounders from 1500 to 1612, were among the exceptions. Inability to produce or rear children, business failure and upward mobility combined to remove the majority from the scene.

James Fretwell (b.1699) was born into the timber trade. He believed that his great-grandfather, 'the first of whom I have heard any mention made . . . was a carpenter by profession'. His grandfather's 'chief business was buying and selling timber'. Both Walter Rose (b.1871) and George Sturt, 'a small boy in the 1860s', inherited woodworking businesses which had been their grandfathers'. Josiah Wedgwood (b.1730) belonged to the fourth generation of a potting dynasty. George Fishley Holland (b.1889) was 'fifth in a line of peasant potters'. Richard Norman (b.1818) started a Sussex pottery which survived until 1939; his great-great-grandson Wallace William Norman had three complementary spokes to his wheel – pottery, brickmaking and farming – and shifted his workmen from one to the other as circumstances dictated. He was one of the last of his kind: in 1900 there were a hundred or so old-style country potteries; in 1945 there were fewer than a dozen.

INFANCY

In such busy households, babies and small children could expect little of their mother's undiluted attention. Alison Uttley remembered lying on a settle with a board fixed on to the front to stop her rolling off, while the work of the farmhouse kitchen went on around her. The infant's chief carer was not necessarily his mother. Stuart babies, perhaps particularly children of urban craftsmen, were sent away to be wetnursed. As a last resort, when their son Samuel failed to thrive in spite of the ministrations of a medical man and a 'cunning woman', Grace and Nehemiah Wallington (b.1598) put him out to nurse at Peckham. In the same generation Samuel Pepys (b.1633) and his younger brothers and sisters, the children of a tailor and a laundress, were fostered out not far from London; his parents' decision may have been influenced by the deaths of their older siblings – fifth of their eleven children, Samuel was the oldest of four survivors by the time he was 7 – but, perhaps, like other women, Mrs Pepys made a contribution to the family budget which could not be foregone. While housekeeper to her bachelor brother William, Elin Stout (b.1660) mothered her nieces and nephews, regularly taking them on in their most demanding toddler years to relieve her sister-in-law, a farmer's wife. Ebenezer Howard (b.1850), whose father kept a string of sweet shops in London, was sent away to school in Suffolk with his two slightly older sisters when he was 4½.

CHILDHOOD AND YOUTH

Education

Because very young children could make a contribution to the family enterprise, sending a child to school, even a school where no fees were charged, cost money. While acknowledging that reckoning and reading and writing in English helped a man to keep track of his business, many farmers and craftsmen were wary and contemptuous of academic pretension. The rich Mr Tovell, 'would now and then growl' about the 'd—d good' book-learning did. Charles Manby Smith (b.1804), who 'enjoyed the advantage of hic-haec-hocing it for a couple of years' at grammar school, discovered that 'the Latin language [was] not worth sixpence to a journeyman printer'; he was paid at the same rate as those who could not tell the Latin text they were setting from Double Dutch. Richard Jeffries (b.1848), son of a small farmer, was left in no doubt that, as a bookish, dreamy boy, he was 'useless upon the farm'.

Investment in a gentlemanly education signalled the intention of launching offspring into a different station of life. The great age of agricultural prosperity between 1540 and 1640 was a period of educational opportunity unparalleled before the end of the nineteenth century. In the rich south of Cambridgeshire there were schools in virtually every community in which state secondary education is provided today, often staffed by young graduates waiting for preferment. The rollcall of farmers' sons who acquired at least the status of 'pengent' includes John Selden (b.1584), the lawyer and antiquary; William Harvey (b.1578), the medical scientist; and Isaac Newton (b.1642). John Richardson (d.1625), Regius Professor of Divinity in the University of Cambridge and one of the team which translated the King James Bible, was the son of a man who farmed in a very small way. John Ray (b.1627), the 'father of natural history', was the son of an Essex blacksmith. Educated at Braintree Grammar School and Cambridge University, he compiled the first local botanical survey, *Catalogus plantarum circa Cantabrigia*, pioneered the use of comparative anatomy in his studies of insects, birds and fish and – a sign of the times – edited a glossary of English words not generally used in polite society.

After the Restoration the sons of landed and professional men began to monopolise university places, and by the beginning of the nineteenth century parents who sent their sons to Harrow, which owed its foundation to a farmer, no longer expected them to sit alongside 'the wretched farmer's boy reeking of a dunghill'. In late Victorian England access to education was restored and now, for the first time, farmers' daughters had the chance, a very slim chance, of climbing the academic ladder to the middle classes. Alison Uttley entered the Free Grammar School at Bakewell in Derbyshire in 1897, just two years after it admitted girls for the first time; she went on to Manchester University.

Books exercised a fascination to which craftsmen seem to have been particularly susceptible. Thomas Turner (b.1729), a Sussex shopkeeper, confessed that 'reading and study would be in a manner both meat and drink to me, were my circumstances independent'. Opportunities for formal adult education emerged in the nineteenth century. Thomas Okey (b.1852), a self-educated London basketmaker, realised Turner's dream. In order to benefit from the newly introduced university extension lectures, he 'concentrated the business' into the early hours of the working day to free his afternoon for reading in the British Museum. He translated Dante into English and eventually became the first professor of Italian in the University of Cambridge.

CHILDHOOD

Learning a trade

The skills needed by working farmers and craftsmen were acquired by observation and practice. Shrewdness was esteemed more highly than booklearning: in medieval Shrewsbury children were judged to have reached the age of discretion when they could tell a good penny from a bad one. Boys destined for their father's craft began their informal training at a very early age, family circumstances dictated its intensity. Children playing in the workplace watched and copied the actions of skilled adults, the sons of craftsmen soon 'got the feel of the tools' they would use in their inherited trade. Learning by imitation was not achieved without cost. In William Stout's case priority was given to work on his family's farm. He and his brothers, born in the 1660s, were taken from grammar school to help with the ploughing, haymaking, corn harvest and turf cutting. Stout needed private coaching before he began his apprenticeship to an ironmonger. For George Sturt the family's wheelwright's shop was 'a sort of playground'; his 'crinkled' fingernail was a lifelong reminder of a careless hammer blow. From a very early age, like many big sisters, Elin Stout carried a heavy burden of childcare and household tasks while her mother looked to her tasks on the farm.

YOUTH: SONS

From the sixteenth to the eighteenth century boys destined for agriculture became servants in husbandry, living-in farmhands, from their early teens to their middle twenties, changing master every year at the hiring fair. As holdings got larger, it became commoner for farmers' sons to stay at home to learn their craft. Jacob Sanderson was heir apparent to a Cambridgeshire farm in the second half of the nineteenth century. The prospect that the farm would be his one day was his only reward: 'My place was with the men, work as they work, fare as they fare, except pay, which I had none, but food.' Any cash Sanderson wanted had to be earned in his spare time, ingrained habits of thrift ensured that what he earned, he saved. His experience was probably not uncommon. The introduction of compulsory schooling in the 1870s did not remove the farmer's child, or the shopkeeper's, from the workforce. George Fishley Holland (b.1889) found he could tackle almost every job on a farm, ploughing apart, by the time he was 11.

The training of craftsmen was regulated by a written contract between the prospective apprentice's guardian and his master. The long fixed-term bond between master and apprentice was soluble only by death or serious misconduct. Orphans boarded out with families were sometimes taken on as apprentices by their foster fathers; until after the Great War, apprenticeship was the closest formal approximation to adoption. Men without sons, or with ambitions to see their sons rise in the world, selected promising apprentices to marry their daughters and carry on their trade. John Davenant, the Oxford innkeeper, who died in the 1620s, brought none of his four sons up to follow in his footsteps. Davenant hoped that one of his daughters, who were all accustomed 'to keep the bars' and record the 'day's taking' would marry his apprentice – 'if he and she can fancy one another'. Jane, the eldest, did and carried on the business as his widow.

When prospects were gloomy men steered their sons away from their own crafts. George Herbert (b.1814) was the son and grandson of Banbury plushweavers. Plushweaving had been the town's staple industry but trade was slack and Herbert's father had to supplement his earnings by working as a hatter and harnessmaker. He apprenticed his son to a shoemaker because 'he thought shoemaking was a never-failing trade as people must wear shoes'. (He had not foreseen the invention of the sewing machine which undermined the leather craftsman's skills during his son's working life.) George Herbert was shrewd and versatile – he set up as a photographer, kept the best customers from his old trade and 'let the long credit ones go'. Edward Bingham, an Essex potter, apprenticed his son to a bootmaker – in his case because he feared that the boy's taste for producing ornaments, in preference to functional wares, would prevent him from making a living. When the younger Bingham became his own master he opened a pottery at Castle Hedingham which he ran from 1864 until 1901. Although his pots now command high prices, he had to take work as a teacher and sub-postmaster to make ends meet.

The experience of an apprentice exiled under a strange roof was inevitably quite different from that of a boy who stayed at home to learn a trade familiar since infancy – as some families recognised. Before James Fretwell's brother was apprenticed to a Doncaster grocer at the beginning of the eighteenth century, he went on an exploratory visit to 'see how he liked the business' and the family of which he would become a temporary member. Even when the master was chosen with care, the relationship could be uneasy. Cultural differences set masters and apprentices at odds. William Stout, reared by pious and frugal farming parents, was horrified by his master's wife's extravagant ways: unlike his industrious mother, Mrs Coward abdicated her duties of housekeeping and motherhood and took her ease. Tensions arose when boys reared in servant-keeping households were expected to undertake what they regarded as menial tasks, particularly those of a domestic character.

London gild records suggest that a significant number of Tudor youths failed to complete their apprenticeships. Towards the end of his term, the apprentice was effectively fully trained; he was often expected to take considerable responsibility, sometimes managing a branch some distance away from the firm's headquarters. At this stage those who had come into London from the provinces might opt to go back home and set themselves up in business. Apprenticeships were sometimes curtailed on the master's initiative. As he lay dying in the spring of 1655, the Oxford barber Arthur Allen willed that his apprentice Edward Stroud, who had been running the shop during his illness, should 'be dis-charged from the remainder of his time' on the payment of forty shillings.

Of course, only those with the means to acquire premises and stock could establish themselves as independent masters. During the eight-eenth and nineteenth centuries a growing number of time-served men were condemned to remain wage-earners all their working lives.

YOUTH: DAUGHTERS

Girls' education was even more emphatically practical than their brothers'. While William Stout's sister Elin (b.1664) stayed at home to help her mother, many of her contemporaries went into service. (Formal apprenticeships were rare.) Waged work was no disgrace and service represented a chance to accumulate skills and savings to take into marriage. In the eighteenth and nineteenth centuries it became less usual for the daughters of prosperous parents to leave home before they married.

THE CHOICE OF A WIFE

Marriage was a serious business properly tied in with economic independence, responsibility for training the next generation and full membership of the local community. Few Tudor Londoners took this step before they were 28. Leonard Wheatcroft (b.1627), the tailor–carpenter–gardener–schoolmaster–clerk wrote 'verses to [his] well-beloved mistress' but the weight of evidence suggests that, in his search for a wife, the farmer, craftsman and shopkeeper was normally harder-headed; he had as his ideal a mature, thrifty and energetic woman of good stock and repute. Wealthy tradesmen, who had no need for a business partner, sometimes took younger brides.

William Stout measured Bethia Greene, to whom he was powerfully attracted, against his industrious mother and sister and found her wanting. In her prime Stout's mother oversaw the workers in the fields, dressed the corn and carried it to market; in old age she kept house for her eldest son. Her daughter Elin followed her hardworking example in house, farm and shop. Stout had adopted his family's 'rustical . . . deportment and way of living', Bethia's upbringing had given her fashionable tastes. The wisdom of his self-denial was confirmed by her imprudent marriage and unfortunate end. To the plain man it was more important that a wife should be serviceable than pretty. Elin Stout's health was undermined by a tubercular condition which may well have disfigured her, yet, according to her brother, she had suitors because she was known to be diligent and frugal, well-connected and likely to bring a good dowry to her marriage. When the Quaker shoemaker Jonathan Abbatt (b.1829) was courting Mary Dilworth, a farmer's daughter, in the early 1850s, his parents wrote to ask for 'more particulars of this female friend, and what is she, what age, and what is her qualifications for making a poor man's wife, can she wash thy shirt and do all such like work, who are her Father and Mother, what are they, are they a sound and healthy family'.

WOMEN'S OPTIONS OUTSIDE MARRIAGE

Although they had no career prospects as we would understand them, these women were brought up to earn their living. They were well-equipped to run a house and supervise servants for bachelors and widowers, within the family or for wages, and the casualty rate among wives ensured that there were always vacancies for capable housekeepers. Of course, provided that she married prudently, the status of a wife was higher than her single sister's and her tenure more secure.

THE CHOICE OF A HUSBAND

The criteria for a desirable groom mirrored those for a bride. Young women and their friends looked for mature men of means and reputation. William Stout's refusal to subsidise a niece who married a penniless youth just setting up in trade and his handsome endowment of her elder sister who matched herself with a solid farmer expressed the matrimonial principles of his kind.

MARITAL ROLES

The Stout women were not exceptionally industrious. Brewing, baking, responsibility for the kitchen, the dairy and the poultry yard were the farmwife's lot and continued to be the responsibility of her descendants as long as this way of life survived. Her duties were summed up by East Riding JPs in 1593 when they laid down the wage rate for a maid 'that is hired with a gentleman or a rich yeoman, whose wife does not take the pains and charge' of housewifery upon herself. Mrs Stout sent just such 'a good maidservant of long experience' to instruct a young daughter-in-law in 'the method of housekeeping' and living within her means. A good husband supported his wife in her work: in the summer of 1647 Adam Eyre made 'a place' for his wife's poultry and rode '6 mile' to borrow 'a pan for [her] to brew in'. Her labour gave the farmer's wife a measure of independence. Harry Cramp remembered that 'eggs were mother's currency'; with them she paid 'for the knitting of socks and scarves, the making and altering of dresses', for the chimneys to be swept and other odd jobs about the house.

Mary Hardy (b.1773), the daughter of a prosperous farmer, revelled in hard work: she kept lodging houses and inns. Her diary records her enthusiasm for bouts of physical labour: in April 1791 she borrowed a washing mill 'and washed three weeks linen without a workwoman'. At the end of the nineteenth century Mary Ann Loosely (b.1842), the wife of a builder–cabinetmaker–undertaker, not only managed a household which included apprentices as well as her own five children, but also regularly worked as a glazier in the family firm.

Such work could undermine a woman's health: nineteenth-century doctors described the aches and unrelieved fatigue experienced by women who milked and made cheese. Concern for the well-being of female kin led men to modify their spartan work ethic. The frugal William Stout hired charwomen to spare his sister Elin the heaviest work in the house, the weekly wash and the brewing that took place from time to time. Jonathan Abbatt, who recognised that his wife-to-be was leaving 'a comfortable home where every want is amply provided for one where thou may have to practise economy', hoped that 'by engaging some one each week to do the washing and rough cleaning . . . to arrange to leave thee comparatively speaking at ease'.

Some wives had profitable sidelines. In Shropshire, at the end of the seventeenth century, Mrs Grestocke's cakes were so celebrated that hostesses entertaining guests from her neighbourhood counted on receiving one. Women played a key part in building, manufacturing and distributive empires. Josiah Wedgwood relied on his wife's taste: 'the approbation of my Sal' was required before a prototype went into production. In the nineteenth century Grestocke could have become a household name: the commercial biscuitmakers Huntley and Palmer built on a similar tradition of home-baking for sale. Jesse Boot's grandmother was a village herbalist; his father carried her expertise into an urban environment. When he died in 1860, 10-year-old Jesse and his sister joined their mother in the business, gathering herbs in the country outside Nottingham, serving in the shop and making pills. Recognising that 'the herbalist and chemist at that time was very much out of date', Boot 'decided to enter the proprietory medicine business in 1874'. His wife, who had worked in her father's bookshop, encouraged him to add stationery and fancy goods to the standard chemists' lines. For more than twenty years she was an active partner, buying stock, selecting female workers and overseeing staff welfare.

Mrs David Greig's *Life and Times* gives a detailed account of the early stages in the development of a chain of retail provision merchants from the point of view of the founder's wife. Greig's wife, Annie Deacock (b.1862), was brought up at her father's dairy in Holborn. One of her earliest memories was 'of going home from school and standing on a chair to serve milk'; it was an experience she wanted to spare her children. In 1879 her parents moved out to Hornsey. Until her elder brother brought a wife into the business, Annie and her sister took turns as housekeeper–assistant in the shop in Holborn and mother's aide in Hornsey. Like Jesse Boot, but at an earlier stage in his career, David Greig benefited from his wife's training in her family business. Her ability to sum up Atlantic Road's trading potential contributed to the success of their first shop in Brixton. As long as they lived on the premises, Annie Greig took responsibility for opening up the shop while her husband was at market 'laying the foundations of his business success . . . for the principal thing in business is to buy well'. She prided herself on her own buying skill and took pleasure in telling the story of a purchasing coup in which she bought eighteen hundred 'lovely great Irish eggs' on her own initiative and, having cornered the market in this attractive commodity, 'sold them at a good price'.

For families like the Deacocks, the move to the suburbs simultaneously eased the wife's burdens and took the family into the middle classes. The Deacocks' five-bedroomed house in Hornsey was called 'Nottingham' in honour of Mr Deacock's birthplace. They kept a carriage. Mrs Deacock made concessions to the suburban code, leaving cards and holding 'At Homes' once a month. But her old habits died hard. 'Plain and substantial was our fare and we fared well on it', her daughter recalled. Their new neighbours kept three servants, the Deacocks managed with one maid and a char once a week: 'Mother, the maid, the char and the eldest daughter at home were responsible for the work, and most of the washing, ironing, mending and making was done at home.' In 1894, Annie Greig, moved in her turn from rooms above the shop to a house named 'Montrose', which was her mother-in-law's home town. She missed the stimulus of the commercial world; in her suburban exile she harnessed her energy and business acumen to the cause of crippled children.

PARENTHOOD

A farmer or craftsman hoped that his wife would be fertile; Richard Gough noted that John and Elizabeth Dod 'lived very lovingly together, though they had no child'. 'Geld wife', the Yorkshire dialect phrase for a childless wife, underlines the stigma of barrenness. Sons and daughters were an important element in the labour force and vehicles for their parents' ambitions. When man, wife and children pulled together a good deal could be achieved with little capital. The complex economy of a couple with twelve children supporting themselves on a fourteen-acre plot near Hawkser in Yorkshire at the beginning of the twentieth century suggests the range of enterprises which could be based on a single smallholding: the family kept a handful of cows and a small flock of sheep; they carted their vegetables to Whitby; the father walked his stallion round the districts serving mares. Their hard work and thrift paid dividends. The parents were able to retire with a comfortable nest egg and all the children were given trades. Their much more successful contemporaries, the Greigs, did not put their sons and daughters behind the counter: they were raised to be gentlemen and -women. Ross Greig, born over the shop in 1890, won scholarships to minor public schools; his father had Eton in mind for him but settled on Harrow on the advice of the headmaster of his son's preparatory school. His younger brother Sam (b.1900) was still at Harrow when the Great War ended; he and his father had agreed that he should 'join up as soon as he left' but they fell out over whether he should take a commission, as his father wished, or 'go into the ranks', as Sam would have preferred. To Annie Greig's mind, the end of the war was fortunately timed to settle 'the differences between them in the best possible way'. Cissie Greig (b.1891) went as a day girl to the local high school and then to Paris to be 'finished'. Her younger sister Mary went to Roedean. During the Great War the Greigs' older daughters volunteered for work in a hospital kitchen. It was their first experience of 'heavy domestic work'.

MARITAL RELATIONSHIPS

A harmonious working partnership seems to have been the basis of a good marriage. John Banks, a seventeenth-century Quaker farmer, praised his wife's good temper, hard work and thrift:

> We lived comfortably together for many years and she was a careful industrious woman in bringing up her children in good order . . . a helpmeet and a good support to me . . . She was well-beloved amongst good friends and neighbours.

David Greig's Golden Wedding toast echoes Banks's tribute. He applauded Annie's reliability, and her practical and managerial competence:

> Never once in all her life have I known her late – never . . . Another characteristic of hers is that she is a wise spender. I have never known her short of money during fifty years. Not only is she an excellent manager, but she is an excellent needlewoman. She made most of the girls' dresses when they were young and laundered them. That was why she was never short of money! Four girls are a heavy charge on the laundry account when they are young and wear white.

Richard Gough, Stuart chronicler of Myddle in Shropshire, condemned women who, directly or indirectly, wasted their husband's wealth. Thomas Hayward's wife was

> highly bred and unfit for a country life, besides she was shrewd with tongue . . . He had little quietness at home which caused him to frequent public houses . . . and being generally well beloved he often stayed too long. . . . This Thomas Hayward sold and consumed all his estate and was afterwards maintained in charity by his eldest son.

Judith Downton 'proved such a drunken woman as hath scarce been heard of; she spent her husband's estate so fast that it seemed incredible'. Downton lost his farm; his widow survived on parish relief until 1735.

Ill-temper, perhaps exacerbated by ill health, was another cause of friction. In 1647 Adam Eyre and his wife were on uneasy terms. On 8 June he wrote:

This morn my wife began, after her old manner, to brawl and revile me for wishing her only to wear such apparel as was decent and comely, and accused me for treading on her sore foot . . . which to my knowledge I touched not; nevertheless she continued in that ecstasy till noon; and at dinner I told her I purposed never to come in bed with her till she took more notice of what I formerly had said to her.

Eyre tried to placate her – he ran errands and, in July, bought her an expensive hourglass but, as he recorded in his journal for 6 August:

This night my wife had a painful night of her foot, which troubled me so much that sleep went from me. Whereupon sundry wicked, worldly thoughts came in my head, and, namely, a question whether I should live with my wife or no, if she continued as wicked as she is; whereupon I rose and prayed God again to direct me.

His prayer was answered with a quiet sleep; a year later he was still contemplating separation. The termination of a marriage was a matter of the utmost gravity; like most couples, the Eyres were parted by death.

WIDOWHOOD

A wise man looked for a wife who would make a capable widow and keep his business in good order until his son was old enough to take over. Until they were swept away, the manorial and borough by-laws governing inheritance reflected this principle. Yet widows' active participation in business must not be exaggerated: between 1660 and 1730, few widowed Londoners carried on a trade that 'was not suitable to their sex'. In the sixteenth and seventeenth centuries, while the gilds remained strong, childless widows, often significantly younger than their first husband, came back on to the marriage market, still vigorous but now endowed with their customary third share of their husband's property. They were excellent catches for men on the threshold of a career. Not infrequently widows matched themselves with a former apprentice of their husband, a young man whose vices and virtues were well known and who had been accustomed to defer to the mistress of the house.

In the countryside custom opposed the widow's remarriage. A second marriage, it was feared, would be at the expense of the children of her first. In consequence, a widow's life-interest in her husband's tenancy often depended on her remaining single and chaste. In a number of manors widows charged with incontinence (very often, no doubt, by those with an interest in their deprivation) were subjected to humiliating rituals to purge their fault, being compelled, for instance, at Enborne in

Berkshire to ride into the manor court on a ram, facing backwards 'with his tail in her hand', and recite a doggerel confession:

> Here I am
> Riding upon a black ram
> Like a whore as I am
> And for my Crincum Crancum,
> Have lost my Bincum Bancum;
> And for my tail's game
> Am brought to this worldly shame;
> Therefore good Mr Steward, let me have my lands again.

At Kilmersdon in Somerset the woman faced forward and repeated:

> For mine Arse's fault I take this pain,
> Therefore, my Lord, give me my land again.

Where custom did not protect their children, careful fathers made their own arrangements. Andrew Brewer, a Lincolnshire man who made his will in 1601, left his son and daughter 'to be brought up by my wife; but if it please God that she marry again, and, that upon her said marriage she shall dislike to do so' the children – and their portions – were to pass into other custody.

Yet 'a woman left with a farm was in a sorry plight'. So were her children. Mrs Holland was widowed in the 1890s, she had no maid and when she went to market, though he was only 5 or 6, her son William was left to feed the farmhands. When she decided to concentrate on dairying, he milked the cows and delivered the milk before he went to school in the morning and after he came home in the afternoon. In the winter he had to feed the stock and muck them out too.

Widows whose endowment was in cash played an important part in the local economy, where they represented one of the few sources of credit. Joshian Makin, who died at Clee on South Humberside in 1615, apparently spent her last days with relatives or friends; her whole estate consisted of her clothes, small change in her purse, 'a little trash' and her capital lent out, in all probability, to her neighbours. This sum, which amounted to 95 per cent of her property, gave her a continuing stake in the community.

Widows sometimes stepped into their husband's role, in the parish as well as in the family business. Long before the wives and sisters of landed, professional and business men were eligible for election to public office, they held office in their parishes, as campaigners for women's civil rights pointed out: George Crabbe's description of an efficient woman's public life was cited in the *Women's Suffrage Journal* in 1876:

No parish business in the place could stir
Without direction or assent from her
By turns she took each duty as it fell –
Knew all their duties and discharged them well.

Crabbe had someone very like his aunt-by-marriage Mrs Tovell in mind.

As the widowed Thomas Turner (b.1729) noted when he considered the pros and cons of remarriage, no servant could be trusted to attend to a man's business in his absence as conscientiously as a good wife could. In consequence when women died their husbands swiftly remarried. In Earl's Colne in Essex between 1580 and 1740 the average time between losing one wife and acquiring the next was five months. Turner deplored marriages made 'from lucrative and avaricious views, or else to satisfy a base and inordinate appetite', his 'choice' combined a good character – 'very industrious, sober . . . and seemingly endued with prudence and good nature' – with prospects of 'some fortune'.

Turner was childless. Arthur Allen left three children under age when he died in 1655. He put his affairs into the hands of his 'trusty and wellbeloved friends': Roger Fry of the University of Oxford, 'gent.', and John Paynton of the City of Oxford, 'gent.'. A month later he added Mr Robert Gilkes and Mr Matthew Loveday, both innholders. Small legacies to his sisters and his neighbour Frances Frogley, women who might be expected to take an interest in the welfare of his 'poor children', underline his anxiety to do the best he could for them. Young orphans were often downwardly mobile: many of the literate Stuart labourers were the sons of tradesmen who died too early to secure their futures.

SUMMING UP

Working farmers and independent craftsmen had recognised standing in the local community. A few were wealthy. Manual work marked them out both from the landowners and the middle classes. When they employed servants, they were kept for use rather than ornament. Their rank was persistently eroded as prosperous men opted to invest in the education and gear which would confer a superior status, and as poorer men lost their independence and were reduced to labouring; in upland areas of England a depleted population of traditional farmers and craftsmen survived into the twentieth century. Patterns of inheritance varied in accordance with local custom and economic circumstances. Where it was customary to divide land and stock, agricultural holdings were liable to shrink beneath the point of viability. Craftsmen's strategies reflected the market for their goods and services. Where it was buoyant, several sons might be brought up in their father's trade. Where it was poor, self-interest and, among the urban craftsmen, gild regulations might restrict the number of recruits. The acquisition of practical skills began early and, in hard or busy times, took priority over booklearning. Apprentices and servants in husbandry lived under their master's roof. From an early age girls relieved their mothers of routine but often heavy domestic tasks. Conventionally, farmers and modest craftsmen married to secure both a successor and a partner for their business. The farmer's wife had responsibility for the dairy and the poultry yard. The craftsman–retailer needed an assistant and supervisor for his shop. Women welcomed help with the heaviest household tasks; some were gratified at the prospect of indulging an appetite for fashionable clothes and furnishings but there is evidence that those who had helped to build up a family enterprise and found themselves cut off from it were frustrated by their confinement to the domestic sphere.

NOW READ ON

Margaret Spufford: *Contrasting Communities: English Villagers in the Sixteenth and Seventeenth Centuries* (Cambridge: Cambridge University Press, 1974).

Mildred Campbell: *The English Yeoman Under Elizabeth and the Early Stuarts* [1942] (London: Merlin Press, 1967).

Alice Clark: *The Working Life of Women in the Seventeenth Century* [1919] (London: Routledge, second edition, 1992).

Ann Kussmaul: *Servants in Husbandry in Early Modern England* (Cambridge, Cambridge University Press, 1981).

Mary Prior: 'Women and the Urban Economy: Oxford 1500–1800' in *Women in English Society, 1500–1800*, edited by Mary Prior (London: Methuen, 1985).

Francis W. Steer: *Farm and Cottage Inventories of Mid-Essex, 1635–1749* [1950] (Chichester: Phillimore, 1969).

Yeomen and Colliers in Telford: Probate Inventories for Dawley, Lilleshall, Wellington and Wrockwardine, 1660–1750, edited by Barrie Trinder and Jeff Cox (Chichester: Phillimore, 1980).

The Autobiography of William Stout, 1665–1752 edited by J. D. Marshall (Manchester: Manchester University Press, 1967).

Richard Gough: *Human Nature Displayed in the History of Myddle* (Fontwell, Sussex: Centaur Press, 1968).

The Diary of Thomas Turner, edited by David Vaisey (Oxford: Oxford University Press, 1984).

William Cobbett: *Cottage Economy* [1822] (Oxford: Oxford University Press, 1979).

George Sturt: *A Small Boy in the Sixties* [1927] (Hassocks, Sussex: Harvester, 1977).

George Sturt: *The Wheelwright's Shop* [1923] (Cambridge: Cambridge University Press, 1963).

Alison Uttley: *The Country Child* (London: Faber, 1931).

H. St. G. Cramp: *A Yeoman Farmer's Son* (London: John Murray, 1985).

5

MIDDLE-CLASS FAMILIES

DEFINING CHARACTERISTICS

This chapter is concerned with middle-class families and their pre-decessors, households headed by clergymen, lawyers and medical practitioners, administrators and businessmen who aspired to live like gentlemen but owed their prosperity to their professions rather than inherited acres.

The number of such households rose sharply as a result of the remodelling of the Church in the middle of the sixteenth century. Priests were given permission to marry in 1549 – around one in ten in the diocese of York and one in four in Essex had done so by 1554. Under the Catholic Queen Mary they 'were commanded to leave and forsake their concubines and harlots and do open penance'; under Elizabeth the right to marry was restored. Although popular hostility to married clergy was slow to evaporate, more than two-thirds of Elizabeth's bishops had wives.

The Church of England became a family business. The Revd Richard Battelle (b.1619) had four ordained sons and two ordained grandsons; his eldest son succeeded him as headmaster of Hertford Grammar School, a younger son was a junior master there: teaching was a common by-employment. Other Anglican dynasties lasting three or four generations were noted in letters published in *The Times* between 3 December 1988 and 17 January 1989. R. Josiah Pratt, whose letter launched the correspondence, cited his own grandfather, great-grandfather and great-great-grandfather who served St Stephen's, Coleman Street, in the City of London, from 1824 to 1911. Three generations of Witts followed each other as rectors of St Peter's, Upper Slaughter, Gloucestershire. Mayfield in East Sussex was held by four generations of Kirbys, fathers and sons, between 1780 and 1912. From 1763 to 1922 Phillack in Cornwall was served by four generations of Hockins. At Offwell in Devon the rectory was held by Coplestons from 1773 to 1954; between 1804 and 1935 the living descended from father to

96

son. There were Leirs at Ditcheat in Somerset from 1699 until 1917; Mr Tripp, rector from 1917 to 1946 was the son-in-law of the last Leir incumbent. Where a family had the patronage of its own living, as the Hastings of Martley in Worcestershire did, the succession was guaranteed: James Hastings used his wife's fortune to buy the advowson in 1791; his great-grandson was incumbent during the Great War.

The legitimation of clerical marriage coincided with a huge rise in the number of university-educated clergy. Until the middle of the nineteenth century ordination into the Anglican Church remained an attractive option for university graduates: at that point about 40 per cent of Oxford men were entering the Church. Victorian and Edwardian academics, men of letters, publishers and administrators were often the literal, as well as the metaphorical, descendants of the parsons.

By comparison with the Anglican clergy, other professions were poorly organised. Men trained in different traditions had little sense of solidarity; indeed they were often bitterly antagonistic. The university-educated physicians, concentrated in London and major provincial cities, were the elite of the medical hierarchy. Surgeons were tainted by their association with the barbers' trade, they sliced like butchers and stitched like cobblers; naval surgeons were not commissioned officers until 1843. Apothecaries were shopkeepers, akin to grocers; worse, they lived 'by the turds of gentlemen'. Competition from practitioners without formal training helped to undermine the medics' standing and many patients kept medicine chests and briefed themselves from texts like *Physic for Families* (1674) and *The Household Physician*, which went into a second edition in 1900. Victorian concern with public health conferred a new authority on medical men; in private practice they succeeded in persuading men able to afford their services that the frail physical and mental constitutions of their female kin required constant medical supervision from adolescence onwards.

Banking and brewing were among the more prestigious mercantile pursuits.

The richest and most pretentious of the middle classes vied with peers in their lavish style of life. The Cupola House, one of the finest domestic buildings in Bury St Edmunds, was built and furnished in the height of taste by a rich apothecary at the end of the seventeenth century; the aristocratic tourist Celia Fiennes singled it out for praise. The obstetrician William Hunter (b.1718) amassed a magnificent library and collections of coins and shells that were amongst the best in Europe. His Scots origin and his unencumbered bachelor status may well have helped him to get on in society. From the eighteenth century employers with pretensions encouraged their workforces to celebrate family anniversaries as the landowners' tenants did. Matthew Boulton (b.1728) laid on a works party when his son came of age. The fifth birthday of

Stanley Baldwin (b.1867), son of an ironmaster, was celebrated in lordly style with tea and games: the workers' wives, suitably primed, presented the young master with commemorative and edible gifts. To mark the Golden Wedding of Sir Robert Ropner Baronet MP and his wife on 1 March 1908 the staff of the North Shore Shipyard in Stockton-on-Tees commissioned a congratulatory inscription decorated with the Ropner arms, portraits of the couple and a view of their home – precisely the sort of tribute that aristocrats' tenants presented to members of their landlords' families.

From the sixteenth to the twentieth century, well-endowed country parsons were able to live in a style that matched that of the modest country gentleman. Once the religious crises of the sixteenth and seventeenth centuries had subsided, parsons had security of tenure, their income from glebe land kept in step with agricultural profits. Their education and tastes were similar to the neighbouring squires': antiquarians, naturalists and sportsmen were as likely to be found in the parsonage as in the manor house. Parsons of this stamp survived into the twentieth century. James Hastings succeeded to his father's living in 1907; 'gardening, local antiquities, campanology, but above all cricket' were his chief interests. As late as 1928 the incumbent of Buxton in Norfolk was entertaining shooting parties on his glebe. The characteristics that bonded the parson and family to the country landowners tended to separate them from the other ranks of rural society. Clough Williams-Ellis recalled the isolation of his anglophone family home set in a wasteland of Welsh-speaking nonconformists: their ' "neighbours" all seemed to be a half-day drive away'.

Books provided novices with instruction in all aspects of correct behaviour and use of language. The *Book of Kervinge* (1508) recorded some graphic terminology, still current in the late eighteenth century – one 'broke' a deer, 'spoiled' a hen, 'disfigured' a peacock, and 'tamed' a crab. From the beginning of the eighteenth century, periodicals carried columns of advice on etiquette. Batty Langley's *City and Country Builder's and Workman's Treasury of Designs*, published in 1741, offered provincial builders and their clients a digest of polite architectural styles. In 1747 R. Campbell Esq. published a comprehensive guide to metropolitan careers designed for 'Persons of All Ranks who are Entrusted with the Settlement of Youth'. Dr Johnson's *Dictionary* (1755) laid down 'correct' spellings and pronunciations. *The Complete Servant* (1825) was written by Samuel and Sarah Adams, who had spent a lifetime in domestic service, 'to assist Masters and Mistresses of families in arranging their establishments, advising them of their own duties and enabling them to estimate the merits of valuable servants'. Novels supplied models of behaviour in high society. None of these sources was infallible – as his acquaintance with the aristocracy grew, Disraeli (b.1804) silently corrected blunders in his early novel *Vivian Gray*.

Josiah Wedgwood (b.1730) whetted this appetite for 'doing the right thing', he produced cameos, busts and urns in the antique mode for those who could not afford the Greek or Roman originals which the aristocracy collected. Wedgwood priced his pottery high and enlisted 'proper sponsors' – he christened his cream-coloured earthenware 'Queensware'. He also strove to satisfy his customers' appetite for novelty in form and glaze, as he wrote in 1759:

> White stoneware was the staple article of our manufacture, but this had been made a long time . . . The next staple article . . . was an imitation of tortoiseshell but . . . the country was grown tired of it . . . I had already made an imitation of agate which was esteemed very beautiful . . . but the country had been surfeited with varie-gated colours.

Nuances of language and behaviour were even more telling social markers than the paraphernalia of the drawing room. To instruct an American guest, Gertrude Jekyll (b.1843) compiled a list of 'quality' words: 'waistcoat' and 'great-coat' were acceptable, 'vest' and 'overcoat' were not; people of quality did not 'take' tea, they 'had' it.

Despite the social and cultural differences running through the middle classes, their family strategies were not dissimilar. In contrast to the landowners, the middle classes did not routinely practice primogeni-ture, although seniority was frequently acknowledged. Mrs Gaskell (b.1810), praising a prospective son-in-law, commended his 'thorough approval of his father's plan of dividing his property among his seven children instead of making an eldest son'. The will of Robert Waring Darwin (b.1766) implies the existence of a sliding scale in which both birth-order and gender played a part. Darwin left his elder son Erasmus (b.1804) £20,000, his younger son Charles (b.1809) £15,500 and his unmarried daughters Susan (b.1803) and Catherine (b.1810) £10,000 each; the three elder children shared his Lincolnshire farmland and the sisters were given tenure of the family home while they remained unmarried.

It is not clear why the middle classes, who followed aristocratic fashions in other respects, rejected primogeniture. Men active in the expanding territory of the professions, administration and business had less need for caution than the landowner and the commercially-minded farmer who sought to protect the integrity of their estates. It may be that landowners' sons, victims of the system which gave the lion's share to the heir, reacted against the custom which had penalised them. The descendants of those tradesmen and farmers who customarily endowed as many young relatives as their means allowed may have carried the tradition into the middle classes. However, Beatrice Webb's account of the division of the estate of a wealthy plebeian cousin who died in 1892 suggests that her family at least had learned to keep their generosity within bounds. In the absence of a will,

> no less than eighty thousand pounds was divided . . . in equal portions among her next-of-kin, who happened to be two groups of surviving first cousins; consisting on one hand of eleven wage-earners . . . and on the other, of the relatively well-off sons of Grandmother Heyworth – the only daughter, my mother, being dead. The eleven wage-earners met together, and, after prayer, decided that it was against Christian brotherhood and natural equity for them to monopolize this unexpected heritage to the exclusion of the children of the deceased first cousins; and they proceeded to divide their share in equal amounts among themselves and some thirty of the younger generation, whose parents, being also first cousins of Mrs Ashworth, were dead. . . . Needless to say, the 'men of property' did not follow suit.

Finally, the division of family fortunes may have been an insurance against the high casualty rates among professional and business men. Whereas landed wealth was secure, at least until the 1870s, middle-class men lost fortunes at an alarming rate. In London between 1660 and 1730, Peter Earle has calculated, 'the commonest end to a business career was death, but bankruptcy must have run retirement very close in second place'. The grandfather of the historian Edward Gibbon was ruined in a stock market crash in 1720. In spite of his 'mature age' – he was in his middle sixties – he set to and 'erected the edifice of a new fortune'. Marianne Thornton (b.1797) witnessed the crises which brought the family's bank to the brink of disaster in the 1820s ('the case seemed desperate – so much that even ladies were allowed to meddle with it'). Her young brother Henry set the bank on its feet again, with the assistance of his family's powerful allies. Molly Thomas (b.1866), whose father was a stockbroker, recalled the fluctuations in his income: the family 'wavered between great affluence and extreme poverty'. 'During one of the depressed financial times' the Thomases retreated for several years to 'a tiny cottage' in Epping Forest. Experiences like this help to explain the awe with which female dependants regarded the men who controlled their destiny: Octavia Hill (b.1838), who assumed a major responsibility for her family's finances in her middle teens, was nicknamed 'brother' by her sisters.

Professional men and government servants could reap rich rewards. Thomas Willis (b.1621), an Oxford graduate, began his medical career as a 'piss prophet' in marketplaces, diagnosing ailments on the strength of urine samples, and ended it as adviser to the 'great men of London', with a country house in Surrey and the widow of a Wiltshire gentleman for his second wife. Samuel Pepys (b.1633) was the able and ambitious son of a tailor and a laundress, educated at St Paul's School in London and Magdalene College, Cambridge. The diary he kept in the 1660s plots his progress from a single room, where his wife prepared their food and washed their dirty linen, to an apartment lavishly furnished in the height of metropolitan taste with a staff of three or four women servants, a coachman and a footboy. In under a decade of service at the Navy Board his wealth increased four hundred-fold. But, like businessmen, professionals could come to grief. The early chapters of the *Autobiography* of Anthony Trollope (b.1815) log his family's calamitous descent. His father, educated at Winchester and New College, Oxford, was a barrister, a man of 'some small fortune', when he married a parson's daughter in 1809. He was, as 'those quite competent to know' assured his son, 'an excellent and most conscientious lawyer but plagued with so bad a temper that he drove the attorneys from him'. His expectations of an inheritance disappeared when 'an old uncle' married and had a family. He tried farming and failed. Then 'he had an idea that money might be made by sending goods, such as pin-cushions, pepper-boxes and pocket knives, out to the still unfurnished States'. This American venture also failed. Anthony Trollope was the victim of his father's miscalculations. Before he was taken away from Winchester, he was humiliated as a pauper before the boys, the masters and the college servants. Sent to Harrow as a day boy, he found himself 'despised by all [his] companions'. The fortunes of the Trollopes looked up only when his mother seized the initiative.

Nor was the Church a sanctuary from the cares of the world. As Campbell noted in his careers guide in 1747, 'there is not a more helpless thing in nature than a poor clergyman'. The misfortunes of the Victorian cleric Biscoe Wortham demonstrate that a flying start was no guarantee of immunity. Wortham was the son of a landowning parson; in 1870 he was vicar of Shepreth in Cambridgeshire. His financial problems began when he fell out with his father and lost his allowance, moved to a remote and decaying parsonage in Devon and ran into the expenses of childrearing. He went abroad to recoup his fortunes but the school he set up in Bruges failed. He spent six years as a locum, minding other men's parishes, until he found a living in England. Shortly afterwards he was falsely accused of 'certain improper acts' with a farmhand; forced to resign, he uprooted his family for the seventeenth time since their return from Belgium.

During the Great War inflation outran fees and salaries and called into being such agencies as the Professional Classes War Relief Company and the Professional Classes Special Aid Society. Not even the most eminent were exempt. The war, which diverted the energies of the advocate F. E. Smith (b.1873) and the architect Edwin Lutyens (b.1869) from their practices, left them financially embarrassed. Smith's family who, before the war, had divided their time between a London residence grand enough to have a ballroom and a house in the country, depended on subsidies from wealthy friends. The winter of 1917 saw Lutyens' income reduced to a trickle; private commissions had dried up and his work on the War Graves was unpaid.

Concern to launch their children, secure their own future and provide for their widows and unmarried daughters led men to save hard. In Victorian England it seems to have been quite common for professional men in their prime to set aside as much as a third of their annual income. Life insurance became a popular form of investment. Ernest Shephard (b.1879), the illustrator of *The Wind in the Willows* and *Winnie the Pooh*, had five spinster aunts, four of whom lived together in a substantial London house 'with a lot of maids' – the fifth had moved to Bournemouth – all on the reserves their father, an insurance broker, had built up.

When men failed to make adequate provision, their children inherited debts of honour. James Hill (d.1871), a corn merchant and banker from Wisbech in Cambridgeshire, bankrupted himself as a result of his commitment to radical causes: he launched a campaigning paper – the *Star in the East* – set up cooperative stores and planned an agricultural commune. In her teens and early twenties his daughter Octavia laboured and scraped for almost a decade to pay off the debts he and her mother had incurred. She carried a passionate hatred of borrowing into her philanthropic work, determinedly helping only those who helped themselves.

A man's ability to spare his mother, sisters, wife, daughters and indeed remoter female kin from menial work in the home and paid employment outside it was such a point of honour that it might be taken as the definitive characteristic of the middle classes. John Coleridge dismissed out of hand a proposal that his sister Nancy should take work serving in a milliner's shop after their father's death in 1781:

> I would rather live my life on bread and water than see my sister standing behind a counter where she is hourly open to the insults of every conceited young man that may chance to purchase a yard of ribbon from her.

For a conscientious man, the burden was formidable. Charles Darwin's ally Thomas Henry Huxley (b.1825) supported his widowed sister and his elder brother's widow and niece as well as his own wife and seven children. His health broke under the strain: in 1873 eighteen better-placed friends, led by Darwin, subscribed £2,100 to enable him to get the 'complete rest' he required to re-establish his health. In spite of a tense relationship with his sister-in-law, Anny Thackeray (b.1837), who nick-named him 'the cold bath' because of his 'chilling criticism' of her 'little schemes and fancies' and his rooted objection to her marriage with a much younger man ('I positively loathed it'), Leslie Stephen (b.1832) felt it his duty to give her the money to buy a house and to resist her later attempts to repay it. It is hardly surprising that Herbert Fisher (b.1865), 'the eldest son of a large family, not too well provided for', found it hard to 'shake off a sense of anxiety as to his future'.

Women paid their dues to their protectors in a currency compounded of deference, housekeeping duties, and ambassadorial service in polite society. Their lives were often arduous and frustrating. Not only were women excluded from the paid workforce, they were, increasingly, removed to a distance from the workplace. With the important exception of Anglican parsons, who were – in theory – to be found in every parish in the land, the middle classes were concentrated in towns. When the urban atmosphere became unpleasant, those who could afford it moved their families out. Rich Tudor Londoners were pioneer com-muters. In the provinces the mercantile exodus began much later: in Leeds it started in the 1770s; prosperous York families did not withdraw from the centre of their city for another century.

Professional men who were tied to their work built houses which clearly differentiated residential from business premises. The country doctor who built a house and consulting rooms at Burwell near Newmarket in about 1900 gave it two façades. A carriage sweep leads to the private front overlooking the garden; parallel paths led patients to the surgery and delivery boys to the kitchen door on the utilitarian street front.

SOURCES

Material for the study of the family life of the middle classes is generally fragmentary and scattered. Francis Galton's compilation, *Noteworthy Families (Modern Science): An Index to Kinships in Near Degrees Between Persons whose Achievements are Honourable and have been Publicly Recorded*, was based on responses to a circular sent to Fellows of the Royal Society in 1904 and published in 1906. Families like the Stracheys could trace their descent back to the seventeenth century but many of the Fellows were unable, or, maybe, unwilling, to give detailed information about their ancestry. *The Boutflower Book*, published in 1930, aims to tell 'The Complete Story of a Family of the Middle Class Connected with the North of England'. *The Book* was the outcome of detective work in clerical libraries, antiquaries' collections, the publications of Record Societies, newspaper files, poll books and apprenticeship records, the archives of the Admiralty and the India Office, the registers of two

Cambridge colleges and twenty-eight parishes. Clergymen are relatively easily traced and the Boutflowers' descent was rich in parsons. *The Book*'s compiler was ordained, so were his brother Charles, vicar of Terling in Essex, his father, vicar of Appleby in Westmorland, his maternal grandfather, who was headmaster of the preparatory school Gladstone attended, and his great-grandfather John Boutflower X, vicar of Seamer in Yorkshire.

Accounts of individual lives, celebrating spiritual, intellectual or material achievements are more characteristic of the middle classes. Personal testimony abounds; the readership for which it was intended varies. The Yorkshire parson John Shaw (b.1608) addressed his autobiography to 'the son of [his] old age', born when he was 55 and therefore unlikely to be 'in a capacity to learn anything considerable either concerning [his father] or from him' at first hand. What John Shaw would have taught the boy *'viva voce'* he, therefore, set down on paper. The diary which Samuel Pepys wrote in shorthand was meant for his eyes only; when he feared he was losing his sight, he abandoned it. The papers of the famous stood the best chance of survival. Pepys's diary was preserved because his library passed into the custody of Magdalene, his old Cambridge college. The correspondence of the Victorian great and good formed the raw material for the memorial volumes of *Lives and Letters* with which their admirers, usually close relatives or colleagues, celebrated their achievements. Although notable women often acted unconventionally by the standards of the day, there are exceptions. Mrs Gaskell's letters provide an intimate portrait of the day-to-day experience of a middle-class provincial family in the first half of Queen Victoria's reign. And Mrs Linley Sambourne's diary and household books, the basis of Shirley Nicholson's portrait of *A Victorian Household*, give a rare insight into the life of a woman who derived great satisfaction from the round of 'At Homes' which many of her better-known contemporaries despised.

THE MEANING OF CHILDREN

For middle-class people children were an insurance against mortality. As well as, or instead of, income or goods, professional men passed their learning on to their sons – and less often their daughters. The text of the sampler Prisca Philips sewed in 1700 sums up this philosophy:

> Look well to what you have in hand
> For learning is better than house or land
> When land is gone and money is spent
> Then learning is most excellent.

Family duties were the female vocation. Girls were therefore useful, but the taboo against paid employment meant that a large family of daughters could be burdensome.

To nineteenth-century scientists, children were natural subjects for observation. Darwin began to collect information about infant behaviour in the months leading up to the birth of his first child in December 1839. Later he compiled 'Babbiana', to keep his wife up to date with their children's doings when she was away. His notes formed the basis of 'A Biographical Sketch of an Infant', a pioneering essay on child development published in the recently-founded journal *Mind* in 1877, as its subject approached his fortieth birthday. Darwin monitored the child's displays of affection – the earliest perhaps significantly directed towards his nurse – and his emerging sense of humour: 'when he was 110 days old he was exceedingly amused by a pinafore being thrown over his face and suddenly withdrawn'. In the 1880s Darwin's cousin Francis Galton devised a 'Life History Album' to enable parents to combine a photographic record with a written log of their child's mental and physical development.

INFANCY

Following convention, many Stuart parents put their children out to nurse. The poignant memorial to Anne, daughter of the Revd Thomas and Judith Consant, in 1606, indicates that even longed-for babies were consigned to wetnurses: the Consants had waited thirteen years for a child. The middle classes, with their respect for expertise, were, perhaps, the group most likely to take note of printed advice on childcare and education. Seventeenth-century parents were the target of treatises encouraging mothers to breastfeed; nevertheless, wetnurses continued to be employed. Mr Watson of Hampstead recognised the human cost in his diary in the 1840s; on learning of the death of the child his daughter's nurse had left behind, he wrote:

> it is a melancholy reflection that our own child's life should be sustained, as it were at the expense of the life of another infant . . . The same thing happened also with Mrs Cooper who suckled our Margaret.

Manuals which argued that the rearing of her children was an intelligent woman's true vocation proliferated from the 1880s. It was in this climate that the compilers of Heal's *Nursery Book*, published in 1914, advanced the claim that children had only recently been brought down from the 'attic or some other room not thought sufficiently good for any other purpose, furnished with things discarded from other rooms' into a 'carefully chosen, well-lighted and well-planned nursery' in the heart of the family. In fact, little chairs for children are recorded from the sixteenth century. Paediatricians, pedagogues and entrepreneurs all had vested interests in the continual stimulation of parental appetites for advice on the best possible ways of bringing up a baby.

CHILDHOOD

John Locke (b.1632) is often identified as an early advocate of more humane childrearing practices. The novelty and humanity of his advice have been grossly exaggerated. He followed traditional authorities in emphasising the need to subdue the small child's will:

> the wants of fancy children should never be gratified . . . the very speaking for any such thing should make them lose it. Clothes, when they need, they must have; but if they speak for this stuff or that colour, they should be sure to go without it.

Another passage in Locke's *Thoughts Concerning Education* rams the disciplinarian message home:

> A kind and prudent mother of my acquaintance once was . . . forced to whip her little daughter, at her first coming home from nurse, eight times successively in the same morning, before she could master her stubbornness and obtain compliance in a very easy and indifferent matter. If she had left off sooner and stopped at the first whipping, she had spoiled the child forever and, by her unprevailing blows, only confirmed her refractoriness, very hardly afterwards to be cured; but wisely persisting till she had bent her mind and suppled her will (the only end of correction and chastise-ment), she established her authority thoroughly in the very first occasion and had ever after a very ready compliance and obedience in all things from her daughter; for as this was the first time, so I think it was the last time she ever struck her.

Note the circumstances in which the eight 'whippings' were adminis-tered: 'at first coming home from nurse' (the child was still very young and had just been removed from her foster mother); 'the matter' was 'very easy and indifferent' (trivial and insignificant). Only after the mind had been 'bent' and the will 'suppled' (the spirit broken) was it advisable to introduce a regime in which the child was encouraged to learn through play. The rising sales of toys and children's books in and after the eighteenth century – often cited as evidence for a growing concern for children – may have more to do with commercialisation.

Childrearing practice varied. The wealthiest parents, living in large houses, able to support a big domestic staff, had the choice of following aristocratic practice, seeing their offspring seldom. In such circum-stances children were vulnerable to ill-treatment by servants. It never occurred to the young Edwardian Belinda Norman-Butler to complain when her nursemaid hit her, shut her up naked and deprived her of food. Some parent–child relationships were oppressively close. John Ruskin (b.1819), the only child of a sherry merchant, never escaped his parents' stifling embrace. Until he was 10, his mother was his teacher; he was 14 before he went to school. His mother accompanied him to Oxford where she saw him daily. Caroline Hill (b.1809) used methods which would still be widely regarded as dangerously radical at the end of the twentieth century. Living in poverty apart from her husband, she brought up four daughters according to the principles laid down by the Swiss educationalist Pestalozzi in the eighteenth century. Miranda (b.1836), Octavia (b.1838), Emily (b.1840) and Florence (b.1843) were encouraged to read but not given regular lessons; the sisters spent a great deal of time in the fresh air.

Occupation affected children's access to their fathers. Lawyers on circuit, officers in the armed forces and other servants of the state were separated from their families in the course of duty, sometimes for long periods. Men building up businesses might, like Matthew Boulton (b.1728), find 'the longest day not long enough'. This comment was made on a day spent at his Soho site where he lived close to his works. He was often away. Affectionate messages to 'the General of Soho', his son Matthew II (b.1770), and 'the Fair Maid of the Mill', his daughter Anne (b.1768), were conveyed in letters written as he travelled about promoting the sales of his engines. Without a private income, Thomas Henry Huxley (b.1825) 'had to struggle to keep his head above water for the first fifteen or twenty years of his married life, he had scarcely any time to devote to his children'. Because he went out early and came back late he called himself 'the lodger'. His younger children and grandchildren saw much more of him.

Parsons, scholars and writers who worked at home often did so with their children at their elbows. The four daughters of the naturalist John Ray (b.1627) helped him to collect the specimens on which he based his *History of Insects*; he called the caterpillars they caught after them: Katherine's Eruca, a moth now known as the Lilac Beauty, was successfully reared in 1695. William Thackeray (b.1811), who brought his daughters up singlehanded, used them as models for the illustrations he produced for *Punch*; they washed his woodblocks too. Much of Charles Darwin's scientific work was carried on with his children at his side.

These children could not avoid exposure to their father's profession. As soon as he could walk Arthur Machen (b.1863) accompanied his parson father 'on such parish visitations as were fairly within the stretch and strength of short legs'. As a small boy, Charles Kingsley (b.1819) played preacher: 'His delight was to make a little pulpit in his nursery, arranging chairs for an imaginary congregation and, putting on his pinafore as a surplice, give little sermons.' Before he embarked on his formal medical training at Guy's Hospital, indeed before he had committed himself to a career in medicine, Richard Kay (b.1716) assisted his father in such operations as 'opening John Schofield's thigh which was accidentally broke'. More surprisingly, he deputised for him in the consulting room and took responsibility for prescribing drugs: 'giving Father an account . . . of the patients I have been concerned for today . . . he blamed me very much for prescribing as he fears a few grains too large a quantity of calomel'.

Boyhood was characterised by a prolonged period of formal education; the contrasting female curriculum is covered in a later section of this chapter: see YOUTH: DAUGHTERS, p. 113.

The boy's first steps in learning were often a maternal responsibility. John Locke praised women who acquired academic skills in order to pass them on to their small sons. Tactics varied. Osbert Lancaster (b.1908) recalled his mother's 'brilliant educational methods'. With the aid of chocolate letters he 'learned to read at a very tender age'.

> Such letters as I recognised I was allowed to eat; later, when my knowledge of the alphabet was faultless, I was entitled to such letters as I could form into a new word. Although never strong in arithmetic, I soon grasped the simple fact that the longer the word, the more chocolate, and by the time I could spell the word 'suffragette' without an error this branch of my education was deemed complete.

Mrs Lancaster's technique was not original; gingerbread alphabets were sold in the eighteenth century:

> And that the child may learn the better
> As he can name, he eats the letter.

Fathers also played an active part. Anthony Trollope's father tested his rote learning of Greek and Latin every morning while he shaved, underlining each 'guilty fault' by pulling the boy's hair 'without stopping his razor or dropping his shaving brush. No father was ever more anxious for the education of his children', Trollope observed, 'though I think none ever knew less how to go about the work.' Clough Williams-Ellis's father gave up his Cambridge Fellowship for a college living when he married late in the nineteenth century: 'the bringing up – or rather the schooling – of his five . . . sons was the true vocation of his later years'. 'Up to the public school stage' he taught them himself; with the assistance of a Cambridge graduate who acted as 'governess-in-chief', five and a half days a week 'long and firmly were [their] miserable little noses held to that drearily trundling grindstone'. The weight clerical fathers placed on education is suggested by the case of a Stuart clergyman charged with absenteeism, who responded that he had moved into

Leicester to enable his sons to attend the Free Grammar School, evidently confident that his bishop would accept this as adequate justification for the neglect of the remainder of his flock.

YOUTH: SONS

Discipline was high on the agenda of Stuart parents and governors. Richard Routh was among the candidates for a schoolmaster's post who were required to demonstrate their ability to wield a cane – a delinquent boy was provided – in support of their application. Academic achievement was not necessarily the schools' goal. Restricted entry rather than the intellectual rigour of the curriculum was the primary defence against the dilution of the ranks of privilege. Until 1855, the Winchester scholarship examination was 'a farce – a few lines of Ovid to be repeated, one or two lines to be construed, and a traditional question, "Can you sing?" with its traditional reply: "Yes, sir: All people that on earth do dwell." ' In spite of his father's bullying, Anthony Trollope left Harrow ignorant of the multiplication tables and unable to read French, Latin or Greek; his 'writing was . . . wretched', his spelling 'imperfect'. He learned to 'read and enjoy the Latin classics' in adult life.

The examinations which controlled entry to the upper ranks of the Civil Service and commissioned ranks in the Army, from the middle of the nineteenth century, were exclusive because they mirrored the public school curriculum. A public school education also enabled boys to shed the regional accents which by the 1870s had become a social handicap. (Girls, in whose education much less money was invested, were more likely to retain local accents and turns of phrase.) The public school world was riven with snobbery. The outsider had a rough ride. Michael Longson (b.1911) arrived at Eton to discover that the provincial tailor who kitted him out had made the mistake of supplying trousers without turn-ups, an idiosyncrasy reserved for the grandees of the school. The public school world was stratified. Demarcation lines were visible in the calendars of sporting fixtures – teams were willing to accept challenges only from establishments they regarded as their equals. Among adults the slang peculiar to individual schools was a more effective marker than the Old Boys' tie.

In higher education, a similar hierarchy existed. The Birmingham industrialist Joseph Chamberlain sent his son Austen (b.1863), who was destined for a career in national politics, from Rugby to Trinity College, Cambridge, where he would rub shoulders with the aristocratic youths who would be his future parliamentary colleagues; he saw the vocational curriculum of Mason's College, Birmingham, as more appropriate for his younger son Neville (b.1869), who was intended for the family firm. F. E. Smith (b.1873), the son of a provincial estate agent, failed to win a scholarship to Harrow but made up for lost opportunities as an undergraduate at Wadham College, Oxford, where he counted Earl Beauchamp and Lord Balcarres among his closest friends.

Shortage of funds could interrupt a poor youth's studies. Ralph Josselin (b.1617) was 'forced to come from Cambridge many times for want of means' though he eventually graduated. Samuel Johnson (b.1709), son of a bookseller from Lichfield in Staffordshire, left Oxford prematurely when his money ran out – his doctorate was honorary. His father's bankruptcy prevented John Coleridge (b.1719) from going to university at the conventional age; after a decade of strenuous saving, he went up to Cambridge in his late twenties, a married man with several children. Childless clergymen earmarked endowments for their kin; local patriots left funds to support boys from their home town – most of these closed scholarships were abolished when college statutes were overhauled in the 1850s. Other boys depended on individual sponsors. Edward Benson (b.1829), Archbishop of Canterbury from 1886 to 1896, owed his degree to the patronage of the Bursar of Trinity College, Cambridge, who not only supported him but, in keeping with the middle-class code, took responsibility for his sisters' dowries. Hardpressed parents were sometimes prepared to accept assistance from dubious sources. Canon Copeman, with several sons to bring up, was apparently willing to turn a blind eye to the potential risks of the connection between his son Charlie and the homosexual don, Oscar Browning (b.1837). Having caught Browning's fancy as a chorister at King's College, Cambridge, where Browning was a fellow, Charlie remained the object of his lavish indulgence throughout his adolescence. As an undergraduate he had the handsome allowance of £100 a year. Later he went into practice as a solicitor.

The privileges of education might be bought at great psychological cost. The hardships of life in the public school were frequently outdone by the wretchednesses of the preparatory school which took small boys straight from home. Leaving his 'happy home' to go to school was a 'wrench' which plunged Henry Liddell (b.1811) into a 'black and hopeless misery' more intense and enduring than any he had known before or since. Charles Kingsley's wife Fanny found parting with her first son 'almost unbearable', it was 'the first real grief and trial' of her married life. Wives, in their turn, may have paid a price. Man and boy, Charles Darwin (b.1809) was uncommonly easy in women's company; he recognised this as one of the benefits conferred by his unusual experience. At the age of 9 he became a boarder at 'Dr Butler's great school at Shrewsbury', which was barely a mile from his home. In his own opinion, this gave him the best of both worlds. He had 'the great advantage of living the life of a true schoolboy' but he 'very often ran

[home] . . . This', he believed, 'was in many ways advantageous . . . by keeping up home affections and interests.'

The restricted access routes to middle-class occupations meant that parents had very little option but to subject their sons to the prolonged and often painful ritual of preparatory and public school education. The willingness of victims of savage beatings, poor food, fagging, bullying and sexual abuse to expose their sons to such an endurance test testifies to the value placed on educational conformity. In 1850, when their eldest son William was rising 11, Charles and Emma Darwin were 'very full of the subject of schools'. On the one hand, Darwin 'could not endure to think of sending [his] boys to waste seven or eight years in making miserable Latin verses'; on the other, he 'could not help being much afraid of trying an experiment on so important a subject'. In this instance, they opted for 'the old stereotypical stupid classical education' at Rugby; their younger sons were sent to a more progressive school. Those who sought to reproduce Darwin's accidental good fortune were commonly frustrated. The parents of Leslie and Fitzjames Stephen sent their sons as day boys to Eton. Leslie Stephen (b.1832) was unhappy and left prematurely; his elder brother Fitzjames stayed the course; his physical prowess, which won him the telling nickname 'Giant Grim', was his shield. The occasional preparatory schools, like the one Richard Strachey (b.1902) attended, which treated their pupils as members of a tolerant extended family, did nothing to toughen their boys in readiness for the next stage – Strachey found himself a miserable outsider at Rugby.

Surmounting the educational hurdle did not mark the end of the youth's initiation. The most fortunate went straight into the family business, joined the family practice, was installed in the living or took up the position which had been earmarked for him. Galton's collection of *Noteworthy Families* includes some striking examples of occupational succession and achievement. He listed four generations of scientific Darwins (in 1904 the brothers George (b.1845), an astronomer, Francis (b.1848), a botanist, and Horace (b.1851), an engineer, were all Fellows of the Royal Society), three generations of geological Woodwards and three generations of architectural Scotts. When Galton constrasted the 'hereditary genius' of his noteworthy scientists with the 'social influence' which 'helped' members of aristocratic families to achieve prominence, we may confidently conclude that he was undervaluing the privileged access to education and employment which the scientists' children enjoyed.

There was a powerful dynastic tendency among clerks at the Bank of England. Between 1799 and 1949 there were seven examples of five-generation families, fourteen families with four generations of service and fifty-two with three. It is probable that the decision to restrict the proportion of Sons of Clerks admitted at any election to one-sixth, which was taken in 1799, the first year covered by the survey, depressed the total. The Bank admitted women to its service in the twentieth century: three representatives of the fifth generation were female.

Other young men benefited from professional patronage. Just as aristocrats without direct heirs grafted successors on to their family trees, professional men without sons bequeathed their practices to favourite pupils. The Warwickshire attorney Thomas Ashton left Randall English, his clerk, the gown, desk, law books and horse that were the essential tools of the seventeenth-century lawyer's trade. The surgeon William Hunter (b.1718) benefited from the patronage of James Douglas, in whose house he remained for nearly a decade after Douglas's death.

Professional adoption became less common as vocational training was institutionalised but patronage remained important for Victorians. With an elder brother able to introduce him to editors, Leslie Stephen 'started as a journalist with many advantages'. Clough Williams-Ellis's 'large and varied assortment of relatives and connections, a number of them quite rich enough to be helpful' was a crucial resource in the early years of his architectural career. Almost as soon as he embarked on his professional training, a second cousin made him 'a sort of ADC' to his builder. Shortly afterwards, 'through family jobbery', he obtained 'a small architectural commission'. The lean years of his career were larded by the hospitality of affluent acquaintances – he owed his entry to London society to contacts he had made as a student at Cambridge. 'As an indefatigable dancing man, and an appreciative and generally amiable dinner or house-party guest', he was 'handed on from hostess to hostess – often as just a plug to fill a sudden hole left by the last-minute failure of some more prestigious guest'; he lived on 'a mixed and irregular diet of alternating quails and kippers'.

Herbert de Fraine (b.1870), the son of the proprietor of *The Bucks Herald*, was conscious of his good fortune in obtaining a director's nomination to an untenured clerkship in the Bank of England: 'These were the days of large families' – de Fraine was one of eight – 'and if a middle-class father could not afford the expense of training for a profession, and the delay in earning, it was with the utmost difficulty that he could find an opening for his sons, who might sometimes drop to artisan level.' De Fraine's acquaintances drifted into schoolmastering or badly paid clerkships of various kinds. 'Agriculture, although one hoped one might one day rent a farm or become agent on a big estate, might offer only a farm labourer's life.' De Fraine owed his own nomination to the Bank to his father's religious and political affiliation: 'My Director . . . Baron Addington, was a devout churchman and Tory . . . my father owned a Church–Tory newspaper.' This patronage came in the nick of time; Addington died later that year. Even so de Fraine was not on an equal footing with the sons of better-off men: when, after two

112

and a half years at the Bank, he took the examination which conferred pensionable status, he found himself competing 'with a new intake of men whose fathers had been able to give them several years' further education, while we were already working and, incidentally, forgetting much of what we had learnt at school'.

Those without beneficial connections faced lean years while they built up their practices. Arthur Conan Doyle (b.1859) was reared 'in the hardy and bracing atmosphere of poverty'; his three sisters went out to Portugal as governesses and sent their salaries home to support the family while he trained. He set up in general practice in a Portsmouth suburb on the strength of a rented house, 'possibly tenth-hand furniture' for the consulting rooms – the rest of the house was bare – and a 'fair consignment of drugs on tick'. He polished his own brass plate and found that, on a diet of bacon, bread and tea, he could 'live quite easily and well on less than a shilling a day'. To help his mother, he took on his 10-year-old brother, Innes, who reported that 'the patients are crowding in. We made three bob this week. We have vaxenated a baby and got hold of a man with consumption.' Conan Doyle recollected how

> Month followed month and I picked up a patient here and a patient there until the nucleus of a little practice had been formed . . . I mixed with people so far as I could for I learned that a brass plate alone will never attract. Some of my tradespeople gave their custom in return for mine.

An epileptic grocer 'meant butter and tea to us'. At this stage in his career a mother or sister willing to act as his ambassador would have been an asset; it was his wife's money which eventually enabled him 'to embrace the decencies, if not the luxuries of life'. Professional men without substantial resources looked to marriage as a means of acquiring capital and connections.

YOUTH: DAUGHTERS

Before marriage, and if she failed to marry, up to the 1860s, and in some circles much later, home was a daughter's proper sphere, her proper style was modest and retiring, at school or at home she was instructed in ladylike deportment and dress, needlework and other accomplishments. In a majority of families her academic education was a very low priority. Mothers were often too busy to dedicate regular hours to daughters in the schoolroom. The teachers in the tiny schools the genteel preferred, and the governesses they brought into their own households (and generally paid less than the cook), were frequently unable to do more than hand down threadbare and superficial lessons to their pupils. Mary Fairfax Somerville (b.1780), an admiral's daughter, spent much of her time learning pages of Dr Johnson's *Dictionary* by heart while caged in a steel contraption intended to improve her posture. Leslie Stephen's daughter Virginia (b.1882) thought of Latin and Greek as passports to an earthly paradise which her brothers enjoyed and from which she was excluded.

A handful of scholarly households reared learned daughters. Bashua Makin (b.1612), daughter of a Sussex rector, studied Latin, Greek, Hebrew and French. Elizabeth Elstob (b.1683), sister of an Oxford academic, compiled an Anglo-Saxon Grammar. According to John Aubrey (b.1626), Mr Lidcot's 11-year-old daughter understood 'arithmetic and algebra, trigonometry and the use of globes' and attended meetings of the Royal Society: 'They do impute all to her early education.' The tradition of classical education at home persisted into the twentieth century. The author of *Postgate's Latin Grammar* brought his children up to speak precise Latin. When his 6-year-old daughter Margaret (b.1893) mistakenly asked for *the* beef instead of *some* beef, he put 'the whole sirloin' on to her plate.

In the nineteenth century commitment to a sound academic education spread. The scientist Thomas Henry Huxley was determined that his daughters 'should not be brought up as man-traps for the matrimonial market'; he planned to give them 'the same training in physical science as their brother will get, as long as he is a boy' – the qualification is significant. Yet Huxley feared that

> other people would not follow his example and five-sixths of women will stop in the doll stage of evolution to be the stronghold of parsondom, the drag on civilisation, the degradation of every important pursuit with which they mix themselves – 'intrigues' in politics, and 'friponnes' in science.

By 1870 a tiny minority of young women were able to follow something like the masculine curriculum at school and university – 'something like' because academic study at full strength was generally considered too taxing for the female constitution, too daunting to suitors and a poor preparation for their nurturing roles as wives and mothers. (Reservations about the Victorian girl's physical capacity to cope with a strenuous curriculum may have had some foundation in fact. The medical notes compiled by Dr Frances Hoggan in the 1880s suggest that many girls had to contend with poor health. Of the 335 pupils she inspected, 329 'had problems ranging from curvature of the spine, to weakness, delicacy, anaemia, languor, rupture, acne, knock-knees, lung congestion, flat chest and heart mischief'.)

Marriage remained the preferred career, and entry into paid employment was widely frowned upon. At Oxford, on the eve of the twentieth century, women students were still divided into 'those who meant to earn their livings' and 'Home Sunbeams'. Elizabeth Wordsworth (b.1840), Principal of Lady Margaret Hall from 1879 to 1909, warned parents that her girls did not marry well; defenders of higher education for women stressed that these graduates' less academic sisters were almost equally prone to spinsterhood. Nevertheless, Miss Words-worth's views were widely shared: on 14 February 1913 Miss Parfit received a Valentine 'C/o Messrs Johnsons' Dyeworks' in Abergavenny. The postcard, depicting, in the foreground, a pensive 'girl graduate', in gown and mortar board, and, in the background, a young mother and her baby, pointed out that

> Science and Philosophy
> Are very well in their way
> But the knowledge of good cookery
> Might make you a MA.

Commitment to women's education tended to be concentrated in families with an academic bent and feminist tendencies. Two of the brothers of Eleanor Sidgwick (b.1845), Principal of Newnham, held Cambridge Fellowships; three of the brothers of the historian Eleanor Lodge were professors; Pernel Strachey (b.1876) came from a formidable family of intellectuals; Philippa Fawcett, who came top in the Cambridge University Final Examinations in Mathematics in 1890, was daughter of a prominent campaigner for women's suffrage and niece of Elizabeth Garrett Anderson (b.1836), the pioneer of medical education for women; Theodora Calvert (b.1898), one of the first women called to the Bar after the Great War, was a niece of Margaret Llewelyn Davies, General Secretary of the Women's Cooperative Guild which gave working-class women a political platform, and great-niece of Emily Davies, co-founder of Girton.

The grounds on which the Hopkinses opposed their daughter Katherine's ambition to read History at Cambridge reflect the thinking of less progressive parents. Her father:

> did not approve of women invading his own university. And he took a poor view of my announcement that I wanted to go to Cambridge in order to equip myself to do a proper job. Paid jobs, mother explained . . . when taken by girls who did not need them were really a form of abstracting the bread from the mouths of girls who really did need the money.

This principle did not apply to her brother. Eventually, on the understanding that she would confine herself to part-time teaching for the Workers' Educational Association, 'or something of that kind', her parents gave in.

Even after a girl had gone up to university, home duties remained paramount. Nellie Benson was summoned home from Oxford when her father became Archbishop of Canterbury in 1886. F. E. Smith's sister Clara was recalled from University College, Liverpool, to provide emotional support for her widowed mother. Katharine Hopkins's hopes were dashed by her father's decision to stand for Parliament. When Helena Sickert's father died soon after her graduation, not only did she come home but, since her mother 'had never slept alone', she 'felt obliged to share her bedroom and . . . had no privacy, night or day'. An established career did not exempt a daughter from her responsibilities to her home and her mother in particular: in 1882 Louisa Lumsden, founding headmistress of St Leonard's School, St Andrews, resigned, ostensibly to care for her invalid mother; friction with colleagues clearly affected her decision. Lumsden's fragmented career – she gave up her post at Girton in 1873 and was to leave the University of St Andrews in 1900 – points to a temptation to retreat behind the stereotype when life in the public sphere became difficult.

If study was a luxury, the nursery and the sewing box were a girl's bread and butter. At the age of 4 Violet Birchall (b.1878) was in 'sole charge of Lindaraja' (who was 17 months younger) for two hours every morning; this was policy, not necessity – the Birchalls had no fewer than nine servants in 1881. Before the introduction of the sewing machine, all needlework was done by hand: shirt-, handkerchief- and dressmaking occupied many hours. As reading was for boys, sewing was for girls an essential skill. *The Mother's Home Book*, published in 1879, declared that: 'Nothing can be more pitiable than to see a female . . . unable to ply her needle, her case being somewhat similar to that of a male . . . who does not know how to read.' While Helena Sickert was at Notting Hill High School she was expected to spend every Saturday morning 'sewing: mending my own clothes and helping my mother to mend the boys' and men's clothes and the house-linen'. Little wonder that, when she came to write her autobiography in her late sixties, and memories 'tumbled out, helter-skelter', she 'was reminded of dealings with a bag of mending wools, not too carefully kept'. The diaries kept by Jeanette Marshall (b.1855), the daughter of a prominent medical man, suggest that, throughout the year, she regularly spent three or more hours a day working on her wardrobe.

Mothers varied in the attention they gave to their daughters' training in housewifery. Some girls were unacquainted with the simplest domestic task. Vera Brittain (b.1893), whose father was a paper manufacturer, studied for her Oxford entrance exam in a chilly room rather than impose on the servants by asking them to lay a fire; it did not occur to her that she might, by observation or by trial and error, learn to do it for herself. Instruction in household management may well have been commoner than training in household chores. This letter from her mother suggests that Marianne Gaskell (b.1835) served a comprehensive apprenticeship in preparation for hiring, firing and managing servants (the Janes Mrs Gaskell mentions are the outgoing cook and her successor):

> *After* one Jane is gone and before the other comes, will you speak to Sarah, before Jessie, and tell her I wish her to mind what *Jessie* says to her, about *personal cleanliness and tidiness in her bedroom*, and that I feel sure from what I know of Jessie that she will always speak kindly to her *(mind you say this* BEFORE JESSIE:) of course; she is to receive all directions *about her work* DOWNSTAIRS from the cook; but she is to be willing & grateful for instructions about her *upstairs* work (study, schoolroom, steps passage etc) from either Hearn [the Gaskells' long-serving nurse] or Jessie. I hear *Sarah wants new and* LONGER *gowns.* Her large legs seem to have made a great impression; and her *rough manners* on Florence. Please see after her always being respectful, and nice-mannered. *Her mother is;* & you might tell her how much I was struck with her in her mother's pretty ways, and gentle voice. And will you ask Hearn to see about her having longer *petticoats, and new* dark print gowns, *with frills round the neck,* and tidy sleeves etc; as well as some *lighter* prints (say lilacs) for Sundays.

THE CHOICE OF A WIFE

Contemplating the possibility of his wife's death, Richard Rogers (b.1551) considered what he would forfeit:

> Forgoing so fit a companion for religion, housewifery and other
>   comforts
> Loss and decay in substance
> Care of household matters cast on me
> Neglect of study
> Care and looking after children
> Forgoing our boarders
> Fear of losing friendship among her kindred.

When Charles Darwin (b.1809) weighed the pros and cons of marriage in 1838, children were at the top of his list of benefits, followed by lifelong companionship and affection, a home and a housekeeper, and 'female chitchat'. (Would this last item have featured on the agenda of a man denied Darwin's happy experience of sisters and female cousins?) The chief disadvantages he noted were the 'expense of children', the sacrifice of freedom and the 'conversation of clever men'. The argument was clinched by the contrast between a 'nice soft wife on a sofa with a good fire and books and music' and life as a 'neuter bee'. Darwin's notes highlight the cultural gap between men and women. Some men addressed the issue by prescribing courses of reading for their wives to be. When, with her mother's consent, Edward Benson (b.1829) fixed on his 11-year-old second cousin Minnie Sidgwick (b.1842) as his future bride, he assumed the role of her tutor.

Having decided on marriage, Darwin considered 'When?' His conclusion was 'soon for otherwise bad if one has children – one's character is more flexible – one's feelings more lively and if one does not marry soon, one loses so much pure happiness'. Thus, with generous settlements from his own father and his father-in-law, Josiah Wedgwood II, which, in his own phrase, made him and his bride, his cousin Emma, 'as rich as Jews', Darwin embarked on a long and satisfying partnership.

A sound joint income was a prescription for marital security. Premature marriage could blight a young man's career. Couples of slender means endured long engagements: sensible men postponed marriage until they were confident that their 'trade would carry two'; families intervened when it looked as though romantic impulses might prevail. The Victorian army took steps to protect young officers; at regimental balls they were discouraged from dancing with marriageable women; if they formed undesirable attachments, they were posted out of harm's way.

Leonard Huxley (b.1860) turned his back on the Law to marry. He took a teaching post at Charterhouse, an option which compared very poorly with the Bar as far as status and potential earnings were concerned. In the opinion of Benjamin Jowett, Master of Balliol, where Huxley had taken a Double First, 'he was ending where he would have been beginning at the Bar'. The commission to compile the official *Life and Letters* of his father launched him into a literary career in middle age.

Arthur Hughes (b.1857) and Molly Thomas (b.1866), whose mothers were impoverished widows, became engaged in 1887 but did not marry until 1897; by then Hughes's legal practice was large enough to permit him to lease a flat, engage a maid and support a wife and child. Men who deferred marriage for ten or a dozen years, until their wives-to-be had fulfilled their home duties, were admired.

WOMEN'S OPTIONS OUTSIDE MARRIAGE

The prospects of women whose male relatives failed in their duty to support them at home, assist them to a suitable match, or, in the 1880s and 1890s, pay for professional training, were bleak. Many were reduced to mercenary dependency. The paid 'companion' or governess offered her services in exchange for the board, lodging, moral protection, and small cash allowance normally provided by her own kin. The

Census of 1851 indicated that there were more than half a million 'surplus' women in England, a significant proportion of them from the middle classes. When the Revd James Thomas, headmaster of a country grammar school, died in the 1880s his daughters had 'one outlet, and one only – to go into a private family as a governess, which was a terribly crowded profession'. One

> found herself, at the age of sixteen, in a remote part of Wales, looking after four extremely unpleasant children for £12 a year. Although this was the worst of her experiences, in most of the jobs she had she was ill-paid and grossly over-worked.

She was never paid more than £25 a year 'and on this she was expected to change for dinner every night'.

The governess, trapped in the uncomfortable terrain which separated the gentlewoman from the servant, was not a good match. Isabella Fane's condescending comment, made in the 1830s, suggests the difficulties she might encounter: 'Mrs Torrens is reckoned a *sweet* woman, but she is so like a governess that one cannot get on with her.'

Older spinsters, like Catherine Porten, who fell on hard times in her forties, transported their domestic competence to the public sphere. Miss Porten, loath to live as a poor relation, ran 'a boarding house for Westminster School' in the 1740s. Over a century later Oscar Browning's Eton connections helped his mother and sister to recruit pupils to the school they launched to compensate for the loss of their unearned income.

In the early 1870s, recognising the quickness, patience, docility and low financial expectations of women brought up in middle-class homes, the Post Office began to recruit them as clerical workers. Entry to other branches of the public service followed.

Nursing became an option for genteel orphans and daughters of impoverished families. A district nurse noted that, in contrast to 'almost every employment for which the average woman is fitted', 'the profession is not at present overcrowded'. She emphasised the intimate relationship between nursing and home duties:

> a majority of women are married sooner or later, and a very large proportion of the minority will ultimately be withdrawn from the paid labour market to be absorbed by such duties as keeping house for a widowed father, bringing up motherless nieces or nephews, or taking care of elderly relatives. Knowing that whatever occupation she chooses, it will only in a small percentage of cases be her life-work, and that that life-work will probably be of a purely domestic nature, and require much nerve and physical strength, many sensible girls will have a strong bias towards a profession which ensures all the means of a healthy life, and gives instruction

in so many subjects that will always be of use to her, and at the same time enables her to provide against a solitary and unaided old age if that should be her fate.

By the beginning of the twentieth century there were several schools for 'Lady Gardeners'. An article describing Swanley Horticultural College referred to the 'natural genius of women' for this work: 'The care of young plants calls forth, in a modified degree, that mother instinct which finds its highest fulfilment in the infant nursery.' Their promoters emphasised 'the healthiness of an open air life'. Unfortunately, the neediest and most deserving, 'the orphan daughters of professional men', could not afford the fees.

Women accomplished in the arts and crafts played a part in widening occupational horizons. Peter Rabbit, who first appeared in an illustrated letter to a sick child, was Beatrix Potter's passport to independence. Potter (b.1866) displayed considerable commercial flair, encouraging Sandersons to produce fabrics and wallpapers based on her illustrations and promoting a whole series of profitable 'side shows' – teasets, games, painting books, toys, bookshelves and slippers. She used her earnings to set herself up as a farmer when she was nearly 50. Gertrude Jekyll (b.1843) was outstanding among the middle-class craftswomen who migrated from the private to the public domain. Examples of her embroidery and metalwork were commissioned by friends and acquaintances of friends. She advised her friend Barbara Leigh Smith (b.1827) on the decoration of Girton; her scheme for her brother's flat led to an invitation from the Duke of Westminster to act as 'umpire-in-chief as to the furnishing' of Eaton Hall, in 1875. The first gardens she designed were for her family; in 1918 she was chosen to design the settings for the graves of those who had fallen in the Great War.

Good works among the respectable poor paved the way for more systematic social work and social investigation (paid and unpaid). Writing in 1889, Octavia Hill (b.1838) recalled that 'long ago', in her youth, 'hardly a woman I knew had any opportunity for devoting time to any grave or kindly work beyond her own household or small social circle. Now there are thousands who achieve it.' Mary Merryweather was among the early paid welfare workers; arriving in Braintree in 1847, she found employment as a 'moral missionary' to Courtaulds' work people, taking a role which, in earlier generations, had been filled by Courtauld women.

With the widening of the gentlewoman's territory, as Octavia Hill observed, 'customs . . . altered in a marked manner; it used to be difficult for a girl to walk alone and it was considered almost impossible for her to travel in omnibuses or third-class trains'. Nevertheless the independence of unmarried women was severely constrained. A Fellow of Newnham who stayed overnight in a London hotel with a woman friend in 1876 needed the services of a 'small boy brother' to act as escort. The women of the Indian Army Nursing Service were required to live under a code at least as strict as a parent would have imposed. As their superintendent explained in 1893:

> I do not hold that a nurse should be debarred, by reason of her profession, from all amusements appropriate to her friends, and to her own rank in life . . . But the fact that they are young women, living without any protection from relations or friends, renders their position in some ways a difficult one. Instead of being more independent, they have practically less safe liberty of action than many a girl living in her father's house.

These examples help to explain why many academic women rejected collegiate life for the dignity and relative autonomy of marriage. Some worked in partnership with their husband – as the historian Barbara Hammond (b.1873) did; others subordinated their work to his – like the economist Mary Paley Marshall (b.1890) – or abandoned it altogether as Molly Thomas did when she left her post in a teachers' training college to marry a barrister.

THE CHOICE OF A HUSBAND

Since marriage was a woman's 'trade', the wedding was the female equivalent of coming of age, completing one's articles or graduating. The relationship between Helena Sickert and her mother was transformed by her marriage:

> A boy might be a person, but not a girl. All my brothers had rights as persons, not I. . . . Once I had a husband, her whole attitude changed and just as, formerly, I could do nothing right, so, latterly, I could do nothing wrong in her eyes.

A wife automatically achieved seniority over her older single sisters and was praised if she did not 'queen it' over them: Mrs Gaskell noted with pleasure that her daughter Florence continued to take 'her place as *third* daughter at home, runs errands &c.'

Until it was acceptable for young women to have an independent social and working life, they depended on parents and brothers to introduce them to prospective husbands. Women without brothers or 'good dear . . . mamas' devoted to matchmaking were at a grave disadvantage. Born into a family which did not go into Society, Beatrix Potter (b.1866) was arrested in the schoolroom with her menagerie of mice, rabbits and hedgehogs until her middle thirties. As the surplus of middle-class women grew in the second half of the nineteenth century, even socially-active women who allowed their 'chances' to slip by found themselves graduating, in their late twenties, into a society dominated by unmarried middle-aged women.

Conscious of the responsibilities a husband assumed on marriage, parents of daughters favoured a man of means and maturity. Romantic love was welcome when it blossomed between well-matched couples who already enjoyed their families' blessings. Although 'kindness would not suffer him to prohibit' it, 'prudence forbad' Thomas Mulso 'to approve' the marriage of his daughter Hester (b.1727) to a struggling lawyer; they remained unofficially engaged for a decade, marrying in 1760. Her biographer attributed their unhappy marriage to poverty.

> Poverty is inimical to felicity; but married penury, worst of woes, is inevitably calamitous. Pecuniary difficulties long protracted the union of Miss Mulso with Mr Chapone, who at last died in [financially] embarrassing circumstances. Much may be borne; but to court long, wait for wealth, wed late and fare ill, seem more than the griefs to which flesh is heir.

It was Mrs Chapone's mature opinion that 'young women' were 'in every way unqualified to choose [husbands] for themselves'. William Thackeray (b.1811), an indulgent father, warned his daughter Anny (his 'dearest Fat'), who was born in 1837, that there was little joy in 'hanker-[ing] after a penniless clergyman with one lung'.

The formal engagement of Thurstan Holland (b.1836) and Marianne Gaskell (b.1835) in 1865, 'after an attachment of many years' – from 1858 in fact – was, as Mrs Gaskell noted,

> opposed firstly because they are cousins (*second*), and secondly because she is eighteen months older than he – and also because he, though the son of a rich man, has *eleven* brothers and sisters, and has to make his way in that most tedious of all professions *chancery* law. He is a barrister now of three years standing, and making nearly £100 a year; but this is all swallowed up by necessary expenses, chambers and the like.

In the circumstances, marriage could be only a very distant prospect. Mrs Gaskell saw no reason to delay her daughter Florence's marriage to Charles Crompton, who was a decade her senior and was 'getting on very fast in his profession'. Leonard Messel's greatest allies in his courtship of Maud Sambourne (b.1875) were her father, a leading contributor to *Punch*, and her mother, a stockbroker's daughter. As Maud acknowledged at the time of her marriage, they promoted the match, guiding her 'to the gate of happiness when [she] was blindfolded'.

Parents of means often made substantial investments in their children's marriages in the form of dowries, or by meeting the expenses of confinements, or underwriting the running costs of the new household, sometimes for years, and paying the school and college fees which bought a boy's way into the professions. Formally-drawn settlements were a prerequisite of marriage.

When daughters defied convention, families felt justified in drastic action. Edith Lanchester's decision to set up home with an Irish railway clerk in 1895 so outraged her father, an architect, that, with the support of his sons, he had her committed to a private madhouse. The doctor who certified her cited 'illicit intercourse with a man in a station much below her own' as evidence that 'overstudy' had unhinged her. The Commissioners in Lunacy set her free, acknowledging that, though 'very foolish', she was 'perfectly sane'.

PARENTHOOD

At the time of their wedding in 1881, Arthur Thorndike, son of a General in the Royal Artillery, was a curate; Agnes Bowers was the daughter of a consulting engineer with the Union Castle line. When Arthur suggested, on his vicar's advice, that they might be happier without children and the attendant doctors' bills and school fees, Agnes responded with a whimsical undertaking 'to give her husband and terrible little family . . . a pig-a-back when they feel fatigued', and launched a fantastical exchange about the names of the nine children she planned and he 'rather dread[ed]'. On balance, he declared, he found the prospect of boys less daunting because they 'could earn their own living and carry on the family name'. Thorndike was not alone in worrying about the cost of children. In the last quarter of the nineteenth century the difficulties they were experiencing in paying school fees and meeting other family obligations seems to have moved some middle-class couples to attempt to limit the size of their family. The Sickerts settled in Bedford in 1868 with the object of educating their three sons 'very cheaply at the excellent school'. Two more came along after their move to London. For the next five years at least Eleanor (b.1830) and Oswald Sickert slept apart; she with 'the babies', he 'in a tiny dressing room'. By the 1880s, thanks to the development of rubber technology, new barrier contraceptives were available, but it is likely that the traditional methods – withdrawal and abstinence – were as, or more, commonly used.

Mrs Beeton maintained that, without a nurse, the mother of young children could not expect to entertain guests at home or go out into society. A letter written by Mrs Gaskell in the summer of 1845 gives an impression of the daily round of a mother of four small children (born in 1834, 1837, 1842 and 1844) in a servant-keeping household. Her elder daughters, aged 11 and 8, were already junior colleagues. It is unlikely that earlier mothers got off more lightly.

Sunday morning
Willie asleep everyone else out

. . . I am so busy and so happy. My laddie is grunting so I must make haste . . .

. . . I have Florence and Willie in my room which is also nursery, call Hearn [their nurse] at six, ½ p[ast] 6 she is dressed, comes in, dresses Flora, gives her breakfast the first; ½ p 7 I get up, 8 Flora goes down to her sisters and Daddy, & Hearn to her breakfast. While I in my dressing gown dress Willie. ½ p 8 I go to breakfast with parlour people, Florence being with us & Willie (ought to be) in his cot; Hearn makes bed etc in nursery only. 9 she takes F & I read a chapter & have prayers first with household and then with children, ½ p 9 Florence & Willie come into the drawing room for an hour while bedroom & nursery windows are open; ½ p 10 go in kitchen, cellars & order dinner. Write letters; ¼ p 11 put on things; ½ p 11 take Florence out. 1 come in, nurse W & get ready for dinner; ½ p 1 dinner; ½ p 2 children, two little ones come down during servants' dinner half hour open windows upstairs; 3 p.m. go up again & I have two hours to kick my heels (to be elegant and explicit). 5 Marianne & Meta from lessons & Florence from upstairs & Papa when he can comes in drawing room to 'Lily a hornpipe', i.e. dance while Mama plays, & make all the noise they can. Daddy reads, writes or does what [he] likes in dining room. ½ p 5 Margaret (nursemaid) brings Florence's supper, which Marianne gives her, being answerable for slops, dirty pinafores & untidy misbehaviours while Meta goes up stairs to get ready & fold up Willie's basket of clothes while he is undressed (this by way of feminine and family duties). Meta is so neat & knowing, only, handles wet napkins very gingerly. 6 I carry Florence upstairs, nurse Willie; while she is tubbed & put to bed. ½ p 6 I come down dressed leaving (hitherto) both asleep & Will & Meta dressed (between 6 and ½ p) & Miss F with tea quite ready. After tea read to M A and Meta till bedtime while they sew, knit or worsted work. From 8 to 10 gape. We are so desperately punctual that now you may know what we are doing every hour.

Half a century later Molly Hughes claimed to find motherhood an absorbing alternative to her paid work as a lecturer in a teachers' training college:

although I had a servant for housework, I never had a nurse. This was not so much from lack of means as from my preference for looking after the boys myself. There was no kindergarten at hand, and even if there had been one I would not have cared to send them to it.

The Hughes's house at Barnet was well-suited to her educational philosophy.

> There was an attic at the top of the house for the boys' own, to set out their train lines, build with their bricks and romp as they liked. There was a garden to grub in and trees to climb . . . Materials of all kinds were in constant demand for operations in the attic. String, empty bobbins, pieces of wood, bits of cloth, sheets of brown paper . . . The gift of a very large box of plain bricks gave endless pleasure for building purposes. The well-made pieces of hardwood varied in size from a cubic inch to lengths of ten inches . . . it was only as I watched them play that I perceived their . . . value. 'Hand me a six,' one busy builder would cry. 'Can't find a six, will a four and a two do?'

Many of her contemporaries continued to entrust their young children to nannies and nursemaids.

MARITAL ROLES

A wife was steward of her husband's household; she had charge of his children, servants and domestic budget; she was his emissary in the locality. The enduring convention that a man would be older, better-educated and more experienced than his wife licensed him to supervise her performance in every segment of the domestic sphere. Samuel Pepys was highly critical of his wife's shortcomings as housekeeper – they reflected badly on him when they came to the notice of his colleagues.

'Economy', Mrs Chapone believed, was 'so important a part of a woman's character, so necessary to her own happiness, and so essential to her performing properly the duties of a wife and of a mother, that it ought to have the precedence of all other accomplishments.' Scrutiny of the household accounts was a weekly ritual. Mary MacCarthy, describing her late-Victorian childhood, observed that 'the family account-book . . . "Le Grand Livre" played so large a part in my parents' marriage that it must be brought into the picture'. Her father was subject to 'attacks of financial agitation'. 'After one of "Le Grand Livre" conferences extreme general efforts at economy would be made. We would have hardly anything to eat for several weeks – and visitors were treated in the same way.' The family's friends became familiar with the alternations of 'fast and feast'. Doing the tradesmen's books under her husband's school-masterly eye was a weekly penance for Minnie Benson (b.1842). In her own words, she 'dreaded the gloom they always brought' and 'cowardly and improvident . . . put them off and lived in the present'. Debt and recrimination were the inevitable consequences. However, Katharine Chorley remembered the housekeeping books as a 'pleasant source of chaff' between her mother and her father (an able mathematician, bored by long columns of figures detailing the minutiae of transactions with the butcher, the baker, the grocer and the haberdasher).

A few women acquired a reputation as sound businesswomen; when her husband was headmaster of Rugby Catharine Tait (b.1819) 'set' the school's finances 'to rights'. As Archibald Tait ascended the ladder of ecclesiastical preferment, her acumen as an accountant was successively exploited in the service of Carlisle Cathedral, the diocese of Winchester and the archdiocese of Canterbury. As Tait acknowledged, 'having the command and distribution of large revenues, she ever exercised a vigilant control over our expenditure'. Her ability was recognised by the banks.

Women had few opportunities to augment an inadequate income. Plying her needle or undertaking fancy work could bring in a little money. Before establishing herself as a writer, E. Nesbit (b.1858) sold hand-decorated birthday cards and fans. Since the seventeenth century, in spite of their very limited formal education, women had earned money with their pens – passing on their own skills and accomplishments or recycling advice plundered from existing manuals. The nineteenth century offered unprecedented opportunities for writing for profit. Frances Trollope published her first book, *The Domestic Manners of the Americans*, in 1832 when she was 50, 'a late age at which to begin such a career', her son noted. Her literary debut was prompted by desperation. 'She had never before earned a shilling' but 'from that moment till nearly the time of her death, at any rate for more than twenty years, she was in receipt of a considerable income from her writings.' Mrs Trollope's writing was not allowed to impinge on domestic routine; 'she was at her table at four in the morning and had finished her work' before the rest of the household had stirred. Half a century later Mrs Humphry Ward (b.1851) became a 'money-generating fiction machine'; her earnings supported her thriftless husband and three children and subsidised her mother and and her feckless father and brothers.

The presence of servants was essential to the middle-class way of life; managing them was the wife's responsibility. Samuel Pepys's descriptions of the uneasy relationships between employers and servants in the 1660s are echoed in Virginia Woolf's diaries two hundred and fifty years later. Middle-class families did not enjoy the landowners' privileged access to a workforce schooled in loyalty and dependency. Servants working alone or with one or two colleagues were a prey to loneliness; some sought refuge in drink, others in sex; both were sacking offences. With the support of the efficient Lambeth Palace staff, the timid Minnie Benson blossomed into a confident and successful hostess: 'Life is roaring on', she wrote in 1893, 'Dinner of 30 Sat. 55 Junior Clergy yesterday. 40 B[isho]ps tonight.'

In 1900 the 'all-electric house' was a futuristic dream. Many middle-class households still relied on woman power to lug water and fuel upstairs and slops and ashes down. Consequently most early-twentieth-century advice on 'How to live without servants' stopped short of advocating doing 'without help of any sort'. One writer, who had designed a cottage which could be run without a resident maid, admitted that

> There is nothing attractive in scrubbing floors or in cleaning grates, or in washing steps. A married woman from a cottage nearby comes in to do all the rougher work for us . . . The man who works in the garden is a handy fellow, and during the winter he cleans and lights the cooking stove in the hour before breakfast.

At about the same time Mrs Clarke put forward a rather more radical solution to the servant problem. Her argument underlines the budgetary problems of the professional middle classes. 'There are', she wrote,

> numerous families of solicitors, doctors and other professional people of good standing where money is scarce because it comes in so slowly, though it may be perfectly safe in the long run. Suppose there is a family of boys and girls, and that every endeavour is made to educate and push the boys so that they may in their turn enter the professions and keep up the family position and credit. The girls may prove themselves sensible, but never do anything wonderful at school, their minds are not capable of being crammed for examinations, so that they cannot go in for teaching as a career, nor secure the qualifications requisite for positions in the musical profession, besides which all lines of life except domesticity are overcrowded.

Note the restricted options she considers.

> Why should not one daughter, when her school days are over, study cooking, and another, or, perhaps, two, give their serious attention to housework? They would do it a great deal better than the average servant because they would bring more intelligence to bear on it, and would consider the family prestige if there were any grit in them. But if the girls do these things they must not be expected to do them for any equivalent but hard cash.

She recognised that her proposals were unconventional but, siding with the manufacturers of 'labour saving devices', maintained that

> Household work is not what it used to be, gas cookers and carpet sweepers, and such like contrivances, have reduced it to a

minimum; it is not beneath any woman to take her part in the service of her own home, and girls living in their father's house do not lose caste, even if they do open the front door and greet their visitors as they enter. . . . Mere callers might, perhaps, diminish in numbers, but there would certainly be more genuine friends.

As Mrs Clarke implies, servants had a significance over and above their utility. When financial disaster struck in 1908, the Bradys of Stockport in Cheshire found themselves cut off from local society by their inability to receive visits from their friends, the families of other mill owners, and the clergymen, lawyers and doctors who had formed their circle, because they no longer had a maid to open the door.

Wives were their husbands' local representatives. Samuel Pepys was anxious to parade his wife's new clothes, which signalled his wealth to the neighbourhood. By the nineteenth century their responsibilities included the complex ritual of paying and receiving calls. Social blunders, *faux pas*, as they were called, could generate acute embarrassment. Accounts of academic society suggest that it may have been unusually tedious. Eleanor Sidgwick, Principal of Newnham and wife of a Cambridge don, 'at her own parties, in the awful after-dinner interval when the matrons were alone . . . had been known to invite them to cat's cradle with a piece of string'. Naomi Haldane (b.1897) recalled 'going . . . the rounds' in Oxford with her mother, 'leaving the right number of cards and congratulating ourselves when those on whom we called were "not at home" '. Pleas of ill-health justified an abdication of unwelcome duties. 'Sofa mothers', as invalids were known, were so familiar that Naomi Haldane posed the mistress of her dolls' house in the drawing room with her feet up. Marion Sambourne's evident pleasure in the social round serves as a reminder that some women, indeed, perhaps, a majority of women, thoroughly enjoyed their tea parties.

In every generation some genteel women found time to undertake good works in the community. The obituaries of seventeenth-century clergy wives indicate that charity was a well-established duty. By the second half of the nineteenth century, middle-class women were influencing policy and developing and demonstrating their own capabilities at local and national levels. 'The two great restrictions of time and money' meant that these roles were generally the preserve of well-off, older or childless women.

MARITAL BREAKDOWN

If the fragility of their fortunes put middle-class marriages under stress, there were strong forces which held couples together: professional men depended for their income on a reputation for probity and discretion;

middle-class women had little to offer on the labour market and scarcely more tolerance was shown to the woman whose marriage foundered than to the daughter who dishonoured her family by 'living in sin'. Annie Herapath Furrell (b.1854) and her children were ostracised by her family when her husband divorced her for adultery in 1881. Her mother equated her misconduct with her brother Spencer's – he was declared bankrupt in 1888 – she cut them both off without a penny. Nevertheless, between 1770 and 1857, when divorces were rare, expensive and socially damaging, a high proportion involved members of the middle classes. Military and naval men made up 21 per cent of petitioners and 29 per cent of co-respondents. Prolonged absences on service appear to have put these marriages under intolerable strain; civilians posted to India were also inclined to divorce.

WIDOWHOOD

The widow's principal duty was to bring up her children. Few were equipped to earn a living. If her husband had not provided for her, she was dependent on her sons or more distant kin. Women left to maintain a household on a much reduced income were among the keenest advocates of the new opportunities which opened up for girls in the later nineteenth century. Molly Hughes was one of the early beneficiaries. In the first months of her widowhood she was 'crazy with grief', reserve had prevented the articulation of her love for her husband, even when he lay dying. 'Fortunately', she felt, there was very little money': 'the necessity to work kept [her] going'.

Sir Leslie Stephen (b.1832), the agnostic editor of *The Dictionary of National Biography*, composed his *Mausoleum Book* as a private memorial to his two dead wives, Minny Thackeray and Julia Prinsep. Letters were the relics of his marriages which he cherished most dearly. Of the casts of Minny's hands, taken after her death (a common Victorian memento), he wrote: 'I do not like such things.' The 'Julia Prinsep Stephen fund', to 'put nursing on a permanent footing' at St Ives, where the Stephens spent their summers, was, he believed, an apt reflection of his second wife's charitable works and thus 'the best memorial of my beloved'. His daughters Stella and, later, Vanessa succeeded to their mother's household duties, including the weekly presentation of the housekeeping books. Widowers, and other single men, could almost always find a relative ready 'to be absorbed by such duties'.

SUMMING UP

The licensing of clerical marriage, the rising demand for professional services and the emergence of a consumer society swelled the ranks of families headed by 'unlanded gentlemen'. Since an academic education and access to patronage could open the door to a middle-class occupation, many fathers could afford to be evenhanded in the treatment of their sons. However, the rising cost of education may have encouraged the late Victorians to seek to limit the size of their families. During the Great War professional confidence was dented as incomes dropped. Middle-class men had a duty to maintain female relatives; unmarried women owed an overriding duty to their family, substituting for missing wives and mothers. The foundation of academic schools and women's colleges in the second half of the nineteenth century did little to dispel the prejudice against paid employment even among the minority committed to developing the female intellect. By the middle of the nineteenth century there was a significant and conspicuous 'surplus' of unmarried gentlewomen. Conventionally, men married late. Parents expected their daughter's suitor to be in a position to provide not only for his wife and children but for his widow and orphans too. Within marriage male and female roles were sharply distinguished. The married woman was her husband's steward, responsible for reconciling the thrifty management of his household and income with the promotion of his pretensions.

NOW READ ON

Peter Earle: *The Making of the Middle Class: Business, Society and Family Life in London 1660–1730* (London: Methuen, 1989).

The Illustrated Pepys: Extracts from the Diary, selected and edited by Robert Latham (London: Bell and Hyman, 1978).

Linda Weatherill: *Consumer Behaviour and Material Culture in Britain 1660–1760* (London: Routledge, 1988).

Edward Gibbon: *Memoirs of My Life* [1796], edited by Betty Radice (London: Penguin, 1984).

W. D. Rubinstein: *Men of Property* (London: Croom Helm, 1981).

Charles Darwin: *Autobiography* [1892], edited by Gavin de Beer (Oxford: Oxford University Press, 1974).

The Correspondence of Charles Darwin, edited by Frederick Burckhart and Sydney Smith (Cambridge: Cambridge University Press, 1985–).

Gillian Darley: *Octavia Hill: A Life* (London: Constable, 1990).

Deborah Gorham: *The Victorian Girl and the Feminine Ideal* (London: Croom Helm, 1982).

Leonore Davidoff: *The Best Circles: Society, Etiquette and the Season* (London: Croom Helm, 1973).

Patricia Hollis: *Ladies Elect: Women in English Local Government 1865–1914* (Oxford: Clarendon Press, 1987).

Shirley Nicholson: *A Victorian Household. Based on the Diaries of Marion Sambourne* (London: Barrie and Jenkins, 1988).

Barbara Caine: *Destined to Be Wives: The Sisters of Beatrice Webb* (Oxford: Clarendon Press, 1986).

M. Vivian Hughes: *A London Child of the Seventies* (London: Oxford University Press, 1934).

M. Vivian Hughes: *A London Girl of the Eighties* (London: Oxford University Press, 1934).

M. Vivian Hughes: *A London Home in the Nineties* (London: Oxford University Press, 1937).

Vera Brittain: *The Testament of Youth: An Autobiographical Study of the Years 1900–1925* [1933], with an introduction by Shirley Williams (London: Virago, 1978).

Ernest Shephard: *Drawn From Memory* [1957] (London: Penguin, 1975).

6

THE INARTICULATE
The families of the labouring poor

DEFINING CHARACTERISTICS

The wage labourer's status was low. Society put a premium on economic independence; he was an employee; in old age and when his children were young, he was frequently in receipt of charity or subsidised by rates paid by his better-off neighbours. His work was punishingly heavy, dirty and undignified, he was caricatured as a yokel, a bumpkin, a clodhopper. Church services ritualised the labourer's subordination. Richard Gough (b.1634) held it 'a thing unseemly and undecent' that the labouring poor should occupy pews in front of their betters. As a small boy Joseph Arch (b.1826) watched the Sunday procession to the altar:

> First up walked the squire to the communion rail, the farmers went up next, then up went the tradesmen and shopkeepers, the wheelwright, and the blacksmiths; and then, the very last of all, went the poor labourers in their smock frocks.

Cliff Hills (b.1904), from Great Bentley in Essex, 'came to the conclusion that church-goers were something like railway carriages were at one time – first, second and third class'. The vicar 'didn't seem to have any time for the lower classes. Mother and her friends would pass out of the Church door, the vicar would . . . smile, perhaps not that even . . . I thought my mother was worth a handshake as well as the rich.'

As farmers opted to endow one son at the expense of his brothers; as the enclosure of commons deprived those without land of their own of the chance to build up a small flock of sheep or herd of cows; as handicrafts were ousted by machine-made goods, the labouring population grew. This was a long-drawn-out process with periods of remission. Handloom weavers, whose craft was challenged by the 'Dutch' ribbon loom in the seventeenth century, enjoyed an Indian Summer of prosperity when spinning machines were introduced at the end of the

eighteenth century, and were finally broken by competition from pow-
ered looms in the 1840s. That hungry decade also saw an influx of
refugees from famine in Ireland. In the 1880s Jews in flight from Eastern
Europe added a new dimension to the working-class population of
London and the industrial cities of Yorkshire and Lancashire.

When tradesmen died leaving sons still at school, the boys might be
forced to turn to labouring to survive. In Stuart England perhaps one
labourer in ten could sign his name, a significant proportion of them
were orphaned early.

The population surge which occurred in the sixteenth century had
serious results. The cost of essentials – bread, fuel, shelter, clothes –
rose. Wages fell behind prices. Work was harder to come by.
Unemployed, 'masterless' men, especially the homeless vagrants, were
assumed to be a serious threat to law and order – the unpaid parish
constable offered little protection.

Regulating the poor

The cities and, following their lead, Parliament took steps to tackle the
problem. Parish officers were empowered to flog 'workshy' vagrants
and pack them off to their home parishes. Rates were levied from the
better-off to support the infirm and others defined as genuinely needy
and deserving – this parish dole was never intended to do more than
supplement voluntary giving. Knitting, lace- and pinmaking schools
were set up to drill poor children in habits of industry and give them a
trade – though not one which offered the prospect of a secure income.
Others were shipped across the Atlantic, thus removing a threat to good
order at home and meeting the labour-hungry settlers' need for servants
in the colonies.

Obsessed by the nightmare of supporting pauper families in perpe-
tuity, parishes dug deep to meet lawyers' bills for suits that might
absolve them from the responsibility. Writing at the start of the eighteenth century, Richard Gough recorded eight cases between Myddle in
Shropshire and other parishes. Myddle lost the first but, and Gough
thanked God for it, none of the others. The parish succeeded in off-
loading a woman whose soldier husband had deserted her and their
newborn child; they foisted a blind old man on his reluctant son-in-law
and shipped an abandoned baby back to its place of birth (having
pursued scanty clues to identify the parish responsible).

By the end of the eighteenth century agricultural labourers' wages
were too low to keep three or four children; parish rates were used to
top them up. There was a widespread tendency to reward the thrifty. At
Empingham in Rutland awards were made to labourers who succeeded
in 'bringing up four children or more (the youngest of which was

fourteen years of age)' without soliciting relief from the parish: five were achieved between 1785 and 1795. In the 1820s in the Hernhill area near Faversham in Kent, as Barry Reay explains:

> The overseers' day book shows a whole range of welfare payments for . . . food, tobacco, tools, clothing, fuel. The occasional doctor's bill was covered; women were hired to nurse, care and wash for the elderly, the infirm or the heavily pregnant. The parish paid for funeral costs including payments for beer.

The fundamental principle of the New Poor Law enacted in 1834 was that subsistence in the workhouse should be harsher than poverty in the outside world. The threat of confinement effectively discouraged the poor from applying for help from official sources. Inmates were subject to a prisonlike regime. Men and women were kept apart; graves were marked with a number, not a name; at Gressenhall in Norfolk in 1838 the governors deprived able-bodied men and the mothers of bastards of the meat and pudding which marked Christmas Day in the workhouse. The Dissection Act of 1832 exposed the remains of paupers who had no family or friends to bury them for use in medical research or teaching. Dread of dissection encouraged the habit of saving to meet the cost of funerals.

Throughout the nineteenth century the labouring family was the target of legislation excluding women and children from the mines, regulating the hours they could put in in factories and compelling school attendance. Compulsory schooling, imposed from 1870, focused attention on the pitiful physical condition of many poor children. Their eyes were dim, their hearing dull, their teeth rotten, their scalps verminous. Tommy Morgan (b.1892), who grew up in London, knew that he would be sent home if he faked ringworm by pressing a button into his throat. Progressive urban authorities set up infant welfare clinics and supplied cheap milk. Middle-class women, confident of the cultural and emotional superiority of their own homes, launched playschemes for the 'deprived' children of the London poor. By February 1909 there were, according to a *Times* leader on the subject, 'twelve play centres in London open on five evenings a week' where 'the younger children learn[ed] singing games and these', the leader writer noted with interest, had 'a strong civilising effect on them'.

In 1908 State pensions were introduced for those who satisfied stringent criteria of age, respectability and need. The definition of respectability included lifelong independence of statutory poor relief. On the eve of the Great War a widowed mother who had reared fourteen children 'on the washtub' was refused a pension because she had had 'a bit from the parish now and again'.

Earnings

As late as 1851 more labouring men worked on the land than in the building trades, the mines or factories; in the second half of the nineteenth century the balance altered radically. At Elmdon in Essex two-thirds of the men were farmworkers in 1861. The agricultural depression of the 1870s hit the village hard. The population dropped. Boys born in the 1880s and 1890s were less likely to settle in Elmdon, to go on to the land or to marry local girls. Big cities became a feature of the landscape, sucking in tens of thousands of people every year. The uncelebrated skills of digging, carrying and heaving translated easily from fields and farmyards not only to the town but to the cross-country work of cutting canals and constructing railway lines.

Apart from the stockmen, whose beasts needed daily attention, few labourers could depend on regular round-the-year employment and earnings. Families pieced a living together; season and weather determined their income. The improving landlord who set out to rid his land of thorns, briars and rubbish and enrich it with marl provided employment. Until late in Victoria's reign there was work for able-bodied men, women, children and old people on the harvest field. Sheep dipping and shearing paid well but did not last long. Labourers 'gardened by moonlight', kept poultry, rabbits and pigs, which were popular because they ate things which other beasts could not digest: a salt pig 'was a better picture than an oil painting because . . . you could take it down and have your piece of it'. A pig-keeper might become a part-time butcher, as Stephen Reeves (b.1860) did at Elmdon. There was work in the woods felling, chopping, hurdle-making. Molecatching could be profitable; poaching and hunting with permission for birds regarded as vermin provided for the pocket and the pot. Unwritten rules governed what was fit to eat: blackbirds, thrushes and sparrows were, starlings were not. Songsters were caught for sale as caged birds. Some locations offered special opportunities: the villagers of Headington Quarry near Oxford made the most of the university's proximity, selling beef dripping bought from the college kitchens and supplying fossils for collectors' cabinets. Men took up their spades to dig wells, cut drainage channels, extract sand, gravel, clay and copralites (fossilised dung used as fertilizer). Some nineteenth-century farmworkers were winter migrants, leaving East Anglia for Burton-on-Trent to work in the breweries or to fish for herring. There was money to be made from trapping and shooting even in industrialised areas like the Potteries. In the town, as in the country, the handy home shoemender or barber could build up a local trade.

Spending

The labourers' dreams of plenty were modest. The fantasy of a Stuart beggar-boy 'who said if ever he should attain to be a king, he would have a breast of mutton and a pudding in it, and lodge every night up to his ears in dry straw' was not far removed from the picture of heaven with 'mountains of pudden and rivers of broth' conjured up for a Yorkshire congregation in the twentieth century.

After food, fuel and shelter were the labouring family's priorities. Until the nineteenth century Lincolnshire households burned cowpats; strangers complained of the smell. Writing in the 1820s, William Cobbett stressed the importance of free fuel: in Salisbury, where it had to be purchased, families took turns to light a fire and provide hot water for three or four neighbours: 'What a winter-life must those lead, whose turn it is not to make the fire?' Artificial light was less important: tapers made from rushes and mutton fat supplied the necessary glimmer.

Low rents seldom purchased accommodation in good repair. Stuart tax collectors readily accepted that hovels blew away in strong winds; two hundred years later Dorset labourers were living in 'dwellings worse than the wigwams of American Indians'. The picturesque thatched cottages beloved of Victorian and Edwardian watercolourists were cramped, dark, damp and unsanitary. Only a tiny minority of lucky and well-behaved agricultural labourers occupied model dwellings like those erected on the Duke of Bedford's estates from the middle of the nineteenth century. And, if rural housing was bad, the accumulation of human and other waste made urban conditions worse. In 1840 a Leeds man described the smell in his living quarters as 'bad enough to raise the roof of his skull'. Fear of contagion prompted action to improve the sanitation of towns from the 1860s but the labourers' low and irregular earnings made the housing problem intractable. In London in 1882 half the dockers' families lived in a single room; almost one in eight shared their room with another tenant. Rent was the first charge on the decent family's income; 'moonlight flittings' provided a way out for less respectable town dwellers; frequent moves prevented households from building up links with the neighbours, shopkeepers and charity workers who might provide assistance when times were bad.

SOURCES

In spite of their numbers, the experiences of the labouring poor are peculiarly difficult to recover. Descents and histories were handed on by word of mouth. As Lord Rhodes, a Labour MP for twenty years, recalled, his family, of yeomen and clothiers turned into factory hands by the industrial revolution, but always living in the valleys of Saddleworth in Yorkshire . . . had preserved its pedigree orally, he himself being taught as a child that he was 'Hervey of Jack's of Bill's of Jack's of Joe's of John's of Thomas's of Dean Head.' Soon after election to Parliament he introduced himself at a meeting at the far end of his constituency by reciting this; when an old white bearded man rose and corrected him, saying that Thomas was not of Dean Head but of Dean Head Clough.

Traditions of this sort are rarely public property.

Few poor men and women attracted a biographer's attention. Those that did were exceptional people. In 1831 Robert Southey, the then Poet Laureate, published his *Lives of the Uneducated Poets*. Three of his subjects were labourers, plucked from obscurity by literary patrons: John Taylor (b.1580), a Thames waterman, Stephen Duck, 'formerly a poor thresher in a barn', and John Bryant (b.1753); Ann Yearsley (b.*c*.1755) was a milkwoman. Even in the nineteenth century autobiographies are rare. Again, they are the work of exceptional men and a tiny handful of women: redeemed sinners, entertainers, political activists and models of self-improvement are prominent among them. Issues of leisure and literacy aside, the majority who led humdrum lives must have shared the opinion that 'there was nothing special about my experiences worth putting in a book'. The *Memoirs of a Female Vagrant*, the life story of Mary Saxby (b.1738), were intended as a horrible warning, the second edition was published by the Religious Tract Society. 'Lord' George Sanger (b.1827) wrote of his *Seventy Years a Showman*; poachers' tales were popular. Titles like *Life as a Farmer's Boy, Factory Lad, Teacher and Preacher* (by Adam Rushton, b.1821), *From Crow-scaring to Westminster* (by George Edwards, b.1850), *From Workhouse to Lord Mayor* (by G. H. Barker, b.1860) and the series 'How I Got On', published in *Pearson's Weekly* in 1906, tell their own story.

Evidence of the childhood experience of ordinary men and women born to labouring parents in late-Victorian and Edwardian England is available, a proportion of it in print. The Cooperative Women's Guild put together an account of its members' experience under the title *Life as We Have Known It* (1931); in the late 1950s local history groups sought out 'Memories of Villagers'; but it was the systematic collection of survivors' spoken reminiscences from the 1960s that transformed the study of labouring lives.

With limited personal testimony at our disposal, we are heavily dependent on the often hostile and uncomprehending accounts of literate observers. Most of these are informed by the twin assumptions that waged employment represented a surrender of personal liberty and that manual labour was degrading. To many of their betters the appearance and aura of the poor were positively offensive. Like craftsmen, labourers were cruelly marked by their work; they walked as though they had a heavy weight tied to each leg. In the 1970s old men whose backs had been permanently bent by the sacks they had carried were a common sight in the corn-growing villages near Cambridge. From the sixteenth century until the outbreak of the Second World War many labouring families lived in a world of rags and cast-offs. The fleabitten were spotted all over like a plum pudding. Their smell offended those who had an adequate supply of clean clothes and employed servants to do their dirty work: the Revd Charles Kingsley (b.1819), author of *The Water Babies*, a champion of deprived children, was regularly driven from the village school by 'the heat and the smell'.

Families and individuals who fell foul of authority were most likely to leave a documentary trace. Widespread distress also excited interest. Sir Frederic Eden (b.1766) was moved to investigate the condition of labouring families by the situation produced by the high wartime prices of 1794/5. The crisis inspired the 'Speenhamland system', which provided income support tied to the price of bread. Eden adhered to the conventional view that 'their own improvidence and unthriftiness' was a root cause of the labourers' poverty; it would be 'far more useful to teach them to spend less, or save a little than to give them much more'. The poor should forsake beer and tea – 'the deleterious product of China' which had become the southerners' 'most usual beverage' – and go back to the 'cheap and savoury soups' which formed the basis of the thrifty northern diet, Friendly Societies would help the poor to help themselves. Nevertheless, Eden acknowledged that even in favourable circumstances, with normal prices, labourers lived in straitened circumstances. On Lord Harcourt's estate at Nuneham in Oxfordshire, in spite of the potato gardens, free firing and schooling and allowances for such larger families 'as behave well', there was 'great appearance of poverty'. There was no Friendly Society. At Clyst St George in Devon, 'prior to the present scarcity, a labourer, if his wife was healthy, could maintain two young children on his 6s a week . . . without parish relief'. In Eden's view, and he spoke for the great majority of the propertied, poverty was the proper condition of the poor; those who behaved well could look for the help they deserved.

Hard years in the 1830s and 40s produced a storm of pamphlets, books and government reports on the condition of the labouring classes. Members of the Manchester Statistical Society pioneered door-to-door surveys of poor households. Novelists turned their attention to the deprived: Charles Dickens published *Oliver Twist* in 1839; Mrs Gaskell's *Mary Barton* came out in 1848. But it was the work of Henry Mayhew (b.1812), who travelled 'into the poor man's country' and brought back 'tales of terror and wonder', all of them supported by 'some voucher for their credibility', who first broadcast the life histories of the London poor. The analyses of poverty in London and York carried out by Charles Booth (b.1840) and Benjamin Seebohm Rowntree (b.1871) at the end of the century provided authoritative demonstrations of need. There was, nevertheless, a striking continuity between this and earlier work. Adopting a position not far from Eden's, Rowntree distinguished between primary, or unsurmountable poverty, and secondary poverty which, with unremitting effort and relentless self-denial, could be avoided.

Before the middle of the nineteenth century few English painters put members of the labouring classes in the foreground of their work. George Stubbs (b.1724) frequently portrayed grooms and stable-lads attendant on his equine subjects; he painted 'Lord Torrington's Hunt Servants' in the 1760s and, twenty years later, 'Reapers' and 'Hay-makers'; there are no hints of physical privation. George Morland (b.1763) threw a harsher light on the state of the poor but the engravers who prepared his work for a wider market softened his originals to make them more appealing. Frederick Shields (b.1833), a Manchester artist, based 'One of Our Breadwatchers' on studies made on a visit to Somerset where he 'worked for three days in a snow-covered ploughed field sharing the privations which his little model and many other boys and girls endured for the poorest wage': a small child is huddled in a rough shelter which gives little protection against the snow as she scares the birds from the winter corn. The 'Breadwatchers' image has charm as well as pathos. Uncompromising accounts of hardship were con-demned. Henry Wallis's 'Stonebreaker', slumped dead at his task, was regarded as 'a subject almost too painful for a picture' when it was exhibited in 1858: 'defects in nature should not be brought within the sphere of art'. Thirty years later opinion was divided: *The Times* denounced George Clausen's bleak portrait of a boy 'Bird-Scaring' as 'ugly' and 'uncouth' but *The Graphic* commended it as 'a very true type of English rustic character'. From the middle of the nineteenth century, photographers produced powerful, though not objective, accounts of hardship and more palatable images of picturesque poverty.

THE MEANING OF CHILDREN

Ann Yearsley, a milkwoman, began her literary career in the 1780s with a tribute to the benefactor who rescued 'her six little infants and herself (expecting every hour to lie in)' from 'the extremity of distress'; her mother had already died of want. The first edition of her poems netted £350 which was put in trust for her benefit and the benefit of her children. She fell out with her trustees because she wanted the fund 'equally divided according to the number of her children, and subject to their demand as each arrived at the age of twenty-one'. In the view of her middle-class biographer 'the proposal was improvident'; we have no means of knowing whether her proposal reflected values shared by other labouring parents. There is, indeed, anecdotal evidence that parents sometimes discouraged a son or daughter from marrying, as a bolster against their own loneliness and need in old age. Poverty made a luxury of sentiment.

The birth of a child could strain the human and financial resources of the labouring family to breaking point. Badly nourished women were ground down by hard physical work on either side of their delivery. A new baby was an extra mouth to feed. Their need for attention got in the way of earning a living; in the Cambridgeshire fens mothers used opium to pacify their infants in the fields. Successive births put pressure on living accommodation. When a baby died, the parents' grief might be muted. The Cambridgeshire farm labourer James Bowd (b.1823) described how he and his wife, wracked by debt,

> had another increase in our family and this proved to be another son and this haded [added] another expense so that we seemed so shut in we could not see any way of escape but this James William Bowd for that was his name did not live with us long he died on the eleventh of June eighteen hundred and sixty one.

The careful note he made of the date James William died suggests concern as well as relief. The tokens and messages left with children admitted to the Foundling Hospital in the second half of the eighteenth century, and the sad secret cache of baby pictures kept by the outwardly dour Selina Cooper (b.1864), confirm that many parents who lost children grieved – though they may have kept their grieving to themselves. Among the poor the argument that a dead child had gone to a better place may have carried extra weight.

CHILDHOOD

Labouring women, especially those with large families – and the poor were the last converts to family planning – had little time or energy for mothering or playing with their children. Jack Lawson recalled his mother's ungovernable temper. She only had 'leisure enough to cuddle . . . her last-born . . . That was a luxury for her and a thing to amuse us.' Mrs Lawson was not exceptional. Miss Loane, an Edwardian district nurse who observed the labouring family's struggles with sympathy for both mother and child, remarked on the latitude the youngest enjoyed. Soap was so precious that,

> Few boys and girls under twelve venture to touch the soap, even

for the most lawful purpose, without express permission, and to 'borrow a rub' of it to make bubbles is a piece of 'darin'' which none or only youngest children would dare to commit.

But a late child could be an unwelcome child, growing up, as Kathleen Dayus (b.1903) did, with a sense of being surplus to her mother's requirements.

The fate of the displaced ex-baby, too young to fend for itself, was regarded as particularly pitiable. To ease a mother's burden, when she had a new baby on her hands, an older child might be 'loaned out' to kin or neighbours. John Bryant (b.1753) was fostered by his grandparents for the best part of four years after his sister's birth; when he returned to his parents, he pined and fell sick. Arthur Harding, born in the East End of London in 1886, left home and started sleeping rough at the age of 9: 'It was no good: we couldn't all sleep in that room and everyone's attention was going on the new baby.'

Food was high on the child's list of priorities. James Orton, a boy labourer interviewed in Kent in 1843, declared that 'I had rather work than play; you get more victuals when you work.' Men and women born in Victorian England recalled frequent squabbles over shares at meal-times and the punishments meted out to quell disputes. Jack Lawson (b.1883), a miner's son from West Cumberland, relished the memory of an exceptional meal:

> A plateful of sausage curled round and round in a little pool of fat. It smelled good and looked beautiful on that plate set on a snow-white tablecloth. Never had I seen so much sausage on one plate. And it was all for me. If Mrs ——, our next-door neighbour, had only given me a liberal supply of fat and plenty of bread to dip in it, I should have thought it a feast, but that plate filled with sausage, set before me, and apparently all for me, held me spellbound. That dinner riveted itself on my six-year-old mind.

Dietary standards were not uniform, as the recollections of two women born in East Anglia at the beginning of the twentieth century demon-strate – their fathers were both ploughmen. Mrs Queen's family existed on bread, tea and vegetables. Mrs Morris's, living on a paternalist estate, often had a stew made of home-reared rabbits with dumplings for their dinner and eggs or bloaters for their tea; the family's better start went beyond food, the children were under less pressure to bring money into the house and one of Mrs Morris's sisters became a schoolteacher.

Children wore hand-me-downs. At the close of the nineteenth cen-tury bought footwear remained an unattainable luxury for the poorest. Jack Lanigan (b.1890), whose widowed mother took in washing, went to school in Salford with sacking on his feet; Kate Taylor (b.1891) trudged the Suffolk lanes to her part-time job on a farm with her feet bound in rags. Her journey was longer but, as a city boy, he was probably worse off – a woman member of the Manchester School Board argued against the salting of icy streets because of the distress it caused barefoot children. A Birmingham newspaper sponsored a boot and shoe fund; a by-law prevented pawnbrokers from accepting them as pledges.

To keep their heads above water, most labouring households needed all the income in kind or cash that could be got. Girls, and, if no girl was available, boys would be pressed into service as babyminders to free their mother to earn. In the past children often made their first direct contributions to the household budget at an age when the children of today are starting school. In the West Riding, on the eve of the Great War, for the Garrows, although 'well off for labouring people', with a high-earning father and a mother who was 'thoroughly competent and reliable' and 'somewhat more capable than the majority', the extent of their Sunday dinner depended on their 3-year-old. A researcher recorded the source of their Yorkshire pudding:

> They are all on cordial terms with the farmer for whom Mr Garrow works; and often when he is going on a quest for eggs, he takes little Bobby Garrow with him. This means an egg in the small boy's hand when he returns, and a Yorkshire pudding on Sunday. They never buy eggs.

Harry Snell (b.1865), growing up in Sutton-on-Trent in Nottingham-shire,

> knew the location of every crab-apple and sloe tree for miles around the village and precisely the place where watercress or mushrooms might be expected. [He] used to search the hedgerows for herbs which were believed to possess healing qualities, and knew exactly where the Trent would be likely to deposit timber.

The hedgerow harvest was welcome for consumption at home and as saleable goods. Many hawkers were children. Watercress, mushrooms, horseradish, groundsel to feed caged birds, holly for Christmas decoration, firewood, flowers, fruit and vegetables were sold door to door.

John Atkinson (b.1814), a parson's son, thought human scarecrows had 'a jolly life, involving no work of any kind but just to halloa . . . from time to time and kick up a hullabaloo', but, as Harry Snell testified, a day in the fields with only the sun to tell the time by could be long and lonely: farmers worked to the rule that two boys were worth half a boy and three boys no boy at all. Lacemaking, strawplaiting and knitting kept children occupied and earning – in the early nineteenth century one Yorkshire boy described heaven to a tourist as a place where it was always Sunday and there was no knitting.

Until 1840 small boys were sold to chimney sweeps for use as human flue brushes – Mrs Cooper, a widow, turned down the offer of 'two golden guineas' for her son Thomas (b.1805). From the eighteenth century the factories had new uses for small hands. Dexterity, not great strength, was needed to crawl under machines to tie broken yarn in cotton mills or wedge clay or run with newly moulded plates to the drying room in the Staffordshire pot banks. Readers may instinctively condemn parents who exposed children as young as 5 or 6 to the risks of accident and abuse in a working environment. In a world of harsh choices, keeping children out of danger was less important than keeping them out of the graveyard or the workhouse. We should not assume that parents sent their children to work with a glad heart.

The calendar provided opportunities for begging for treats and pennies. In Salisbury boys went 'a-shroving' for

> An apple or a dumpling,
> Or a piece of truckle cheese
> Of your own making,
> Or a piece of pancake.

In London in July Victorian children urged passers-by to 'remember the grotto', built of oyster shells begged from fishmongers and sherds of coloured china. The grottoes were lit by candles; though few realised it, they commemorated the feast of St James the Less of Compostella. In November children remembered Guy Fawkes. In the North Riding, boys went begging for cakes, gingerbread and pennies on St Thomas's Day, 20 December. In Oxfordshire Edwardian boys went 'niggering' on Boxing Day. As Mont Abbott recalled,

> One 'ud play the fiddle, another the squeeze box, or the mouth-organ, the bwoons [bones], the triangle or the whistle . . . We'd black-up our faces with burnt cork and go round the outlying hamlets, farms, and pubs a-singing, playing and clathopping.

The proprietors of the small schools which catered for the children of labouring parents in the eighteenth and nineteenth centuries recognised that earning and freeing others to earn were family priorities, and put up with irregular attendance. Church and Board schools were less flexible. Compulsory education enabled a tiny minority of children to escape their labouring destiny. Most ended up in modest white-collar jobs. Kathleen Betterton (b.1913), the daughter of a liftman on the Tube, recalled how, as a bright and willing learner, she soon became 'a teacher's pet'. She won places first at Christ's Hospital and then at Oxford.

By no means every able child had his or her path smoothed by supportive parents or devoted teachers. Many families found the standards of punctuality and neatness which schools sought to impose alien or unattainable. The learning the schools sought to pass on had little obvious relevance and curtailed the time available for the vital business of scratching a living. George Ewart Evans's conversations with men and women brought up in Suffolk at the end of the nineteenth century suggest that 'parents discouraged education because it would make the child dissatisfied with her station in life'. Kate Taylor, 'a bright pauper', the fourteenth of the fifteen children of a Suffolk labourer, refused to behave at school as though she knew her lowly place and found herself the target of a vindictive schoolmaster. Kate spent her working life in service and married a labouring man.

The progressive enforcement of compulsory school attendance from the 1880s did not mark the end of child labour. Demand for field hands is reflected in the attendance registers of country schools. In Kent the timing of the Hopping Holiday varied according to the season. At Tiptree in Essex at the end of the nineteenth century the schools shut when the strawberries were ripe – teachers cooperated with Mr Wilkin the jam-maker because the children needed the money for boots.

Kate Taylor and Cliff Hills (b.1904) both put in a three-hour shift before they went to school in the morning; Cliff did another couple of hours' work at the end of the school day. Kate helped in the house and the dairy and made local deliveries of milk, cream, butter, eggs and chickens in return for her breakfast and ninepence (less than £0.04) a week. Cliff plucked birds, skinned rabbits and hares, cleaned knives, shoes and dog kennels and sifted cinders for a weekly wage of two shillings (£0.10).

In Salford Jack Lanigan earned a slice of bread when he fetched loaves for his neighbours; he begged for bread at the factory gate as the hands came off shift; he turned cartwheels for pennies. Before he left school he was working four hours every weekday evening, a fifteen-hour day on Saturday and another four hours on Sunday morning as a lather boy for a barber. He took home a shilling (£0.05) a week, plus a few tips and scraps from the lunchboxes of customers who remembered him from the factory gate. According to Arthur Harding (b.1886), his 'Mother was a dead cripple . . . father a loafer'. The children earned their breakfasts for the week by going to Sunday School. They busked for theatre queues and traded in whatever came to hand. There were pickings from the market – discarded fruit and vegetables and orange boxes for furniture and firing. Children from 'criminal families' went out with 'a wee bit of a bag' for their loot. They stole from the stalls and delivery vans, to eat, to sell and to take home: 'It was something to make a mother happy, when a child brought something home.' If parents had scruples, stolen goods could be passed off as gifts.

An invisible army of late-Victorian child homeworkers was revealed by the surveys undertaken by the Salvation Army and other campaigning agencies.

YOUTH: SONS

Among the labouring poor, only a handful of parents could hope to educate their children better than their peers, or save the cost of an apprenticeship premium or bequeath the freehold of a cottage, but such triumphs were not unknown. While it remained a rare skill, even the rudiments of literacy were an asset. Joseph Mayett (b.1783) was taught to read by his mother; as a young man he was offered a post as clerk to an illiterate pay sergeant in the Marines. In eighteenth-century Exeter a handful of labourers managed to put their sons to a trade. Edward Southard found eight guineas (£8.40) – probably the equivalent of half a year's wages – to apprentice his son to a barber and peruke maker; John Bulled apprenticed his boy to a druggist. At Headington Quarry in Oxfordshire Pedgell Webb was remembered because he saved enough to give his nephew a trade. Specialist skills were a worthwhile legacy. Joseph Arch, determined to maintain his independence, developed a series of specialisms – hedging and ditching, hurdlemaking and gate-hanging, basic carpentry – to make himself a good all-round workman who would never be at a loss for a job. There was always work for a man who could thatch; farm buildings, hay and corn ricks, walls made from mud or easily-eroded chalky stone all needed protection from the weather.

Many country boys went to work as living-in servants on farms. These servants in husbandry were hired by the year; there was rarely continuity of employment. As they acquired skills, boys moved on in search of higher wages, seeking new masters at a hiring fair. Evidence is scanty but it appears that most farm servants worked a local beat, preferring employers they knew by reputation at least. Whether they did a day's work or not, living-in servants ate. Employers were well aware of the cost of feeding and housing their workers and replaced them with day-labourers when they could. Between 1540 and 1914 the proportion of farmworkers living-in declined, falling sharply in the late-eighteenth and nineteenth centuries. The farmer's savings were partly offset by the rising cost of poor rates.

Farm servants were not the only young workers who lived-in. The early water-powered textile factories, built away from centres of population, lodged their young workers (girls as well as boys) in company dormitories. Many of these children were paupers drafted in from London. Up to 1816 they were classified as apprentices and received no wages; their diet was primarily milk, water gruel and oatcakes; they lodged in barracks.

For those who remained under their parents' roof, earning brought a change of status. Jack Lawson (b.1883) described the transition from child drudge to 'man' which occurred when he went down the pit for the first time:

> Until I was 12 years of age and commenced work in the mine I had to spend most of my time after school hours and during the holidays as a nurse and housemaid. I could legitimately say that I brought up several of my younger brothers and sisters. As a rule I had two in my charge – one to nurse and the other to watch . . . When I wasn't nursing I was washing dishes, dashing pit-clothes, cleaning boots, brushing and greasing pit-boots or cleaning the pit lamps

– the working gear of his father and older brothers. On his first day at work,

> I worked ten hours that day, and my pay for it was tenpence. Still I was a man and I knew it. There was no more drudging at home. I was entitled to as much meat as I wanted, and others were cleared out to make a seat for me. Even mother slightly deferred to me.

Mont Abbott went to work as 'bwoy-chap' to a cowman. At 13 he was 'no longer a bwoy and not yet a man'. His midday 'tucker' reflected his status: 'more often than not it would be bwoy-chap's grub, bread-n-lard-onion or a cold end of roly-poly pudden' but on good days he had bread and bacon like the men.

Pressure to earn as much as possible as soon as possible forced many boys into what contributors to a survey published in 1912 called 'blind-alley boy work' as errand boys, van boys, messenger boys, office boys, boy hands in factories. Courtaulds, the textile firm, produced posters to emphasise the very limited possibilities of permanent employment.

Youngsters who lived at home were expected to 'tip up' and content themselves with the pocket money their mothers handed back. A boy who had prided himself on putting food on his family's table might see 'tipping up' as natural, a means of repaying his mother, an opportunity to give a small brother or sister a better start in life. But the mother who nagged, the father who threw his weight about might provoke bitter resentment. Young people who were out of work or whose earnings did not come up to expectations might have their noses rubbed in their failure. Tension between parents and young adults living at home might prompt the breakup of a family.

YOUTH: DAUGHTERS

Domestic service occupied many labourers' daughters in their teens and twenties. Demand for living-in maids held up and indeed increased as the servant-keeping classes expanded in the nineteenth century. Servant-keeping households ranged from the aristocratic to the plebeian. In the great houses girls from labouring families were more likely to be found doing the rough work in the kitchen and the laundry (which was often detached from the house); at the other end of the scale were the households of clerks and small tradesmen who could afford only an inexperienced general servant. Outside factory towns and communities like Headington Quarry, where laundry was carried on on a big scale, the daughters of the labouring poor had little choice. Where there was an alternative it was eagerly embraced.

Hard though their lives might be, maids, like servants in husbandry, were generally better housed and better fed than they had been in their parents' home or could expect to be when they set up a household of their own. Rose Rayner (b.1892), who left home to enter the dowager Countess of Harrowby's service as third laundry maid, was moved to tears by the food in the servants' hall, knowing that the cupboard at home might be completely bare. Girls like Rose often sent money home. When Kate Taylor's father was disabled by a serious leg injury, the family was tided over by her elder sisters' contributions. Familiarity with good feeding could blunt the memory of childhood hunger. As a twentieth-century mother pointed out to her daughter who announced she was leaving 'good service' to marry, 'She'd never know the size of her belly till her feet were under her own table.'

In reality, the attractions of service were muted. Although in theory protected against wrongful dismissal, servants were liable to be turned out without just cause and without warning. Maids were at the mercy of their employers' moods. Pepys's diary gives an intimate picture of an increasingly affluent household of the 1660s; after an initial period of sweet temper and mutual satisfaction, relations between the Pepyses and their maids almost invariably soured. Some went of their own accord, in search of new pastures, others were dismissed for gossiping and gadding about, or thieving from their employers or fellow servants. The diaries of Virginia Woolf (b.1882) reflect a similarly stormy relationship between servant and employer.

Elizabeth Pepys frequently, and with justification, suspected her husband of sexual dalliance with their maids. Men were obliged to respect the chastity of women of their own kind, but servants were considered fair game. Maids were awed or bullied into submission or seduced by what were, to their pursuers, trivial presents and by the remote but not impossible prospect of marriage. According to gossip, the Duke of Chandos (b.1708) took a maidservant from an inn as his second wife. In marrying the daughter of an Oxford ostler, the designer William Morris (b.1834) transported his wife Janey (b.1839) from poverty to affluence – his income was perhaps thirty times greater than her father's. Her younger sister Bessie did well too. Thanks to a legacy from her brother-in-law and her own earnings as an embroideress, naturally boosted by the connection with Morris, Bessie Burden left £1,000 in cash when she died in 1924.

A servant without a place was at risk. The fleeting pleasures of the hiring fair could eat into the wages which servants received at the end of their engagement. Paying for board and lodging rapidly exhausted the store of cash which, if kept intact, would provide the maid with her dowry.

THE CHOICE OF A WIFE

From the sixteenth to the early nineteenth century the age at which labouring men married was remarkably constant: most took this step in their mid to late twenties. The average age of first-time brides went up and down: in hard times they tended to be older. A sensible man looked for a woman with savings to testify to her thriftiness. Of course, sense did not always prevail. 'Love' propelled John Bezer (b.1816) into 'marriage and beggary . . . And bitterly, very bitterly' did he and his wife suffer for their 'folly'. Three months before the birth of their first child Bezer lost his job as a porter: 'That was a horrible day – the birthday of my first boy! Wife, it was thought would die; and I knew why – from sheer starving want.' John Clare (b.1793) was one of the pressed men who married when, in Clare's words, 'amorous intrigues and connections' resulted in an unintended pregnancy. Patty Turner's 'emergencies became urgent'; 'she was unable to conceal [her condition] any longer'; 'the wide mouth of the world was against her' – yet Clare held back. Patty was seven months pregnant when he married her; they did not set up home until four weeks after the child's birth.

THE CHOICE OF A HUSBAND

A woman's earnings were too low to support an independent life. Those who did not marry faced a continuation of their adolescent roles, working as servants or living at home and contributing to the upkeep of a household headed by a parent or sibling.

The labourer's daughter ran the greatest risks of bastard-bearing and more often than not the father was her own 'young man'. If a young family fell on hard times, they could not depend on assistance from their kin. Poor women were therefore urged to subject their suitors to a dispassionate scrutiny:

> If virtuous affection seems to be rising, be sure you instantly
> calculate on the age and temper, religious conduct, and probable

148

ability of the man to maintain a family, before you suffer your mind to be carried away, lest your affections run headlong, and at length are taken advantage of to the complete loss of your comfort. [1825]

Working women expressed similar sentiments in plainer language. Lucy Lock (b.1848), a straw-plait worker, summed her future husband up as 'a steady saving man'. His good nature – 'he will never hit you' – was a further recommendation. Good health was important. James Bowd (b.1823), a Cambridgeshire farmworker, found his lameness 'a great hindrance' in making a living.

MARITAL ROLES

Earning was a husband's chief duty. Managing and, whenever possible, adding to the household income were the wife's responsibility. Naturally, women found it easier to cope with a predictable wage than one which fluctuated. Few found themselves in this fortunate position before the Great War.

The man was the breadwinner but it was his wife's task to feed the family and, first and foremost, the higher-earning males who were allotted the lion's share. One of Queen Victoria's old soldiers, keeping house for himself and five children while his wife was away, 'allowed margarine all round on the same scale as he had always used it himself, with the result of more than doubling the amount spent on it'. (Harry Snell's mother could have 'spread a pound of butter over the whole of the . . . churchyard, and then have sufficient left to cover the gravestones on both sides'.)

Cereals were the staple food of the labouring poor. Bread, porridge, soups and stews formed the basis of their diet. Poor women and their children gleaned grain left on the harvest field. The custom came under attack at the end of the eighteenth century but in good years, in villages like Elmdon in Essex, gleaning was still providing the labourers' families with a year's supply of corn until the Great War. Threshed at home and ground locally, it provided flour for bread- and pudding-making and grain for home-brewed beer. In Norfolk, Kate Taylor's family paid the miller's bill in acorns for his pigs. The mechanisation of the harvest reduced the 'wastage' of grain but gleaning went on into the 1940s. A Cambridge woman, born in the 1930s, gleaned for chickenfeed as a child; her mother had gleaned for the family's flour supply. The quality of the gleaners' harvest varied, as Sam Kendall recalled in his *Farming Memoirs of a West Country Yeoman*:

After a wet harvest, such as was experienced in the year 1860 . . . two knives were required to cut the bread when it came to the table – one to tear or cut and the other to clean the used knife before another portion could be taken from the loaf, as the dough . . . made from the flour produced from sprouted grain fails to 'rise' properly . . . neither will it bake correctly in the oven, but runs more or less into a glutinous sticky mass surrounded by a doubtful-looking crust – the inside of the loaf when baked being stodgy and sticky with a sickly, sweet unpalatable flavour.

Stockmen's wives had access to other sources of 'free' cereals. A man old enough to be of his grandfather's generation told A. G. Street (b.1892)

that in his childhood he was fed on barley bannocks . . . . His father was allowed so much coarse barley meal each month to feed the sheep dogs. His mother used to sift this through a piece of muslin, use the fine sample for the children and the coarse for the dogs.

Bought bread had advantages. It needed no cooking; it could be eaten without dish or spoon. Stale bread could be transformed into a hot dish by dousing it with boiling water. 'Tea kettle broth' or 'hot water mess', flavoured with salt and pepper and, in the best of times, with a knob of butter, is remembered with surprising relish by elderly people from Cambridgeshire and Hertfordshire. An infusion of burnt toast and hot water was used as a substitute for tea. The cereal diet was enlivened by small quantities of strong-tasting accompaniments – cheese, bacon (and bacon fat) and raw onion were common relishes. The mass-production of pickles came in in the 1860s. Jam appeared on working-class tables from the 1870s, as the price of sugar dropped.

Well into the eighteenth century potatoes were more likely to be eaten by the institutionalised poor than by those living in their own homes but, easy to grow and easy to cook, useful for stock as well as human food, the potato became central to the labouring diet. Just before the Great War the Finch family ('man, wife, five daughters aged twelve, ten, nine, six and two'), who had had to sell their gleanings to pay off accumulated debts, got through 49 pounds of homegrown potatoes a week.

Waste food was given away, tainted food was cheap. In Edwardian London the Hardings' status as deserving poor gave them privileged access to waste food from restaurants. Richard Gough, writing at the beginning of the eighteenth century, described how a local ne'er-do-well killed a cow by thrusting 'a wire into her throat so that she bled inwardly' and so tricked the drovers into selling it cheap. Cliff Hills recalled that

Nearly every bit of meat we got was suspect. Dad always smelled it first, but we never seen him put a bit to one side . . . And talk about the flies, I've wondered since why we didn't get some kind of disease because the meat had gone off, the flies were crawling all over the place.

Much of the meat which went into hot pies for sale on the street was 'off'; the strong taste of mace helped to mask the taint.

Local circumstances influenced eating habits. Elizabeth Roberts, who studied the experience of working-class Lancashire women between 1890 and 1940, noted the place of cockles gathered by men and children in the diets of Barrow and Lancaster. In these towns, where a very small minority of married women were in full-time paid employment, there was a tradition of serving soups and stews, which required long, slow cooking, pudding-making and baking. In Preston, where a significant number of married women were employed, there was a much greater dependence on shop-bought pies, tripe and fish and chips.

Seasonal delicacies were often gifts. Labourers' wives took part in a begging ritual just before Christmas to obtain white flour and sometimes fruits and spices to make a pudding.

Credit was important in many budgets. Loans were available from pawnshops, which were first recorded in English towns in the Tudor period, and from unlicensed moneylenders. Anne Deacon (d.1675) ran a pawnbroking business in Limehouse – her clients were more likely to have been shopkeepers or craftsmen than labourers. The number of licensed pawnbrokers increased dramatically in the 1850s and 1860s. They were commonest in London, the ports and the industrial areas of Lancashire and the Black Country. Families depended on their pawnable possessions to see them through the week and it was a black day when 'uncle' was no longer willing to advance the expected sum on a Sunday suit or a pair of boots. Working people treated small items of jewellery, bought when times were good, as insurances to draw on when they were laid off, in the winter or when trade was slack. As a last resort, tokens of respectability were pledged: women pawned their wedding certificates and rings; old soldiers pawned their medals.

PARENTHOOD

On the whole, caring for and disciplining children was women's work. Mothers rarely went out to work full-time but it was assumed that they could and should earn. When Ipswich councillors reviewed the needs of the town's poor in the autumn of 1597, they noted the Brounes' 'wants' as 'firing, clothing, bedding'. Rowland Broune was a labourer; his wife could spin 'but she doth nothing but tend to her children', one of them was a year and the other a few months old. For widows earning was a high priority.

Mothers undertook a great variety of paid work, including child-minding. Married ex-servants were hired by better-off households to undertake the heaviest domestic tasks. Washing was the priority. Both Elin Stout (b.1664), the frugal sister–housekeeper of a Quaker merchant, and Mrs Thomas, wife of an Edwardian clerk, had paid help on wash-day while tackling the other chores themselves. The woman who came in to wash or clean might take discarded food and clothes home. Laundry could become a full-time occupation. It was a trade associated with widows and assertive wives. Neighbours collected money to set widows up in business – a cottage at Wicken in Cambridgeshire, still known as the Mangle House, commemorates a Victorian whip-round. One London laundress, making the Census return, put herself first as 'head of family, mangling woman; John, husband, turns my mangle'. At Headington Quarry, thanks to custom from academic households of North Oxford, laundresses' husbands could afford to be 'an easy going class of men', largely dependent on their wives.

Homework was common. In the sixteenth century knitting passed out of the hands of craftsmen and became the drudgery of poor women and their children who worked stockings for the English and European markets. Handknitting remained a significant source of income in parts of the south-east and in Westmorland and the Yorkshire Dales into the nineteenth century. Women took in sewing. An ingenious Liverpool mother bought coarse old sugar bags and made them over into children's clothes, remembered for their scratchiness. In the north-east women ran quilt clubs, using the weekly subscriptions to purchase materials and provide a steady small income while the series of quilts was completed.

In the late-nineteenth century boxes, soft toys and artificial flowers and party favours were made by women at home. Photographs suggest that very small children worked alongside them. Thomas Holmes described an Edwardian widow he watched

> making cardboard boxes, and pretty things they are. Two beds are in the room, and one contains three, and the other two children. On the beds lie scores of dainty boxes. The outside parts lie on one bed, and the insides on the other. They are drying while the children sleep; by and by they will be put together tied in dozens, and next morning taken to the factory. But of their future history we will not enquire.

> The widow speaks to us, but her hands never rest; we notice the celerity of her movements, the dreadful automatic certainty of her touch is almost maddening; we wait and watch, but all in vain, for some false movement that shall tell us that she is a human and not a machine. But no, over her shoulder to the bed on the left side, or

over her shoulder to the bed on her right side, the boxes fly, and minute by minute and hour by hour the boxes will continue to grow till her task is completed. Then she will put them together, tie them in dozens, and lay herself down on that bed that contains the two children.

The boxes she was making were probably designed to contain some de luxe toiletry.

There was work on the land. In the middle of the seventeenth century on Henry Best's farm women spread muck and molehills, raked hay, cut corn and picked peas. Like other employers, Best bracketed them with 'the weakest sort of men'. More than three hundred years later mothers were still toiling in the fields; as Richard Jeffries noted in an article published in 1875, the appearance of the first 'sweet violet . . . in warm sheltered nooks' signalled the beginning of the labouring woman's working year. At Elmdon in Essex women went stone-picking and gathered acorns for pig food.

At Courtaulds' mill at Braintree in Essex in the nineteenth century the plum women's jobs tended to go to the wives of leading male hands; other working wives were the partners of handloom weavers, whose trade was in decline. Mothers were a sufficiently important element in the workforce for the management to set up a day nursery in 1850. Women were shy of it, preferring to leave their children at home with their fathers, or minders who could take on some of the chores and would bring the baby to the mill to be nursed. By 1875 the bottle had displaced the breast and infants were no longer brought in.

MARITAL RELATIONSHIPS

The character of family life was profoundly affected by the man's occupation. When the occupants of tied accommodation lost their jobs, it 'meant getting out of the cottage as well'. The lot of women whose husbands' work made it impossible for them to establish a permanent home was particularly hard. The Army treated soldiers' wives with ruthless disdain; few were recognised. Women 'taken on to the regimental strength' were usually married to sergeants, corporals and long-serving men of good conduct. Wives 'on the strength' were the regiment's chars and washerwomen, sometimes unpaid; a wife who refused to work could be struck off. Wives not 'on the strength' were left to fend for themselves and their children; unlike civilians, soldiers were not obliged to maintain their families. Widows received no pensions. Navvies were rootless, lodging in temporary camps, which resembled colonial frontier towns. In a society where aliases were common, a navvy who chose to jettison his family was virtually untraceable.

It is possible that husband–wife relationships among the labouring poor were affected by the work women had done before marriage. Maids in well-regulated households enjoyed little freedom; their tasks were often minutely detailed; time off was severely restricted; followers were discouraged. Women who had worked in factories seem to have developed better negotiating skills.

Men who were expected to show deference in public felt the need to be masters in their own home. James Bowd's description of his feelings for his wife – 'I was as fond of my wife as a cat is of new milk' – is well known; his qualifying remarks are seldom quoted. 'I felt as if I dared not tell her how much I loved her because I thought she would be trespising [trespassing] on were I should be and that would be the head of the house.' According to Robert Roberts, who grew up there, Salford men who helped their wives with domestic chores were jeered at as 'mop rags' or 'diddy men'. A concentration of brazen collaborators was known as 'Bloody-good-husband Street'.

There is no doubt that some men took the frustrations and humiliations of their working lives out on wives and children. Alcohol offered 'the fastest road' out of intolerable situations. Arthur Young, writing at the end of the eighteenth century, suggested that the enclosures which had deprived the labourer of a chance to keep the cow, the few sheep or geese, which might serve as his passport to independence, had driven him to drink. His work was punishingly hard; he was frequently paid in drinking places; the comradeship of the alehouse and the opulence of the Victorian public house contrasted with the often squalid conditions in which the labourer lived. The nineteenth-century stereotype of the labourer had drunkenness and brutality as characteristic faults. And, to a disturbing extent, the picture is confirmed by the autobiographies of men and women born into Victorian and Edwardian labouring families. Many wives put up with drunken, violent men. Francie Nichol (b.1889) recalled that her mother waited until she had a son-in-law to take her part before leaving home. The deprivation which she and her daughters embraced helps to explain other women's stoicism: they moved into a bare room, sleeping on sacks stuffed with straw and drinking from jam jars until they acquired enough cups to go round.

MARITAL BREAKDOWN

Poverty put the labouring household under peculiar stress; Olwen Hufton, writing of the poor of France called it 'an acid' which 'corrodes and dissolves human relationships'. Families were liable to break up when times were hard – when work was hard to come by, men left home to look for it. Evidence from the sixteenth and seventeenth centuries suggests that the poorer the migrant, the further he travelled and the more likely he was to lose touch with his kin. For the man or woman on the road, the camaraderie of the tippling house took the place of the family. While illiteracy was common and postage prohibitively expensive, the labourer who left his home district for another part of England might be as cut off as the man who crossed the Atlantic. Among those who responded in 1901 to an advertisement seeking information about Devonshire men and women who had emigrated was a man who had left the county to find work on the railways in Hartlepool and York forty-odd years before and now sought to renew contact with his brothers and their children. 'Sir', he wrote 'if you her on any one off the name of Bayes Kindly let them see thiss Letter as it may be some of my Bruthers or some of there children as i should like to hear from them.'

Keith Snell's calculations suggest that between 4 and 6 per cent of poor men abandoned their wives in the eighteenth and early nineteenth centuries. Desertion seems to have become much commoner as the labouring population moved into the more anonymous urban environment. Poverty probably split more couples than clashes of temperament.

WIDOWHOOD

Women's limited earning power had a particularly damaging effect on the high proportion of children dependent on widowed or deserted mothers. A report prepared for London County Council in 1911 revealed that in one deprived district of the inner city 'approximately one-third of the children' were 'supported by female labour' – older sisters as well as unsupported mothers. In earlier, less closely monitored generations, mortality, migration in pursuit of employment and desertion may well have produced similar situations. The widowed mother's struggles to support her children have already been described. The death of a parent could lead to the breakup of a household. For ten years after John Terry died in 1871, his widow and three of their children lived with her parents in a one-up, one-down cottage in True's Yard in the fishing quarter of King's Lynn; the twins born after John Terry's death were split up – Thirza went to live with her father's family round the corner in Pilot Street.

Only among the old did women fare better than men. Women who won through the trials of marriage and motherhood unbroken and unbowed might achieve the status of community matriarchs. Under the Old Poor Law widows were hired to nurse the sick, care for orphaned children and prepare food for builders working on parish property. Less troublesome and more useful than old men, older widows were more likely to be taken in by kin or even, in textile and pottery towns where mothers of young children were most likely to enter full-time paid employment, to be adopted by families without grandmothers of their own.

SUMMING UP

The number of labouring families grew as the population of England rose and traditional patterns of farming and craft production were undermined. Labouring parents rarely had property to hand on. Their legacies were less tangible: skills; access to patronage; under the Old Poor Law, settlement in a parish which guaranteed relief in hard times. The poor were subject to the scrutiny – and interference – of those whose property gave them a voice in the local community. Big families did not necessarily make big households. Infant deaths took their toll, so did informal fostering-out and recruitment to living-in service. Baby-minding and domestic chores bulked large in girls' lives. Both boys and girls began to earn early; the imposition of compulsory education in the 1870s did not exclude them from the world of work. Less sheltered than other women, the daughters of the labouring poor were more likely to bear children outside marriage. Nevertheless, women of the labouring classes were less likely to remain single than those from other social groups. Whether they were employed on the land, or as porters, dockers, miners or navvies, the earnings of labouring men were often irregular. Mothers who went out to work full-time were rare but mothers' earnings as fieldworkers, chars, washerwomen and out-workers were vital components in many family budgets. The management of a complex and generally inadequate income was the wife's responsibility. To keep the main (male) contributors to the household's economy earning, women often went short of food. In old age the balance was redressed; old women were more likely to be useful than old men and more likely to be taken in.

NOW READ ON

A. L. Beier: *The Problem of the Poor in Tudor and Stuart England* (London, Methuen, 1989).

K. D. M. Snell: *Annals of the Labouring Poor: Social Change and Agrarian England, 1660–1900* (Cambridge: Cambridge University Press, 1985).

Alan Armstrong: *Farmworkers: A Social and Economic History, 1770–1980* (London: Batsford, 1988).

Anne Kussmaul: *Servants in Husbandry in Early Modern England* (Cambridge: Cambridge University Press, 1981).

Robert Malcolmson: *Life and Labour in England, 1700–1780* (London: Hutchinson, 1981).

David Vincent: *Bread, Knowledge and Freedom: A Study of Nineteenth Century Working Class Autobiography* (London: Europa, 1981).

John Burnett: *Destiny Obscure: Autobiographies of Childhood and Family from the 1820s to the 1920s* (London: Allen Lane, 1982).

John Burnett: *Useful Toil: Autobiographies of Working People from the 1820s to the 1920s* (London: Allen Lane, 1974).

The Unknown Mayhew: Selections from the Morning Chronicle, 1849–1850, edited with an introduction by E. P. Thompson and Eileen Yeo (London: Merlin Press, 1971).

Melanie Tebbutt: *Making Ends Meet: Pawnbroking and Working-class Credit* (Leicester: Leicester University Press, 1983).

Patricia E. Malcolmson: *English Laundresses: A Social History, 1850–1930* (Urbana, Ill.: University of Illinois Press, 1986).

Raphael Samuel: ' "Quarry Roughs": Life and Labour in Headington Quarry, 1860–1920. An essay in oral history', in *Village Life and Labour*, edited by Raphael Samuel (London: Routledge and Kegan Paul, 1975).

Carl Chinn: *They Worked all their Lives: Women of the Urban Poor, 1880–1939* (Manchester: Manchester University Press, 1988).

Elizabeth Roberts: *A Woman's Place: An Oral History of Working-class Women, 1890–1940* (Oxford: Blackwell, 1984).

Maud Pember Reeves: *Round About a Pound a Week* [1913], introduction by Sally Alexander (London: Virago, 1979).

Robert Roberts: *The Classic Slum: Salford Life in the First Quarter of the Century* (Manchester: Manchester University Press, 1971).

7

THE LOWER MIDDLE CLASSES
The families of blackcoated workers

DEFINING CHARACTERISTICS

Until the nineteenth century, literacy and numeracy had some sort of scarcity value. There were poor clerks and schoolmasters in Tudor England but men who could calculate, read and write fluently possessed skills which might be used to carry the ambitious forward. Analysing London society between 1660 and 1730, Peter Earle noted the rapid expansion of the population of teachers and, in general, of the

> educated lower middle class, a stratum of society which included book-keepers, clerks, customs officials and similar types of occupation, a world of prototype Pooters striving valiantly to retain some dignity on incomes well below what could be earned by many skilled artisans.

Predictably they left faint traces in Earle's sources and remain on the shadowy fringes of his panorama of middle-class London life. These book-keepers and clerks were, presumably, among the purchasers of John Garretson's pocket-sized *School of Manners*, which went into its fourth edition in 1701, with its parallel texts in Latin and English. As Garretson pointed out, 'in the learned language' it could serve as an exercise for schoolboys, 'in the mother tongue' it 'benefited' those with pretensions to refinement. Households of this rank were among the customers for the cheaper paraphernalia of polite domestic life like prints and knives and forks, which could be purchased for a shilling or so.

Census returns indicate a rapid growth in blackcoated (and indeed white-bloused) employment in commerce, in government and in elementary schoolteaching between 1801 and 1911. On the eve of the Great War there were over 800,000 clerks and nearly a million shopworkers (not all of them members of the lower middle class). Whiteley's, the London department store, had five and a half thousand employees.

Industry generated comparatively few clerical jobs – in 1833 a Lancashire factory with 1,600 workers employed only two clerks.

There is some evidence that employers preferred to take on clerks who were clerks' sons but it was inevitable that, as the demand for clerical workers grew, many were recruited from the families of manual workers. The distinctive formal clothing of the blackcoated worker was widely regarded as a badge of achievement. The work was physically less taxing than the labourer's or the artisan's. Just as important, it was cleaner. While professional men were expected to make provision for their widows and orphans and their own old age, salaried employees were among the first to benefit from occupational pension schemes. But perhaps the most significant attraction was the, at least superficial, resemblance of their tasks to those of more highly esteemed pen-pushers. Edward Thomas (b.1878) recorded his Welsh grandmother's pride in her son's promotion from the workshop to the clerk's stool. His father had 'only been a fitter but he was a clerk with the Board of Trade'. Laurie Lee (b.1914) acknowledged that his father, who began his working life as a grocer's assistant (in the days when grocers were skilled craftsmen) and ended it as a clerk in the civil service, had succeeded 'in his miniature way'; he climbed the ladder from shop to office by dint of years of part-time study and service in the Army Pay Corps in the Great War.

There were, however, big and growing drawbacks to be set against the clerk's advantages. The qualifications for blackcoated employment, though for a long time in short supply, were modest – a neat person, a neat hand, arithmetical competence, deference, reliability. By the middle of the nineteenth century literacy was a widespread attainment. In addition, the clerk faced unprecedented competition from women who were willing to accept lower rates of pay as the price for refined employment. As his skills became commonplace, the clerk's status declined. Nineteenth-century Registrars General had placed clerks in Social Class I; in 1911 they were demoted to Class II. Twenty years later they were consigned to Class III. Blackcoated men were often no better paid than skilled manual workers but their 'uniform' cost more to buy and to maintain. Promotion prospects were severely limited. Many of the best-paid posts were reserved for privileged youths whose passage through the lower ranks of the clerical hierarchy was accelerated by their families' influence. And, far from recognising the blackcoated man as a colleague, the professional was disposed to disparage his pretensions and shrink from his company.

The author of an article printed in *The Cornhill Magazine* in 1862 maintained that the lower-middle-class man condemned himself out of his own mouth:

the manners of an English gentleman have much more in common with the manners of a labourer than with the manners of a commercial clerk or small shopkeeper . . . Their language proves it conclusively. A gentleman and a labouring man would tell the same story in nearly the same words, differently pronounced, of course, and arranged in the one place grammatically, and in the other not. The language of the commercial clerk and the manner in which he brings it out, are both framed to a different model. He talks about himself, and constantly attempts to talk fine. He calls a 'school' an 'academy', speaks of 'proceeding' when he means 'going' and talks, in short, much in the style in which members of his own class write police reports and accounts of appalling catastrophes for the newspapers.

The farming community shared these prejudices. Sam Kendall, who classified himself as a 'West Country Yeoman', wrote contemptuously of the teachers recruited to provide compulsory elementary education for the children of his labourers. They kept 'one eye on their holidays and another on the associations which help to govern their salaries'. As their logs make clear, the village schoolmaster or schoolmistress was often an outsider at odds with pupils and parents as well as the farmers and landowners, all of whom shared a resentment against a new and alien authority and considered it a waste of time to keep strapping boys in the classroom when they could be in the fields.

Like parsons, elementary schoolteachers were to be found in almost every community, but employment in the business world and the civil service was concentrated in a few great cities. The rapid expansion of blackcoated posts in the three decades leading up to the Great War coincided with the construction of small houses to let in places served by public transport. These became the natural habitat of the lower middle classes; some of the newly-developed London suburbs were said to be almost wholly populated by clerks. The areas where blackcoated workers congregated were the targets of derisive comment in the building trade press. Their houses were 'semi-detached boxes', monotonous, repetitive, drably uniform, 'ready-made articles', poor miniaturised imitations of gentlemen's residences, their rooms mean and poky. A satirical Edwardian postcard, entitled 'The Last Workman's Car', shows women and men scrambling aboard an already grotesquely overcrowded vehicle in their determination to secure a cheap fare, their headgear indicates that at least a proportion had middle-class pretensions. Examples of the card exist overprinted 'from Tooting' – and 'from' a number of other unfashionable suburban areas.

The need to keep up a front of prosperity and respectability discouraged many lower-middle-class families from inviting outsiders into their homes. The special status of those close adult friends who penetrated the household defences was acknowledged in the way they were referred to and addressed by children as 'aunt' and 'uncle'.

Glimpses behind the unimpressive façade of the home life of the man on the Clapham omnibus or the tram to Tooting reveal family characteristics of considerable interest. In these small introspective households, male and female territories, though still distinct, appear to have been less clearly defined than in other social groups. Low household incomes emancipated daughters from the 'negative forms of employment' to which many of their better-off contemporaries were condemned. They were well-placed to translate the expanding educational opportunities of the late nineteenth century into comparatively responsible and well-paid jobs which could, sometimes, be combined with marriage and children.

Lower-middle-class parents put a high priority on schooling and informal self-improvement. It was for this market, and for working-class readers, that Lever launched the *Sunlight Year Book* in 1895 and Pears the *Shilling Cyclopaedia*, which they claimed to sell at a loss, in 1897. The *Sunlight Year Book* was described as a 'treasury of useful information of value to all members of the household'. The second, 1898, edition proclaimed itself as a compendium 'including The Calendar and Kindred Matter, Universal History, Geography, Army and Navy, Science, Literature, Fine Arts, Architecture, Commerce, Agriculture, Medical, Sports and Pastimes, the Household, Port Sunlight [the site of Lever's factory and model company village] etc. Also Story by Conan Doyle', literary and art competitions for adults and 'the Little Ones', under 14, with prizes worth as much as £10. Every page carried a slogan promoting Sunlight Soap as the housewife's prop and stay.

SOURCES

The families of blackcoated workers made a statistical mark in the nineteenth century but their reticence and lack of property combine to preserve their privacy. The home life of the lower middle classes has not attracted much attention; their apparently humdrum lives lack the glamour of great wealth or the fascination of poverty. George Grossmith (b.1847) and his younger brother Weedon guyed the lower-middle-class clerk's pretensions in their *Diary of a Nobody*, Charles Pooter of The Laurels, Brickfield Terrace, Holloway. The Grossmiths produced an accurate picture of the Pooters' material world, and they captured the lower middle classes' sense of social insecurity. However, their account of the clerk's domestic life is inaccurate. In the absence of other material, we depend heavily on a handful of autobiographies written by men and women like H. G. Wells (b.1866), Edward Thomas (b.1878), Helen Corke (b.1882), Richard Church (b.1893), and indeed Patricia Beer and Michael Green, who were born in the 1920s, all the literary sons and daughters of clerks and shopkeepers; and on the oral testimony of Edwardian children like Sidney Ford and Florence Atherton. According to her son, Sarah Wells (b.1822) belonged 'by nature and upbringing alike . . . to the middle class of dependants who occupied situations, performed strictly defined duties, gave or failed to give satisfaction, and had no ideas at all outside dependence'.

Florence Atherton's father, born into a middle-class Anglican family and disowned when he married a working-class Catholic, sold insurance. The family lived in what Florence Atherton described as 'a genteel poverty'. Sidney Ford's father was a clerk, his mother had been in domestic service before her marriage. Richard Church, the son of a Post Office worker and a schoolteacher, offers an insider's analysis of the modest ambitions which his parents shared with their peers: 'a safe job, a respectable anonymity, a local esteem'. The Churches' visitors, 'few and infrequent', shared 'their social and moral quietism'. Lower-middle-class families liked to keep themselves to themselves.

The outsiders' impressions of suburban drabness are belied by reminiscences of family life among the lower middle classes. Frequently, it seems, a respectable front was achieved or maintained at the expense of the family's physical and emotional health. Behind their front doors families were stressed and broken by men determined to struggle into the ranks of the clerks. Laurie Lee's father abandoned his wife and family who represented the plebeian way of life he had rejected. Other households were made miserable by the eternal campaign to maintain appearances on an inadequate budget. Mrs Wells, wife of a Bromley shopkeeper, 'believed that it was a secret to all the world that she had no servant and did all the household drudgery herself'.

THE MEANING OF CHILDREN

Children who got on in the world 'did their parents proud' and justified their sacrifices, but caution, straitened circumstances and the consequent absence of paid domestic help encouraged a preference for small families. H. G. Wells (b.1866) attributed his parents' decision to sleep apart to a determination to limit their family. His mother's diary suggested to him that she lived in 'perpetual dread of further motherhood . . . "Anxiety relieved" became her formula' for the welcome onset of menstruation.

CHILDHOOD

Children were drilled in correct behaviour. Florence Atherton contrasted her own family's eating habits with those of their neighbours, the Kellens, who had 'no cloth on the table' and ate 'potatoes out of a pan'. Her mother steered clear of the chip shop and 'wouldn't buy a cake out of the shops to put on the table'. Mrs Ford was very particular about her children's table manners. In Leicester in the 1930s mealtimes in the Green household were characterised by ritual affirmations of the family's gentility. 'A milk bottle on the table was a cardinal sin; sugar was picked up with plated tongs; fish could only be eaten with special knives they got as a wedding present.' Except tea, 'all meals were formal . . . with a white tablecloth and linen serviettes, everyone having their own silver ring'. The Greens' mealtime customs and the vocabulary they used to describe them set the family apart not only from the working classes but from the socially-secure middle and upper middle classes too. The fish knives and serviettes on which Mrs Green founded her gentility were precisely the tokens John Betjeman – himself, in childhood, a victim of snobbery – chose to ridicule in his poem 'How to Get on in Society'.

Clothing, also a potent index of status, was another focus of anxiety. Young Herbert Wells was a victim of his mother's powerful 'instinct for appearances' which she lacked the means to support. As a schoolboy, he had to take his coat off gingerly 'because [his] underclothing was never quite up to the promise of [his] exterior garments. It was never ragged but it abounded in compromises. This hindered [his] playing games.' Helen Corke's childhood was blighted by her father's failure in business. Her mother, 'a daughter at home' before her marriage, was obliged to keep a shop. Helen was condemned to wear hand-me-downs passed on by cousins. They were 'at least of good material and cut' whereas her brother's were 'necessarily' the cheapest to be had. His trousers were 'ill-cut, too long in the leg, bagging at the knee'. Mrs Atherton contrived to keep her children 'dressed right through making things do'; she paid for their shoes by sewing for 'a friend that kept a shoe shop', Mr Atherton repaired them. Florence was aware that her parents 'never sent us to school untidy'.

Even quite young children were made aware of their inferiority to the offspring of the professional middle classes. The Wellses felt that 'people who were not beneath [them] were apt to be stuck up and unapproachable'. As a young boy, Edward Thomas was 'conscious' that other children invited to the neighbouring doctor's Christmas party 'were richer or of a different class'. Later his 'shame' of his family's 'slightly inferior social position' encouraged him to exaggerate the size of his grandmother's cottage and credit his cousins with 'horses and stables' when, in reality, they had only a donkey or a pony. The Green boys 'were never allowed to forget that on father's side of the family an ancestor had once been mayor of Leicester and there was a tablet to his memory in the cathedral'. Patricia Beer's parents took great pleasure in a teacher's comment on their daughters' speech which had been stripped of local characteristics.

Parents with these values were naturally on their guard against rough children whose nits, fleas and ringworm or 'bad manners' might contaminate their own. Herbert Wells was 'never to mix with common children who might teach [him] naughty words'. Florence Atherton's father was 'very particular who we played with. We weren't allowed to bother with anyone who was rough and we weren't allowed to bother with anyone that had a fight . . . and we weren't allowed to go down certain streets.' Lack of suitable playmates restricted the lower-middle-class child's social circle from an early age. At school Florence Atherton instinctively avoided contact with the children from the workhouse. One way and another, as Wells observed, the blackcoated family's 'universe of discourse was limited'.

Academic achievement commanded respect; in Mrs Beer's words, it was 'as good as the Squire' as a passport to better things. Job opportunities in shops, offices and elementary schools gave parents an added incentive to put pressure on girls to take their educational chances. Attendance at the elementary schools sponsored by Anglican and non-conformist churches or supported by the School Boards set up as a result of the 1870 Education Act exposed the sons and daughters of black-coated fathers to contact with working-class children; nevertheless, some parents were prepared to reconcile themselves to this temporary evil because it offered a way into the Higher Grade Schools which, for a quarter of a century from 1875, provided a bridge between elementary education and teaching or clerical work for the able and deferential. Others, like the Athertons, were too poor to have a choice. Mrs Wells shunned the Church school which served the working classes of Bromley, opting instead for Morley's Academy which catered for 'the sons of poorish middle class people in the town'. Unlike the old Grammar Schools' or the Public Schools', the Academy's curriculum was commercial not classical. Wells and his school fellows learned no Latin. When he was 4 years old Michael Green (b.1927) was sent to 'a small private establishment for infants' not far from his home. At 8 he 'joined [his] brother Roger at the Wyggeston Grammar School' where the fees were three guineas (£3.15) a term.

The Thomases apparently plotted a sophisticated course, designed to extract the maximum advantage from the range of schools available in London. They started their sons off at the Board School where Edward Thomas's classmates included 'a poor dirty girl who came from an old hovel . . . on the slum frontier' of suburban settlement and put him off the name Lizzie for life. At 10 he was sent to a private school which specialised in coaching boys for entrance scholarships to Battersea Grammar School: he won a free place. When he was 16 he was transferred to St Paul's, one of the great London schools, as a fee-paying pupil. In the course of his schooling, Thomas had ascended the educational and social ladder from the despised Board School to a school of national repute, at very little cost. Success in the scholarship examination was and remained, long after the Great War, of such importance that for Patricia Beer and her contemporaries, sitting the exam 'involved at least something of the striving, heartburning and dedication of the early Christians'. The ordeals of scholarship boys and girls did not end when they passed the exam. At their new schools they were thrust into daily contact with teaching staff and paying pupils who set norms against which the manners and values of their family at home could be tested and found wanting.

Morley's Academy turned out clerical workers for shops and offices. Wells and his elder brothers were destined for the drapery trade. Their mother 'thought that to wear a black coat and a tie behind a counter was the best of all possible lots attainable by man – at any rate by man at our social level'. Her youngest son rebelled. He found a place as a pupil teacher in an elementary school and then as a pupil pharmacist – in this case his ignorance of Latin was a handicap but it was the cost of professional training that proved an insuperable barrier. In Leicester the 'main function' of the Wyggeston Grammar School 'was to produce clerks for banks, insurance offices or local government'.

Perhaps because they had keys in common, typewriters, which came into use in the 1880s, acquired the piano's ladylike aura. Thousands of women became mechanical clerks, developing expertise which went beyond the keyboard to punch-card machines, adding machines and duplicators. The shorthand typist made her appearance at the turn of the century. For reasons that have yet to be explained, the state was faster to employ women than the private sector. In the Post Office, which recruited its first women employees in 1871, more than 40 per cent of clerks were female by 1914. The Great Western Railway, by contrast, hired its first woman clerk in 1906.

WOMEN'S OPTIONS OUTSIDE MARRIAGE

It would be wrong to hail the widening range of female employment as a breakthrough in equal opportunities or occupational integration. The ring-fence which contained women's work was expanded, not dismantled. Categories of clerical work were redefined as women's. Female clerks and typists were segregated from their male colleagues and generally confined to routine, poorly-paid posts. (Contemporaries recognised that 'gentility' was regarded as 'part payment' in kind.) Her earnings were rarely high enough to enable a single woman to set up a household of her own. And in any case, employment did not emancipate daughters from home duties; bonds of obligation tied them to their parents whose sacrifices had kept them at school beyond the compulsory leaving age. Women who remained unmarried often carried a double burden, combining a full-time post with the duties of a daughter at home.

Nevertheless, in comparison with other working women, teachers and office workers were well off. Although until after the Second World War the Civil Service required women to resign on marriage, women who retired into domesticity were rewarded with dowries, which reflected their length of service. If they had what was generally perceived as the misfortune to remain 'old maids', they had a pension to look forward to. Before the Great War women teachers were not subject to a marriage bar and could continue to work even after they had children, making their own private arrangements for maternity cover by hiring a substitute. In 1908 39 per cent of women heads of London schools were married.

THE CHOICE OF WIVES AND HUSBANDS

Among the lower middle classes marriage was not an occasion when much property changed hands; these introverted households paid their own modest way. The matrimonial plans of clerks and schoolteachers were thus of interest only to the couple and the small circle of their close relatives, friends and colleagues. A prudent single man or woman sought in a partner those qualities employers valued: respectability, industry, steadiness.

MARITAL ROLES

The man went out to business; housekeeping and childcare were primarily the wife's responsibilty. At this end of the middle-class spectrum, the servant, if she could be afforded, was likely to be young and untrained. Washing, the heaviest household task, was the first to be consigned to hired help. A young wife without children might have 'time to spare when there are only three rooms to keep tidy and two people to look after', but those who were unable to afford domestic help felt the strain once the children came along. In 1862 Mrs Gaskell, by this time a well-known writer, wrote a letter of advice to a woman, the mother of two small children, who had sent an unsolicited manuscript for comment. She encouraged her 'to economize strength as much as possible in all [her] household labours'. Her advice serves as a reminder of the arduous nature of housework before it was mechanised:

> I hope (for instance,) you soap and soak your dirty clothes well for some hours before beginning to wash [all these clothes would have been made of natural fibres, of course] and that you understand the comfort of preparing a dinner and putting it on to cook *slowly*, early in the morning, as well as having *always* some kind of sewing ready arranged to your hand, so that you can take it up at any odd minute and do a few stitches. I dare say at present it might be difficult for you to procure the sum that is necessary for you to purchase a sewing machine; and indeed, unless you are a good workwoman to begin with, you will find a machine difficult to manage.

The sewing machine, which promised emancipation from the endless drudgery of making and mending clothes entirely by hand, was certainly out of the reach of many purses when it came on to the market in the 1860s.

In the Wells household, 'in opulent times, Betsy would come in to char' but the business limped along and normally his 'mother drudged endlessly in that gaunt and impossible house'.

> Her toil was unending . . . hunting the boys out of bed, seeing that they did something in the way of washing, giving them breakfast, and sending them off in time for school. Then airing and making the beds, emptying the slops [dirty water from the wash basins and the contents of the chamber pots] washing up the breakfast things. Then perhaps a dusty battle to clean out a room; there were no vacuum cleaners in those days; or a turn at scrubbing . . . There was no O-Cedar mop, no polished floors; down you went on all fours with your pail beside you.

In the Thomas household maids came and went. Mrs Thomas experimented with Mother's Helps, who were addressed as 'Miss Blank' and worked alongside their employers rather than for them. The weekly washerwoman was a permanent feature of the Thomases' kitchen.

Then there was the mending and the cooking to be done. *The Ingle-Nook Cookery Book* (1910), compiled by Mrs Stuart Macrae from recipes sent in by readers of *Cassell's Saturday Journal*, was designed for 'the thrifty and economical housewife who is bent on making the most of every penny which she is able to expend on food'. Her benchmarks were 'a shilling dinner [£0.05] for a family of six, or a savoury supper for four persons, to cost not more than eightpence [£0.03]'. Mrs Macrae set out to inspire her readers with the spirit of enterprise:

> There is a certain fascination in concocting meals from odds and

ends which only those who practise it know; and there is plenty of opportunity for this to be done when there are children. Every crust of bread, every dry fragment of pudding, tiny scraps of everything left over, must be carefully saved, and it will be found that nothing is ever useless; indeed it is surprising to find how, after growing accustomed to this planning and contriving, one can make use of scraps that the average person would throw aside.

To the section on 'The Schoolchildren's Dinners' Mrs Billson of Balham contributed 'Egg and Potato Sandwich and Banana Turnover'. 'The ingredients required' for the Egg and Potato Sandwich were 'three small eggs . . . half a pound of cold boiled potatoes, a little meat and drip-ping'. To make the turnovers, she split the bananas lengthwise and encased the halves in 'a little light pastry'. Both these dishes were baked. Arranging 'to cook all either inside [the oven] or out' was a mark of the 'Ingle-Nook' cook. Tips for saving gas sent in by Mrs Noakes of Leicester, one of eighteen readers quoted in this section, suggest the strains imposed on women striving to achieve 'standards' on a stringent budget:

> I arrange a square of bricks round my gas ring, then I have a piece of sheet iron on top with some small holes drilled through. In this way I keep three saucepans boiling, of course bringing each one to the boil right over the top of the ring joint.

Lavinia Church returned to her teaching post within a few weeks of her sons' births, leaving them in the care of 'a young woman named Harriet', who 'knew how to deal with children, having practised lifelong on her younger brothers and sisters'. As soon as she could be dispensed with, Harriet was let go 'and the price of her wages and keep went towards the quarterly allotments for the building society'. Now,

> Mother ran the house, doing her shopping on her way home from school. She made the beds at lunch-time (it was then called the dinner-hour) and frequently scrubbed the kitchen floor after the midday meal, before going off to the afternoon session at school. In the evening she had the rest of the cleaning to do, the household sewing for four, the supper to get and the rest of the tasks that usually keep the mother of a family busy from morning to night.

These accounts of the lower-middle-class housewife's lot in Victorian and Edwardian England tally with Michael Green's recollections of his mother's daily round in the period between the wars:

> Mother had little leisure. She simply worked all the time . . . [She] spent hours in food queues . . . and achieved prodigies with ingenious recipes but we were forced to eke out butter with mar-

168

garine, the ultimate disgrace of someone pretending to be middle class. Only poor people ate margarine then . . . [Her] days were spent cooking and cleaning, the evenings mending, darning and looking after her children. The petty economies of her life seem impossible today. Sheets were turned side to middle, socks darned again and again; clothes patched until they hardly held together and when they fell apart the pieces were carefully saved for further patches . . . [In the Green household] no food was ever thrown away unless it was actually putrid (which as we had no refrigerator sometimes happened). Even then mother hesitated to waste it. Stenching pieces of flesh would be brought out of the larder for inspection in hot weather and sometimes father, who had an iron stomach, volunteered to eat them. Stale bread re-appeared as bread pudding, or baked in the oven as a snack for the boys. Bones went on for ever in stock, the very bacon rinds were pressed into service, carefully cut off and fried crisp later for their fat and then served as a separate dish. The result of this economy was a wonderful variety of dishes such as bubble-and-squeak made of leftovers.

PARENTHOOD

Blackcoated fathers seem to have been unusually involved in childcare. Mr Ford played boardgames at home and took the children out to fly kites. More surprising was his willingness to take the babies for outings in the pram. Mr Atherton cooked, cleaned, washed, saw after his children's physical needs and mothered them (to his daughter Florence he 'was more like a mother beside Mother'). In the Atherton family, leisure activities centred on the church and involved the whole family group. It is improbable that many men were as ready to immerse themselves in domestic duties as he was.

Richard Church's autobiography gives a sense of the more than material benefits conferred on his family by his working mother. His parents' combined income from her teaching and his work in the Post Office enabled the Churches to buy their house, to acquire not one but two pianos, to enjoy the freedom of the road on a fleet of bicycles, and summer holidays in a rented country cottage. Both their sons were given an education which opened the way to more prestigious employment.

MARITAL RELATIONSHIPS

A cluster of factors may have fostered the collaborative style of some lower-middle-class marriages. Clerks were less likely than the labourers to come home physically exhausted; they were less likely to bring work back with them than their managers or employers. As an insurance agent, Mr Atherton had considerable freedom to organise his own working hours. He had married 'beneath' him and may have been anxious to compensate his wife and children for lives which were less materially privileged than his boyhood had been, but, kind-hearted or conscience-stricken as he may have been, there were sound practical reasons for his taking a share of 'woman's work': his wife shared the traditional male responsibility for earning. Teachers married to teachers were bound by a shared professional training and experience; two-teacher schools, especially village schools, were sometimes staffed by a husband and wife team. Typically the woman taught the infants, the man the older children; he was the head.

MARITAL BREAKDOWN

The tension between keeping up appearances and making ends meet put lower-middle-class marriages under strain but the very same forces bonded man and wife. When Sarah Wells left her husband, whose business had collapsed, she was in the unusual situation of being able to go back into service as housekeeper at Up Park where she had been a lady's maid before her marriage. Other marriages ended not in separation but in physical or emotional collapse. Richard Church dwells on the stress his mother was under. 'Having to live two lives in one', carrying the responsibility for 'handling some sixty slum urchins from the wilderness of Pimlico' during school hours and managing the introspective household of 'lower middle class . . . human hedgehogs', broke Lavinia Church's health.

SUMMING UP

The families of blackcoated workers emerged as a numerically significant social group only in the nineteenth century. Compared with owners of property and men with more specialised skills, they had little to hand down to their children. Blackcoated workers were rarely able to afford the living-in servants whose presence was necessary to secure the middle-class status they aspired to. Although their anxiety to mark themselves off from the working classes led parents to prefer a private education, the children of blackcoated workers were perhaps the chief beneficiaries of the expansion of elementary education which gave access to jobs in offices, shops and elementary schools. Women usually retired from paid work when they married – indeed some employers operated a marriage bar; long-serving female staff might be eligible for dowries. Without servants and inclined to 'keep themselves to themselves', these families were unusually insular. There is evidence that blackcoated men had the time and energy and, in some cases, the inclination to assist their wives with domestic chores. In many respects the blackcoated family conforms to the stereotype of the 'modern family': small, introspective and emotionally self-sufficient.

NOW READ ON

John Earle: *The Making of the English Middle Class: Business, Society and Family Life in London 1660–1730* (London: Methuen, 1989).

Lorna Weatherill: *Consumer Behaviour and Material Culture in Britain, 1660–1760* (London: Routledge, 1988).

John Garretson: *The School of Manners or Rules for Children's Behaviour* [4th edition, London: Thomas Cockerill, 1701] (London: Victoria and Albert Museum, 1983).

Frances Widdowson: *Going up to the Next Class: Women and Elementary Teacher Training, 1840–1914* (London: Hutchinson, 1983).

H. G. Wells: *An Experiment in Autobiography: Discoveries and Conclusions of a Very Ordinary Brain (Since 1866)*, Vol. I (London: Gollancz, 1934).

Dina M. Copelman: 'A New Comradeship Between Men and Women: Family, Marriage and London's Women Teachers, 1870–1914', in *Women's Experience of Home and Family 1850–1940*, edited by Jane Lewis (Oxford: Blackwell, 1986).

George and Weedon Grossmith: *The Diary of a Nobody* [1892].

The Childhood of Edward Thomas: A Fragment of Autobiography, with a preface by Julian Thomas (London: Faber, 1938).

Helen Corke: *In Our Infancy: An Autobiography, 1882–1912* (Cambridge: Cambridge University Press, 1975).

Thea Thompson: *Edwardian Childhoods* (London: Routledge and Kegan Paul, 1981).

Richard Church: *Over the Bridge: An Essay in Autobiography* (London: Heinemann, 1955).

Michael Green: *The Boy Who Shot Down an Airship: The First Part of an Autobiography* (London: Heinemann, 1988).

8

SOURCES FOR
THE HISTORY OF THE
ENGLISH FAMILY

Historical investigation generally is complicated, first, by the uneven survival of source materials; second, by their nature and quality; third, by problems of interpretation. Historians of the family face a particularly severe and stimulating challenge: the range of materials is immense but their quality is variable and debated; the evidence is often oblique. The sources the historian emphasises and the questions she asks of them have a profound effect on her conclusions: personal testimonies of various kinds lie at the heart of this account, and almost inevitably, therefore, there is a sharper focus on the experience of more recent generations. The paragraphs which follow review these sources and others which have been used to reconstruct the experience of families of past times. Generally speaking, historians are more at ease with documentary materials and it is with these that I begin.

PUBLIC RECORDS

Parish registers are a memorial to the bureaucratic energies of Thomas Cromwell, who was executed by his ungrateful master, Henry VIII, in 1540. Cromwell's project, launched in 1538, was designed to record every baptism, marriage and burial which took place under the auspices of the newly-independent Church of England – in theory, that is, every baptism, marriage and burial in the country. Parish registers are a good example of oblique evidence. In recording ceremonies associated with birth and death, parish registers provide evidence of these events at one remove. An unguessable and inconsistent but rising proportion of births in particular went unlisted: frail newborn babies baptised at home might be omitted; when the parish church was hard to get to, in the Essex marshes for example, baptism might be delayed – sometimes a clutch of siblings was christened together. Both the shifting population of the very poor and those whose parents opted out of the Church of England for reasons of conscience – the Catholic remnant and Protestant dissenters (Baptists, Congregationalists, Presbyterians, the Quakers, and the Methodists, who separated from the Anglican church in the eighteenth century) – went unnumbered. And, as the penalties for nonconformity diminished after 1690, the number of dissenters rose: by 1851 nearly half the regular worshippers in England were chapelgoers.

Some parsons were poor record-keepers, making notes on scraps of paper and copying them up at intervals. The registers themselves were vulnerable. There was a market for the durable waterproof skin on which they were written: tailors wanted parchment to make patterns, cooks used it to line pie dishes, dairy women used it to wrap butter, I have come across fragments of manuscript cut up to make tags for keys. Rodents had a taste for parchment too. Curiosity took its toll; registers from the parish of St Aldate's in Oxford went missing after the local historian Anthony à Wood (b.1636) borrowed them. Enemy action in the Second World War brought further casualties. The upshot was that only 400-odd of the 10,000 old English parishes have registers which meet the criteria laid down by the team of demographers which set out to reconstruct the history of the English population from the sixteenth to the early nineteenth century. Sorting the reliable from the unreliable registers was not the end of the researchers' problems; in a society in which a handful of male Christian names were handed down as heirlooms from one generation to the next, it was hard to separate one John Robinson from another. Techniques were devised to cope with this difficulty and to calculate patterns of fertility, marriage and mortality.

Historians working on Stuart England have used the records of ecclesiastical courts to explore the theory and practice of marriage and sexuality; they have used the statements made by witnesses in civil courts to deduce the rate and distribution of literacy and the influence of rank on patterns of migration.

Scattered listings of local populations offer bird's eye views of a tiny sample of communities; a hundred were made for a variety of reasons between the sixteenth and the early nineteenth century. These listings indicate that married couples and their resident children formed the core of a majority of households, that living-in servants were commoner than living-in kin and that the smaller a household was, the poorer it was likely to be. The national Census, introduced in 1801, and repeated at ten-yearly intervals, provides regular snapshots of households. Inevitably it took time to refine the design of the survey and, even in its mature form, the Census had shortcomings. To take one example, Mary Prior's close study of the boatmen's families of Fisher Row in Oxford revealed 'two large families [that] all but entirely escaped the Census'. Between 1848 and 1864 Anne and Robert Humphries had eight children baptised in the parish; their more prolific neighbours John and Mary Howkins baptised fifteen; none of them appears in the 1861 returns.

RECORDS OF PROPERTY HOLDING

From the Reformation to the Great War the family was the chief vehicle for accumulating and transmitting property – until the late nineteenth century land was the securest form of wealth. Perhaps alone among landowners, the Shirleys of Ettington in Warwickshire can document the descent of their estate in the male line from the time of the Domesday survey in 1086 to the present day, but archives of many other landed families covering shorter spans of time survive. In the Middle Ages details of many peasant holdings were stored only in the communal memory; such tenancies proved woefully insecure, even those which were documented were at risk. Like other mercenary Tudor landlords, Richard Kirby used a combination of brute force and legal expertise to menace and eject his own and other tenants; fortunately for the villagers of Landbeach in Cambridgeshire, the Master and Fellows of the College of Corpus Christi had interests in the parish. The contest, which came to a head in 1540, was resolved when the Master of Corpus set the record straight by compiling an authoritative statement of tenants' rights.

Post-mortem inventories survive in quantity from the sixteenth to the middle of the eighteenth century. Drawn up by the neighbours of the deceased, they tend to give a tantalisingly curt and dismissive – 'books and other lumber' – account of the furnishings and stock in trade found in the dwelling houses of landed gentlemen, parsons, professional men, farmers, craftsmen, shopkeepers and even, occasionally, labourers. The great mass of people, who owned very little, are not represented. Inventories document the descent of former luxuries like chairs and clocks to the rank of everyday possessions and give an impression of the furnishings and functions of rooms. However, the interiors they suggest are not always true to life because, quite properly, anything the subject used but did not own was omitted. Farmers' inventories reflect the seasons.

Wills are another precious, though by no means infallible, source. They may give an optimistic account of the testators' wealth. Parents' wills frequently ignore hefty investments in education, training and marriage settlements. Against these defects we must set the weight of evidence that wills provide of the ways in which men and women disposed of their possessions and attempted to secure the future of those they left behind. Elizabethan examples of Latin and English inscriptions on memorial rings left respectively to male and female mourners are pointers to the cultural wedge which education drove between men and women in Tudor and Stuart England. Wills remind us of the frictions which could be generated between widows and their grown-up children. William Sampfield, a labourer, who died at Orwell in Cambridgeshire in 1586, leaving his wife the life tenancy of his own bedchamber, was careful to secure her a legal title to free access to the fire in the main room of his cottage, the fruit of two apple trees in his orchard and room to graze a bullock there.

LETTERS, JOURNALS, DIARIES AND MEMOIRS

Like willmakers, most writers of letters, journals and memoirs belonged to the privileged minority of property owners. However, they were rarer. Anticipating death, prudent people put their affairs in order; wills, once proved, passed into the relative security of public custody. Until the nineteenth century, few labourers could write with ease; at all social levels women's literacy lagged behind men's. Farmers, craftsmen and shopkeepers, many of whom were literate even in the sixteenth century, were brought up to regard writing primarily as a medium for keeping accounts.

Letters can give the reader a sense of closeness to the men and women who wrote or dictated them – all Honor Lisle's letters were dictated, but, far from inhibiting her, her reliance on scribes may explain the conversational tone of her letters. Here she reports on a channel crossing in November 1538: 'I thank God I was but once sick in all the way; and after that I was merry and well.' The reticent may reveal themselves in their own way: Winifred Shute (b.1879) put a letter describing the birth of her first child into code because 'she felt it so delicate a matter'. Mrs Shute's confinement occurred during the Great War, the letter fell into official hands and her confidante was arrested as a suspected German spy. The story has become public because Winifred Shute was the sister of the flamboyant painter Augustus John.

Diarists' methods and motives varied. Thomas Isham (b.1657) wrote a diary in Latin from 1671 to 1673 'at his father's command' and in pursuit of the considerable reward he had offered. Theatrical programmes and reviews enabled Ellen Terry (b.1847) to keep her 'diary with a paste pot and scissors as much as with a pen'. While some diarists wrote to be read, others sought privacy. The apparently happily married Stuart diarist Sarah Savage hesitated to keep a spiritual journal because she could not write shorthand 'characters'. Samuel Pepys used a shorthand well known in his own day, though probably not understood by his wife. To record his sexual fantasies and activities, he adopted a by no means impenetrable 'foreign' language. The eighteenth-century printer's apprentice John Coggs made mundane entries in plain English and cloaked references to his master's family in anagrams; a third category of material is locked in an as yet unbroken code. Beatrix Potter (b.1866) kept her diary in a cypher of her own devising.

Nehemiah Wallington (b.1598), a Puritan Londoner, produced 20,000 pages of autobiographical manuscript which reveal 'little about his childhood and virtually nothing about his schooling or his training in the craft of woodturning. We do not know how he met his wife or how his marriage was arranged.'

Wallington's chief preoccupation was his sense of moral worthlessness. He recorded providential escapes from danger and penalties meted out by God as the interim wages of sin. The material he left is exceptional in its volume, but not in its orientation. Samuel Jeake (b.1652), a merchant of Rye in Sussex, was one of many moved by concern with astrological or 'astral' influences. In an entry for 1666, he stated that

> (being 14 years 14 days 14 hours old) I was taken sick of the small pocks . . . and it seemed from an astral cause; that distemper not being in the town of Rye before nor after for a considerable time, nor I having been anywhere to catch it.

'Diary' suggests a record of events compiled as they occurred but Jeake's account was written up from old notes in the summer and autumn of 1694. Editing of this kind is common.

Internal contradictions and cross-checks with other sources suggest the power of self-censorship and the tricks memory can play. While she was alive, the Sussex shopkeeper Thomas Turner (b.1729) depicted his wife as a shrew; as a widower, he portrayed her as patience personified. Painful episodes may be completely ignored. The drama of Mary Godwin's middle teens – her elopement with Shelley, his first wife's suicide, her step-sister Claire Clairmont's entanglements with both Shelley and Byron, whose child she had – go virtually unremarked in her journal. When Basil Sanders was jilted by the woman he intended to marry in April 1928, all he wrote was 'Began Sep. 5th 1924. Ended today.' Articulate, confiding, reliable diarists are rare and it would be rash to assume that their actions and reactions were typical.

BIOGRAPHICAL WRITING

These cautionary comments apply to biography with equal force. In *As We Were: A Victorian Peepshow*, E. F. Benson (b.1867) portrayed his parents' marriage as a model of Victorian domesticity; other accounts suggest that the archbishop was a domestic tyrant.

Memorial inscriptions, which are to be found in every old parish church, incorporate brief, usually idealised, accounts of the subjects' descent, qualities and careers. They refer, almost invariably, to the propertied classes. Occasionally the devoted service of veteran retainers is recorded: a tablet on the outside of St Mary's Church at Dalham in Suffolk records that

Near this place lies the body of John Keates, labourer of this parish, who died 5 November 1820, aged 89, also the body of Joseph Brett, labourer of this parish, who died 30 January 1822, aged 75. Each of these worthy men served the family of Dalham Hall honestly and faithfully and with little interruption for half a century.

> Who change their places often change with loss!
> Tis not the rolling stone that gathers moss!

Funeral eulogies, some of which went into print, were the inscriptions' oral equivalent, designed to celebrate the dead and to provide an exemplar for the living. Private feelings and family relationships are not necessarily themes to which much space is devoted. Richard Baxter's brief life of his wife Margaret (d.1681) was a 'paper monument' which he hoped would be as 'useful and durable' as a stone tablet; he described her weaknesses as well as her merits, but he 'left out . . . the occasions and inducements of [their] marriage and some passages between her relatives and her which', in his opinion, 'the world [was] not concerned (yet at least) to know'.

Selective coverage is common. Biography written before 1900 may dwell on death; the popularisation of psychological theories in the twentieth century stimulated interest in childhood; since the 1960s the conventions which obliged writers to steer clear of sex and money have been jettisoned. The lesson to take on board is that biographers, like historians, are prisoners of their time and blinkered by their own prejudices.

BOOKS AND OTHER READING MATERIAL

Because it helped to shape their attitudes and influenced the language they used to describe their feelings, it is well worth becoming familiar with the material which the men, women and children of the past knew as readers or hearers – the Bible in particular.

From the 1730s many newspaper column inches were given over to advertising goods and services: manufacturers, shopkeepers, the proprietors of schools and travelling shows believed that it paid to advertise. The copy that they used provides clues about the aspirations of the people who read them – and their sense of humour. Neil McKendrick, who analysed George Packwood's advertisements of the 1790s, lists the genres Packwood used to promote his shaving tackle:

> riddles, proverbs, fables, slogans, jokes, jingles, anecdotes, facts, aphorisms, puns, poems, songs, nursery rhymes, parodies, pastiches, stories, dialogues, definitions, conundrums, letters and metaphors.

As this suggests, Packwood's advertisements were wordy; the pithy slogan is characteristic of illustrated advertisements. The possibilities of colour printing were exploited to the full in the great late-Victorian soap wars. With blithe disregard for the dignity of the Art establishment, Pears added a bar of his soap to Sir John Millais's 'Bubbles' and Lever emblazoned the slogan 'So Clean' on W. P. Frith's painting of a small girl showing off 'The New Frock'.

Written prescriptions

Theologians, educationalists, medical men and arbiters of taste pronounced on such aspects of family life as the proper relations between man and wife and parent and child; much of their advice got into print. The connection between precept and practice is debatable, levels of illiteracy were high and it seems likely that, even among the reading classes, more people owned these manuals than followed their prescriptions. However, Gillian Avery has recently drawn attention to the possible influence of the primers from which children learned to spell. She cited, as an example, the violently anti-papist *Protestant Tutor*, published in 1683, which provided young Puritans with an extensive vocabulary 'mostly scriptural and theological'. Nineteenth-century children ate and drank from plates and mugs printed with mottoes urging piety, hard work and thrift. Isaac Watts's *Divine Songs Attempted in Easy Language for the Use of Children*, published in 1715, were frequently reproduced; so were Benjamin Franklin's maxims:

He that hath a trade hath an estate

Diligence is the mother of Good Luck

and

Silks and satins scarlet and velvet put out the kitchen fire

suggest the tone of the collection.
The old favourite

Early to bed, early to rise – the way to be healthy, wealthy and wise

is also found.

SPOKEN TESTIMONY

The dying statements of the notoriously good and bad were noted down to encourage readers and hearers. The deathbed testimony of Mary

Simpson, a poor godly woman from Norwich, was published in 1649; speeches from the scaffold were regularly printed; but it was in the nineteenth century that poor men, women and children acquired a voice. The small but swelling stream of working-class autobiography is supported by the witness of men, women and children who testified before commissioners investigating the working conditions in factories and mines and on the land. However, it was the development of sound-recording techniques which enabled historians to build up large archives preserving the experience of ordinary men and women in their own distinctive words and accents: after a day's graft and an evening stint digging his quarter-acre allotment, the Suffolk farmworker Sam Friend was so tired that if he'd 'hit a cobweb', he'd 'ha' fallen backwards'. George Ewart Evans, who recorded Sam Friend, published *Ask The Fellows Who Cut the Hay* in 1956. Systematic recording by teams of researchers followed. Important 'life story' collections are held at the universities of Essex and Lancaster and at Manchester Polytechnic. Talking witnesses are able and may be willing to answer many of the questions that historians working on earlier periods ask in vain or approach obliquely.

Unsympathetic commentators have questioned the authenticity of testimony selected and woven together from very long and sometimes incoherent taped reminiscences. And readers of oral history should not allow the pungency of many survivors' recollections to distract them from the possibility that their memories may be unreliable or their experiences atypical. As Steve Humphries wrote of his collaborators in the investigation of *A Secret World of Sex*, which looks at the British experience of pre-marital sex in the first half of the twentieth century, those willing to share their intimate experiences with strangers are almost certainly 'an unusual group'. Historians working with these living witnesses bear a responsibility not shared by those who work with paper sources: the quality of their listening and prompting can draw their respondents out, encourage them to embellish their testi-mony, or shut them up. Steve Humphries noted that 'in a few cases the interviewers seem to have actually backed off [spontaneous] taboo talk', shaming their interviewees into silence; Gwendolen Freeman, whose work as a voluntary collector for a savings bank made her familiar with the back streets of Birmingham in the 1930s and 40s, was conscious that the fact that she talked 'lawn tennis' came between her and her clients.

Although I have emphasised the importance of spoken evidence for the experience of the working classes, interviews with eye-witnesses in fact lie behind many written histories and biographies – in England this applies as far back as Bede (b.673). The twentieth-century shift from writing to oral communication has dramatically increased the signifi-cance of the spoken medium.

IMAGES

Monuments

Memorials provide evidence of attitudes to death among the well-to-do. On Tudor and Stuart monuments and gravestones skeletons and tokens of decay are used to underline the transience of the flesh. During the eighteenth century images of physical corruption were replaced by more subtle references to death: the broken column, the funerary urn (favoured long before cremation came into fashion); the dead are shown sombre, resigned, more often than not asleep but sometimes seated or standing in attitudes as appropriate to the secular environment of the town hall, park or square.

The earliest effigies in parish churches and cathedrals represent, by means of costume and accoutrements, the rank of the men and women they commemorate and the time at which they lived; the individual's descent and connections by marriage are conveyed in heraldic code. Influenced by Italian examples, sixteenth- and seventeenth-century sculptors set out to achieve a physical likeness of their subjects. In the eighteenth and nineteenth centuries, the more elaborate memorials express their subjects' roles and merits in imagery as well as words; the Good Samaritan was a favourite metaphor for philanthropists. John Sibthorp's monument in Bath Abbey alludes to his profession – he was a botanist – and the place of his death, which occurred during an expedition to Greece in 1796: he is depicted as an ancient Greek traveller bearing flowers; a wreath of *Sibthorpia Europea* compliments his father and predecessor as Professor of Botany at Oxford, after whom it was named.

Family portraits

Holbein's annotated drawing of the household of Sir Thomas More, 'united in the common pursuit of piety and learning' (1526/7), was the sketch for the first major portrait of an English family at home. It was More's position as a chief servant of the Crown which brought him into contact with Holbein whose portfolio included most of the leading figures of Henry VIII's Court. More, who died on the scaffold in 1535, was revered as a Catholic martyr. The image of his household became an icon; later versions incorporated further generations of his staunchly Catholic descendants. Other sixteenth- and seventeenth-century group portraits also express the continuity of kinship between the living and dead. Magdalene Aston died in childbirth a hundred years after More's execution. She appears twice in the family portrait commissioned by her husband: on her deathbed, with the black-draped cradle of her dead baby by her side, and alive, as though mourning for herself and her child. The scene of birth and death is decorated with symbols of mortality, the starkest is the skull on the cradle hood on which Sir Thomas rests his left hand; in translation, the Latin motto beneath the skull reads: 'Who sows in flesh will reap in bones.' The Astons' rank is emphasised by their coat of arms.

Among the most touching early images of young children are the potter John Dwight's figures of his daughter, who died in 1674, 'Lydia Dwight on her Deathbed' and 'Lydia Dwight Resurrected'.

Group portraits of families became the bread and butter of English painters. Carefully composed to represent the relationships between the actors, to demonstrate their taste, to convey and, perhaps, exaggerate their wealth, they are not to be taken at face value. 'The Graham Children' (1742), William Hogarth's painting of the small son and daughters of George II's apothecary, their pet bird and their tabby cat, is a commentary on the hazards that await the children in the adult world. To take only the most explicit reference, freed from its cage, the bird would be at risk from the cat's unsheathed claws. In the 1760s, Joseph Wright of Derby painted portraits of the Rastall brothers, Samuel (b.1749) and William (b.1745), to hang face to face. The viewer needs no specialised knowledge to decode their message: the boys' relationship is apparent in their matching jackets and occupations; Samuel is shown copying an engraving; his younger brother is leafing through an album of prints, the means to copy are before him.

Queen Victoria celebrated her Golden Jubilee in 1887 by commissioning a portrait of herself with her 'children, children-in-law, and grandchildren', fifty-five in all, 'not . . . stiff and according to *Etiquette*, but prettily grouped'. The appearance of informality was the product of meticulous planning and calculation. The bust of Victoria's husband and consort Albert, who died in 1861, appears on the mantelpiece above and behind the figure of their eldest grandson, the languid Prince Albert Victor, to symbolise dynastic continuity.

The sketches made by the Drummond children supply a rare child's-eye view of family life between 1827 and 1832; their father was a banker with aristocratic connections. The emphasis is on chastisement, humiliation and tears: this may reflect the peculiar experience of the Drummond household. The Jenyns family's unpublished albums of nineteenth-century sketches certainly give a more cheerful impression of life in a landowner's household; they include what seem to have been running family jokes, like the saga of the gigantic cabbage, first shown as a curiosity attracting crowds to the kitchen garden and, finally, making its entrance to the dining room with the footman reeling and groaning under its monstrous weight.

Portraits of farmers and tradesmen were generally the work of less polished artists, some of them itinerant. They express their patrons' pride in their trade: the craftsman is shown in his workshop; the farmer with his prize beasts – in W. Williams's painting 'A Prize Bull and a Prize Cabbage' (1804) a small dog leads the bull, a woman carrying the cabbage brings up the rear of the procession.

Drawings and paintings commissioned by poor families were crude, personalised primarily by their inscriptions and, in the case of serving soldiers and sailors, their uniforms.

Pictures which tell a story

The pictorial life histories of fictional men and woman give an insight into attitudes. Hogarth's etchings illustrate the dominant values of his day. 'A Harlot's Progress' (1732) describes the seduction and downfall of a country girl in London. 'Marriage à la Mode' (1745) is the story of the disastrous mercenary match between Viscount Squanderfield and an alderman's daughter. 'Industry and Idleness' (1747) contrasts the careers of fellow apprentices, Francis Goodchild, who marries his master's daughter and becomes Lord Mayor of London, and Tom Idle, who, turned thief and murderer, is hanged at Tyburn.

Victorian painters provide commentaries on similar moral themes. Augustus Egg's three-canvas series 'Past and Present' (1858) is an essay on the consequences of a wife's infidelity, Egg supplied the following commentary:

Aug. 4: Have just heard that *B.* has been dead more than a fortnight; so his poor children have lost both their parents. I hear *She* was seen on Friday last, near the Strand, evidently without a place to lay her head – What a fall hers has been!

The last picture shows *Her* under the Adelphi Arches with a babe in arms, on the verge of ending it all in the Thames; the text on the posters rams the message home, 'VICTIMS . . . A CURE FOR LOVE'. William Frith's 'The Road to Ruin' (1887) traces a gambler's progress from the University, via the racecourse, to suicide, in five episodes; his victims are his wife and children. Sex is the woman's downfall as money is the man's.

Photographs

The discovery of photography was published in January 1839. William Fox Talbot, the Wiltshire landowner who pioneered the art in England, described it as 'photogenic drawing'. Technical limitations made it impossible to take snapshots. Herbert Fisher (b.1865), a great-nephew of the distinguished camerawoman Julia Margaret Cameron, recalled how 'urgent' it was 'to escape being photographed, for the exposure . . . was a sore trial to the patience of a child'. Retouching, to smooth wrinkles and slim waists, flattered the vanity of those who could afford it. By the time of the Great War the photograph album was a well-established feature of the middle-class family archive; undocumented albums are tragically incomplete, since photographs without clear captions are liable to be misinterpreted. The proliferation of commercial studios in the 1860s transformed working-class families' opportunities to represent themselves as they wished to be seen, with the aid of studio backdrops and furnishings. Photography was also used to fire the conscience of the nation; Dr Barnardo (b.1845) was among the campaigners who used 'before and after' cards to demonstrate the value of subscriptions to his Home for Working and Destitute Lads.

In Edwardian London 'Animated Family Portraits' were available from the Biograph Studio in Regent Street: a sequence of more than six hundred photographs was used to give an impression 'so lifelike as to border on the marvellous', reproducing the subjects' 'actual gesture, expression, smile'. One 'Animated Portrait' cost roughly what a labouring man could expect to earn in a fortnight.

GOODS AND CHATTELS

While thrift and poverty limited the pace at which new things were acquired, durable and renewable goods and chattels were passed down from generation to generation and from richer to poorer. The relics of celebrated men and women, objects of intrinsic or symbolic value and curiosities are most likely to survive the end of their useful careers and fetch up in public and private collections. Robbed of their context, objects lose much of their meaning; when things were made, why and for whom may be unclear. The relatively modest price-tags often attached today to newly-made goods 'with an authentic feel of the past' give a misleading impression of the ownership of the models from which they derive. Many are mass-produced, by modern methods, from cheaper materials than the originals. Offered for sale in the shops attached to museums and houses open to the public, these reproductions assume a false authority.

MUSEUMS AND HISTORIC HOUSES

Visitors interested in the experience of family life in the past will find relevant material in almost every museum or art gallery, although the concentration is likely to be greatest in museums which specialise in local history, social history, the history of childhood, or the life and possessions of a family or individual. Museums' missions vary. Their prime purpose may be to support scholarly activity, to educate and/or entertain the general public, or to make money. Their priorities shape acquisition policies, the way in which collections are displayed and described, the stocking of shops, the style of catering facilities and so on.

Conventional museums are patently artificial environments: the distance between viewer and object is maintained. Visitors to historic houses, exhibitions of 'living history' and 're-enactments' of past events enter more ambiguous territory.

Old buildings are palimpsests, reflecting shifts of custom and taste. The interiors of only a tiny minority of houses open to the public would be familiar to their original inhabitants. The living rooms of 18 Stafford Terrace, London are exceptional. This was the home of the *Punch* cartoonist Linley Sambourne (b.1844) and his wife Marion (b.1851) from 1874 and, as his photographs, a detailed inventory and other documents confirm, the hall, the dining room, the morning room and the drawing room look very much as they were when the Sambournes lived there. The kitchen and bathroom have been altered out of recognition – kitchens are probably the rooms most susceptible to change and hardest to put back as they were.

The houses in Stafford Terrace were built to accommodate comfortably-off professional families and their three or so servants. Building a great house involved prodigious expenditure; the cost of restoration can be ruinous. Advertisements for the Queen's House at Greenwich invite visitors to 'admire the sumptuous Royal Apartments that recreate the original seventeenth-century splendour'. Compare the recreated furnishings with surviving originals and the gulf between aspiration and achievement will be obvious; lack of funds explains the shortfall but the claim is misleading.

Custodians need to drum up custom. It is assumed that links with famous people will attract visitors. Advertisements for Blenheim celebrate its connection with Winston Churchill; visitors can see the room where he was born, examples of his paintings and a collection of Churchilliana. Literary associations – 'Charles Dickens, a frequent visitor, used [Rockingham Castle] as a model for Chesney Wold in *Bleak House*' – film and television credits are stressed. To compete with other choices for 'family days out', sideshows are added to the main attraction. At Blenheim the 'inclusive ticket covers the Palace Tour, Park and Gardens, Butterfly House, Motor Launch, Train, Adventure Play Area and Nature Trail. Optional are the new Marlborough Maze and Boat Hire.' At Holdenby 'as buzzards and other birds of prey capture the attention in the sky, train rides and a "cuddle farm" ensure an enjoyable day for the children on the ground'. Such ventures testify to the financial problems faced by landowners and their corporate successors, but for visitors interested in the daily life of the household before the decline of landed power and wealth they are distractions.

FEATURE FILMS, 'LIVING HISTORY' AND RE-ENACTMENTS

Although schooled in objectivity, historians recognise that they are not immune to the influence of 'current events and current values', as Lawrence Stone observed in an autobiographical essay:

> My first article, on the life of seamen in the Elizabethan navy, was written in 1942 on board a destroyer in the South Atlantic . . . My book on the family, sexuality and marriage was conceived and written in the 1970s, at a time of heightened anxieties about just these issues, provoked by rocketing divorce rates, sharply declining marital fertility, much greater sexual promiscuity, changes in sex-roles caused by the women's liberation movement, and the abrupt rise in the proportion of married women in the labour force.

Scriptwriters and designers are equally susceptible to the climate of their times and often reveal more about the concerns and taste of their own day than about the past in which their work is set.

At museums and historic sites workers in period costume practise crafts – their products may be on sale as souvenirs. The miller's dependence on the wind, or the time and skill required to make a barrel by hand are instructive. At Kentwell Hall at Long Melford volunteers are recruited to 'live' in a specific year – in 1992 it was 1578, the summer of Elizabeth I's progress through Suffolk – for one, two or three weeks at a time; enthusiasts return year after year and invest time and money in briefing and equipping themselves. Visitors are encouraged to dress up.

'Living history' tends to present a sensationalised, glamorised, non-violent and cleaned-up version of the past. Replayed in real time, the past is not eventful enough to satisfy the paying public: re-enactments of battles and skirmishes are popular; organisers do not subject spectators or participants to the tedium of a siege. The advertised high point of school trips to Kingston Lacy in Dorset 'in 1905' is the arrival of Edward VII 'to plant his tree and in a wholly permissible anachronism [go] walk-about among the excited children'. Anachronism is common and can be dangerously misleading – the royal 'walkabout' is a phenomenon of the very recent past. The promoters of 'battles' seek to avoid bloodshed; twentieth-century actors are unmarked by the privations, diseases and injuries to which, in the past, people were prone; visitors are spared the stench of unwashed clothes and bodies and human and animal waste, they are not deliberately fed tainted food, nor are they expected to use earth closets.

Producers, actors and spectators carry mental baggage from their own day with them into recreations of the past. A Kentwell volunteer playing the part of a 'milkmaid with a pail on her arm' – to use Elizabeth I's own stereotype of an Englishwoman of no importance – will, if she has done her homework, be better-informed about events in 1578 than the queen herself. She will know, for example, that the queen's longstanding favourite, the Earl of Leicester, married secretly at the beginning of the year and would in September 1578 go through a second discreet ceremony, before witnesses, to bind him irretrievably to his by now visibly pregnant wife. But, at the same time, however well she has prepared herself, the volunteer's twentieth-century upbringing and experience will prevent her from looking through Tudor eyes.

WHEN IS A SOURCE NOT A SOURCE?

It should be clear by now that it is impossible to recover the whole and unadulterated truth about events and experiences in the past. Professional historians disagree about the reliabilty of source materials and dispute each other's methods and conclusions. It is hardly surprising that, although there is widespread concern about what is perceived as the creeping blight of nostalgia for a past that never was, there is no clear academic consensus about the line which separates the doubtfully legitimate reconstruction from the thoroughly bogus. Fortunately, curiosity and scepticism are among the qualities which lead adults – and children – to want to find out about the past. Instinctive historians are not content with the rote learning of dates and other 'facts', they want to make up their own minds and are unlikely to be satisfied with the answers in the book. Approached in this spirit, the least rigorous representation of the past can yield food for thought.

INDEX

adultery 55; attitudes to 36, 37, 65; as grounds for divorce 36

advertising: by Lever 35–6, 178, 181; newspaper 177; and soap wars 178

agriculture: accumulation of farms 77; children in 85, 93; economic changes in 77; employment in 135, 145; and enclosures 132, 154; and mechanisation 20, 21; training for 85; women in 153; *see also* farmers; labourers

alcohol, and marital relationships 154

anachronisms, in re-enactments 185

ancestry: pride in 5–6, 78, 81; research into 5–6, 41, 45

Anderson, Michael: household economics approach 8–9, 10; *Approaches to the History of the Western Family* 6–7; *Family Structure* 8

Anglican Church, Archbishops of Canterbury 68, 110, 116, 118, 176

Anglican church, clerical dynasties 96–7

Anglican Church: dissenters from 172–3; education of clergy 97; financial difficulties among clergy 101; life of clergy 96–8; loss of influence 22–3; and parish registers 172–3; and Reformation 15; restoration after Civil War 18; and social hierarchy 39, 41, 132

apprenticeships 52, 145; in factories 145; from labouring class 145; and future prospects 85–6; for landowners' sons 52; relationship with master 86

architects 62, 111; and 'model dwellings' 136; municipal building 22

Aries, Philippe, study of childhood 8

Aristotle's Masterpiece 26

Army, treatment of soldiers' wives 153

Atherton, Florence, on childhood 162, 163, 164, 169

autobiography 161–5, 168–9, 170, 176; by middle classes 104; of landowners 40, 41, 46, 51, 53–4; of plain folk 89–91; of poor 137; spiritual 80, 175–6; use to historians 175–6; Wells, H.G. 161, 162, 163, 164, 165, 167; working-class 179

babies, birth *see* childbirth; pregnancy; feeding *see* breastfeeding; swaddling 27–8; *see also* children; fathers; mothers

Bank of England, dynasties of clerks 111–12

barbers, changes in craft 78–9

Beeton, Mrs, on occupations of mothers 123

begging 151; 'niggering' 143

Benson, Edward, Archbishop of Canterbury 110, 116, 118, 176

Benson, Minnie, marriage 118, 125–7, 176

betrothal 32

Bible, familiarity to readers and listeners 177

Biograph Studio, Regent Street, 'animated' portraits 183

biography 137, 177; attitudes to 46; of poor 137; *see also* autobiography

birth control 26–7, 123, 130, 162

debt 100, 102
demographic approach to family
history 7–8
diaries, value to historians 175–6
diarists 175, 176; *see also* Pepys,
Samuel
diet 14, 17; of labouring class 141,
149–51; of poor 141, 150; tainted
food 150–1; variations in 151; *see
also* breastfeeding
discipline, of children 106–7, 109
Disraeli, Benjamin 56; country estate
39; *Vivian Gray* 99
Dissection Act (1832) 134
dissent, religious 18, 23, 172–3
divorce 36–7, 69, 129; of landowners
65; through Acts of Parliament 65;
see also marital breakdown;
separation, legal
dowagers 60
dowries 44, 55–6, 59, 122; *see also*
marriage settlements
drainage and enclosure: resistance to
77; social effects of 132, 154

earnings: of children 142; of
craftsmen 78–9; of farmers 73–4; of
labourers 135; supplementary 17,
126; of women 101, 126
ecclesiastical courts, use of records by
historians 173
education: adult 84; attitudes to 83;
boarding schools 31, 83, 109,
110–11; of boys 51–2, 69, 83–4,
107–11, 130, 143–5, 164–5; by
parents 107–9, 124–5; compulsory
31, 134, 143–4, 156, 164; cost of 130;
expansion of opportunities 15–16,
83, 114–16; of farmers and
craftsmen 79–80, 83–4, 85; funding
110, 112, 119; gender differences in
31–2, 53, 69, 114–15, 174; of girls
53–4, 69, 84, 107, 113–17, 130, 161,
164; of landowners' children 51–4;
in medicine 78; parents' attitudes to
109, 144; preparatory schools
110–11; public schools 31, 109,
110–11; radical ideas on 107;
scholarship children 165; self-
education 84; stressed by lower
middle classes 161, 164; suspicion
of girls 114–15; universities 23,
51–2, 78, 84, 97, 109–10, 114–16

elderly: employment of 38; provision
for 38; *see also* widows
electricity, introduction of 22, 61
emigration 21, 25
employment: of boys 32, 84, 85–6,
142–3, 144–6; by state 21, 165; of
children 20, 31–2, 84–5, 142–6, 156;
of elderly 38; of girls 32, 86–7, 142,
143–5, 146–8; homeworking 152–3;
married women's 88–90, 103, 152–3;
and motherhood 35, 151–3, 156; of
older women 155–6; and status 146;
of women 24, 33–4, 102–3, 105,
118–21, 151–3, 159, 161, 165; *see also*
apprenticeships
enclosures and drainage: resistance to
77; social effects 132, 154
engineering 20
epitaphs 176–7; *see also* memorials and
monuments
epitaphs 66
etiquette, for middle classes 98–9
Eton College 51, 109, 111

factories, employment of children in
20, 143, 145–6
family: anthropological analysis 9,
31–2, 110; breakdown of 154–5
family archives 41–2, 45, 46, 53, 174
family businesses 74, 82, 85, 89–90, 98
family histories 45, 46, 48, 52, 56, 103
family history: application of scientific
concepts to 6; demographic
approach 7–8; household
economics approach 7, 8–9;
psychohistorical approach 7;
sentimental approach 7, 8
family obligations 25, 53, 102, 103,
104, 130, 146, 147
farmers: aspirations to gentry 76–7;
carrying on other trades 73, 78;
duties of wives 88; lifestyle 72–6;
loss of holdings 78, 94; in Tudor
period 16; *see also* agriculture;
labourers
fathers: attitudes to children 27, 47,
49, 81, 107, 109, 123; and childbirth
63; and children's marriages 56,
58–9, 122; and death of children
29–30, 140; desertion of families
155; education of children 108–9;
provision of dowries 44, 55–6, 59,
122; violence towards family 154